FAIR PLAY

12 women speak

Conversations with Canadian Playwrights

Judith Rudakoff • Rita Much

Simon & Pierre
Toronto, Canada

We would like to express our gratitude to the Canada Council and the Ontario Arts Council for their support.

Marian M. Wilson, Publisher

ISBN 0-88924-221-6

1 2 3 4 5 • 4 3 2 1 0

Canadian Cataloguing in Publication Data

Fair play: twelve women speak

ISBN 0-88924-221-6

1. Women dramatists, Canadian (English) - 20th century - Interviews.* 2. Dramatists, Canadian (English) - 20th century - Interviews.* 3. Canadian drama (English) - 20th century - History and criticism.* 4. Theater - Canada - History - 20th century. I. Rudakoff, Judith D., 1953-   . II. Much, Rita, 1954-   .

PS8177.F35 1990   C812'.54'09287   C90-093596-0
PR9191.5.F35 1990

Cover Design: Christopher W. Sears

General Editor: Marian M. Wilson

Editor: Peter Goodchild

Printer: Les Ateliers Graphiques Marc Veilleux Inc.

Printed and Bound in Canada

Order from
Simon & Pierre Publishing Company Limited/
Les Éditions Simon & Pierre Ltée.
P.O. Box 280 Adelaide Street Postal Station
Toronto, Ontario, Canada M5C 2J4

Contents

Acknowledgments

Special thanks to Myles Warren, who suggested the idea for this book.

This book was completed with the volunteer editorial assistance of Deborah Tihanyi, David Brinton, and Andrea Williams, and the volunteer proof-reading of Marion DeVries.

We would also like to thank Peter Goodchild, Jean Paton, and especially Marian Wilson for their input, encouragement and enthusiasm.

Preface

Women talking to women about play-making. It seems so ordinary, until we realize that despite the hundreds of plays written and published by women in Canada, few achieve even one professional production. It is all the more important therefore that these conversations, providing as they do a context for the works of some of those plays which have reached the main stages, be heard. It is appropriate too that the format of this volume is dialogue rather than a series of prepared apologias. The voices are those of creators and critics, reflecting different viewpoints yet learning from each other. Like so many of the plays discussed, these conversations encircle, probe, embrace polarities and pluralities, seek sustenance in collaboration, make room for other voices, take up fresh images.

Reflected also in these twelve dialogues as in the plays discussed is the need to make connections, to seek relatedness and interrelatedness. The playwrights willingly explore the many different ways of knowing, moving from instinct, impulse and passion to order, control and reason, then back again, breaking down barriers between inner and outer worlds, seeking home in strangeness, learning not only to speak but to listen. Many of them speak about lost innocence, of characters and a world vulnerable and at risk, of having to face their fragments before becoming whole again — and in so doing they refer not only to their plays but to the very act of writing, the need to carve a space with words and images.

For none has finding that space or making the gesture of creation been without sacrifice; for all, empowerment has meant "revisioning" and reclaiming. They write not only out of inner compulsion but for others — for the actors who seek truthful roles, for the audiences who want a world they can acknowledge.

These voices speak to all of us. Listen.

Ann Saddlemyer

Massey College,
University of Toronto

Introduction

As teachers of drama at Toronto universities, both of us have discovered, over the past decade, a distinct and distressing lack of
reliable material to which we can guide students in search of background information, theoretical material or analytical commentary in
their research on Canadian playwrights. Reviews, newspaper interviews, the odd profile: little exists that gives much more than a
cursory or perfunctory overview of a playwright's style, thematic
concerns or influences that have shaped the work in question. In the
1970s Geraldine Anthony's *Stage Voices* and in the early eighties
Robert Wallace and Cynthia Zimmerman's *The Work* provided some
hope that with the burgeoning theatre movement and growing number of produced and published Canadian plays we might also gain a
body of critical and analytical material. However, the book-length
studies devoted to examining specific playwrights have been few and
far between. For those curious about Canada's woman playwrights,
the library shelves yield even less. (Out of the thirty-eight playwrights presented in *Stage Voices* and *The Work*, only five are
female.) The purpose of this collection of interviews with twelve of
Canada's woman playwrights is to help fill this vacuum.

The study, we believe, crosses many borders. Most obviously, it
will appeal to students and teachers of theatre, members of the
profession, and the general theatre-going public. In addition, the
discussions on process will be of particular interest to students and
teachers of creative writing, and the playwrights' views on such
issues as feminism, the elusive Canadian identity and the state of
cultural life in Canada will attract those interested in Women's
Studies, Canadian Literature and even Social Studies. We hope this
work will strike a chord in everyone concerned about the nature of
male-female relationships and the role of women within a cultural
and social hierarchy tailored by men, for men.

Time once was, and not a time too far removed, when artistic
directors might choose a Canadian woman playwright's work for a
season to kill two birds with one large stone. In fact, Carol Bolt
remembers being interviewed years ago, with Sharon Pollock, and
Pollock telling the interviewer just that. Today, the cachet of being
female and a playwright isn't quite so painfully chic.

Though this sort of tokenism is waning, there are certainly still
hurdles to overcome. Noticeably, there are no women of colour
included in this study. This is not to imply that no playwrights exist
in this category; however, as the 1980s draw to a close there are as
yet none who have made the great leap from talent to nationally
produced and/or published playwright. We acknowledge and lament
this situation and look forward to the time when this oversight will

be rectified. (There are also no Quebecois women included, but this is because of a happier situation: there exists such a large body of work and there are so many voices in Quebec today, that we feel strongly that the work of Quebecois woman playwrights deserves a volume of its own.)

The plays of the women included in this collection cover a wide range of styles and thematic concerns. The writers hail from one end of the country to the other and they are at different stages of their careers. Naturally, these discussions, approved and edited by the playwrights, vary in tone and timbre according to the particular background, personality and artistic goals of the individual playwrights. We discovered early in our research that the same questions often triggered totally different responses, responses that frequently led the conversations in directions we could never have anticipated.

What many of the playwrights have in common is a deep and abiding need for balance in order to survive, a struggle towards wholeness in their art. From Sally Clark's balance of Light and Dark to Linda Griffiths' fascination with duality to Banuta Rubess' insistence on "revisioning" history to Judith Thompson's principle of connectedness to Wendy Lill's concern with being engaged by your environment . . . these themes were raised again and again. In addition, many of the playwrights seem to feel an obligation to be hopeful in their work — "incorporating the Shadow to work for you rather than against you," as Ann-Marie MacDonald puts it or, as Joan MacLeod states, "finding the light." A surprising number also regard their life in theatre as part of a spiritual quest. For Joanna McClelland Glass, for example, writing is "salvation." For Judith Thompson, it's a "vocation." For Margaret Hollingsworth, it's a "passion."

Other dominant concerns reflected in the themes that reverberate throughout the body of work created by these playwrights are the exploration of where and what "Home" is, what forces may threaten it and how to maintain and protect it once it is achieved. "Home" for many of the playwrights is a sense of safety, an understanding of personal identity or, quite simply, a sense of control over one's life and destiny.

Another recurring topic was a shared interest in fairy tales: not surprising considering how many of these writers are working at shaping a Canadian mythology, at delineating a contemporary sense of personal identity within a shared cultural mythology and at discovering the links between conscious and unconscious existence.

All the playwrights in this volume are firmly connected to the unconscious Life Force that fuels our daily life. Their unique and individual voices and styles eloquently express the concerns that plague us all. Their work evokes emotional and intellectual and spiritual responses that are directly related to Today, but are also timeless and universal.

The conversations in this volume are, in one sense, framed close-ups of a moment in the development of selected artists. In fact, one of the reasons we chose the conversation/interview format rather than the fixed analytical perspective of critical evaluation was that these are writers who are changing moment to moment, play to play. When Linda Griffiths read her piece eight months after the initial conversations, she was struck by the realization that though the issue of the writer-actor duality (and, in fact, duality in general) was still a primary concern for her, her perspective had shifted.

These are portraits that are without a doubt located in a place, a time and a state of mind. While the truths each playwright articulates and the issues they've been grappling with remain constant, their perspective — and ours — will never again be exactly the same. And somehow, that makes it all even more exciting and immediate. Talking to Sally Clark before *Moo* had opened, before it had been nominated for a Dora Mavor Moore Award for Outstanding New Play, before Tarragon's production of *Jehanne of the Witches* and before Canadian Stage's production of *The Trial of Judith K.* provides a particular and specific insight.

Of course, the plays of these twelve Canadian woman writers stand for themselves. By making information about them more accessible, we ultimately hope to see their plays even more widely and more frequently produced. Each playwright is as visionary, as intense, as inspiring in person as on the page, and there is also a lot of anger, wonder, hunger and passion in these pages. Our greatest hope is that readers won't just be enchanted by these writers, but invigorated. And empowered.

Judith Rudakoff   Rita Much

1. Playwright Linda Griffiths

Born in Montreal in 1954, one of the original writers of the acclaimed *Paper Wheat*, Linda Griffiths performed in ten collectives with Saskatoon's Twenty-fifth Street House Theatre. The first time she performed the character of Pierre Trudeau was in *Les maudits anglais*. She has twice won the Dora Mavor Moore Award for Outstanding New Play and has written and acted for stage, film and television.

They're huge, they're giants . . . two epic characters, and they carry on a mythological struggle. They're King Arthur and Guinevere, and Clytemnestra and Agamemnon, and they play out our pain way up there.

Henry in *Maggie and Pierre*

I sit in a room full of sweet grass and animal skins, with rattles and drums, as if I wasn't carrying a Walkman and a computer the size of a briefcase. Vitaline, I like spike heels. I read Karl Marx and People *magazine.*

Jessica in *Jessica: A Transformation*

Produced and published plays:

Maggie and Pierre. With Paul Thompson. Vancouver: Talonbooks, 1980.

The Book of Jessica. With Maria Campbell. Toronto: Coach House Press, 1989.

Produced plays:

O.D. on Paradise. With Patrick Brymer. Premiere at Theatre Passe Muraille, Toronto, 1983.

Linda Griffiths Interview

by Judith Rudakoff

LG: Actually, I've been starting to believe in the old Paul Thompson school of documentary where you don't use the tape recorder. Remember what you can; do it again. Now I know why he never did use a tape recorder: because then someone's got to listen to the tapes and accept what was said as if it were the gospel truth, when often it is just so much flotsam and jetsam.

I think I'm having my battle again with being a writer and what that means, what the mentality actually is as opposed to just the act of writing. Who is this rude person, "The Writer"? There's a part of me that just wants to run off and do my part as an actor and just hoof it. And, instead of hoofing it, I'm up there in my attic office with these piles of paper, picking out commas, trying to figure out how I got there and how this happened to somebody who just wanted to run away and join the circus.

And I knew that we were doing this interview, and I make up this Woman Writer who loves this stuff, who has a natural-born pickiness and a grasp of the exact right word *and* a thesaurus! (I don't have a thesaurus; I have just got a dictionary. . . .)

And I imagine that this woman combines the academic and a desire to be . . . I don't know; I keep saying "picky." In my imagination, women like this will sit at the kitchen table and write their novel with their husband beating them and the kids screaming. And it doesn't matter to them, because they have this attention to detail, and they're vigilant, and they don't want to go off and drink in the bar all night, or run off to weird places or get themselves into trouble or have adventures. Now, I know this woman doesn't really exist, but I feel that somehow she's there, and I thought, "What am I going to talk about? Am I a writer? Am I an actor? A writer who isn't an actor, or an actor who isn't a writer?"

And then I'm reading a draft of the book I'm working on about the making of *Jessica* and I get to the line where Maria Campbell says, "I am not a writer, I am a community worker." And then I reply, "Well, I *am* a writer, and that's why I wrote *Jessica*." I am a writer: so why isn't this process easier? Why isn't it any more fun? Any time I say I'm either an actor or a writer I feel like I'm lying.

JR: CAN'T YOU BE BOTH?

LG: Yes, of course; but it doesn't seem. . . .

Maybe I possess one part of this imaginary woman writer: the linear mind. (It's fuzzy, but it's linear!) When I went down to Jamaica recently to play Wallis Simpson in a film, I bought a laptop portable computer to take there with me, knowing I would have a lot of time to spare because mine was a small part spread out over four-and-a-half weeks. And when I packed my bags, I left the computer in a box in my living room. On purpose. I just left it. I did, however, take all the *Jessica* transcripts with me.

And when I got there, I walked into the dining room, sat down and just became one of the actors. We got dressed up, someone did our hair, our make-up, we walked out and emoted a little bit: the paperly or writerly side of me went completely out the window. For a while.

And then the writerly part of me would take over, the part that actually liked to be in a room with a pile of paper, reading it and editing so I can finally publish *Jessica* (or take the long swim in Lake Ontario. Other writers publish; why are my plays always out there in oral-history land . . . ?). So I would get out my piles of paper and work.

And, of course, that would only last so long, and then back to the bar.

So there's an example of the contradiction: from this group of people, "the circus," to the attic and me and my writing.

I really get pissed off if I'm not considered a writer: I know that there's no logic to that. It's a kind of a female irrationality. If anyone calls me a creator of things, or some title like that, I'm livid. I know how many hours I've spent on my own, working and editing, when I really want to be out there acting. Those are my only thoughts on coming to the interview. Ask me questions.

JR: THE FIRST TIME I INTERVIEWED YOU WAS IN 1980, DURING THE HEIGHT OF THE *MAGGIE AND PIERRE* ERA. I WENT BACK AND I TOOK A LOOK AT THE PIECE AND THERE WAS ONE STATEMENT THAT REALLY JUMPED OUT AT ME. I HAD ASKED YOU TO DESCRIBE *MAGGIE AND PIERRE*, AND YOU DESCRIBED IT AS THE "STRUGGLE OF MAN, WOMAN, PATRIOTISM, POWER, CORRUPTION, VISION, MOTHERHOOD, FATHERHOOD, CHANGING RELATIONSHIPS, ETC." THAT STATEMENT REALLY DESCRIBES *ALL* OF YOUR WORK TO DATE, DOESN'T IT?

LG: Yes. That's great. I think that's what work like you're doing does: it gives me a context, so *I* don't have to figure out a way to explain my work. At one point I was thinking about the phrase "a so-and-so play"; a Tom Walmsley play, a Judith Thompson play, and I thought, "What the hell would a Linda Griffiths play be?"

It's only now that people can actually look at three of my plays (if they can find a copy of *O.D. on Paradise* . . .). And I don't know what you would say about these three things, actually, because stylistically they're quite different. Not completely, but quite different. What through-lines would you see?

JR: THERE ARE SOME REALLY STRONG ONES. DUALITY, FOR EXAMPLE, IS A THEME THAT IS MOST APPARENT IN *JESSICA*.

LG: Or maybe in *Maggie and Pierre*. That's an example of the duality that I'm trying to express when I talk about being a writer-actor.

In that play, the writer is Pierre, and the actress is Maggie, and those two elements combined, well, if I could have them dwell comfortably within me, that would be fantastic. In me, they're expressed by the same person who wants to leave Toronto and move to Thailand, or Jamaica, or anywhere, and the person who clearly sees that Toronto is a place of great strength for me, the place where most of the people I know and love live. It's constant, that duality.

And I'm back again working with that duality in a very clear way in my collaboration with Maria Campbell: a very bizarre relationship, because with Maria, I become the one who wants accomplishment, the one who looks ahead and plans ahead, while she's the one having the argument with *me* saying, "But don't you see that planning kills something about this whole thing? Don't you see that I can't be like that, but that doesn't mean I don't have a right to work, or I don't have my contribution?"

The duality keeps splitting and shifting: either outside, creatively, or inside, in terms of the yin and the yang, the Dark Mother and the Light Mother. And with *Jessica*, the struggle is both between the two cultures and also between light and dark.

The reading I've been doing (which is, I think, the reading a lot of women are doing) is about trying to understand that dualism and balance. And it's all in the interpretation. Take, for example, the interpretation one might have of the Persephone myth: she's certainly kidnapped, but I would say she wanted to go. And I would say that many people would agree.

In *Jessica*, the political and the sociological levels are also there. But it's my particular definition of those aspects which involves emotions, and which isn't just issue-related (or media-issue-related, in spite of *Maggie and Pierre*). I don't know if I've always had that understanding, but I think I have. It tends to come out as a kind of an anger that is political, an anger at a society that tells you you're worthless. It's a raised fist saying, "That's not true," or "I refuse to accept it as true that you're nothing." And that's how I define a revolutionary statement.

On one level, you could say that *Jessica* is a political play about the oppression of Native people. And yet, as far as I'm concerned, the politic of the play is articulated when Vitaline says, "Magic is revolution." That's politics to me, not Meech Lake. But if I were to write a piece about Meech Lake or Free Trade people would be crying. There would be weeping and gnashing of teeth, and I would include all the extenuating circumstances that aren't strictly journalistic. Political analysis without journalism is an odd way to do it, but that's how I think. And that sense of wanting to take things from real life comes from my experience with Paul Thompson's creative process.

JR: DUALITY DEPENDS ON BALANCE: IT'S NOT THE DARK WINNING, OR THE LIGHT WINNING, IT'S BALANCE. AND WHEN THERE'S A CROSS OVER, AND THE TWO SIDES LOOK AT EACH OTHER, THEN YOU HAVE MOMENTS WHERE YOU EITHER LIVE OR DIE. THAT TYPE OF MOMENT IS APPARENT IN *JESSICA*.

LG: It's amazing that some of the words I *wrote* in *Jessica*, I *said* years later, as if I hadn't written them or thought them before. That has a lot to do with the balance, and the accepting of the conscious and the unconscious at work. That's what I don't understand about writing: how you can know, but not know. Or how you can read something that someone's written, that seems to come from some place of awareness, and then meet the person, and they're a total mess. You think, "How can they write these things, and yet be like this?" That's where maybe there's something else at work than what's consciously known to the person.

JR: WELL, YOU CERTAINLY HAVE A WAY OF TAPPING INTO — WHATEVER YOU WANT TO CALL IT — THE UNCONSCIOUS, THE COLLECTIVE. ALL OF THOSE LEVELS. EURIPIDES GRIFFITHS. . . .

LG: Sibyl Griffiths . . . I'm writing about that process in this book about the making of *Jessica*. The best way I can describe it is that it is like being a sibyl of sorts. Or like making paté! You stuff the goose with all this information which then goes through to the liver (which used to be called the soul) and then you cut her open, once it's all digested, and take out the paté! That's what I did originally with *Jessica*. It's a type of improvisation.

Now improvisation is something that, in a way, I haven't done in a long time. And something that I know I have to do again. It was my source into writing. I didn't suddenly start writing plays on pieces of paper: I started *talking* plays. After you've talked plays for a certain amount of time, you're going to want to write them down. And then you're going to say, I don't have to have six people in the room with me; I'll be all the six people. And then you say, I don't even have to be all the six people, or utter a word — I can do it on my own in front of this piece of paper. And that was the way I moved from improvisation and talking plays to actually writing them. On paper!

JR: I'M QUITE SERIOUS WHEN I CALL YOU EURIPIDES GRIFFITHS: YOU WRITE EPIC THEATRE.

LG: When you do all that work you can't bear it for the play to have less than seven things going on in it!

And yet, when I see such a brilliantly focused piece like Betty Lamberts' *Under the Skin* that was produced in the 1988-89 season at Theatre Passe Muraille, I ask myself, would I have stuffed the bloody thing? Maybe. Restraint is something I'll either learn, or I'll deliberately and completely ignore, and leave to other writers. But I do appreciate focus. Not single focus, but that laser beam intensity.

When I write, or act, I like the sweep. Now Clare Coulter and I are, as actors, often set up as opposites: Clare will feel out a moment, and if there's nothing happening, she won't do anything. I, on the other hand, will stand on my head, I will run around the stage. I'll do anything to make something happen. In a way, it's the same kind of energy that writes my plays: I don't like to have a dull moment. I like my actors to have a good time. I like the environment of the theatre to somehow reflect the environment of the play. Epic theatre, the circus, they're the same to me. No matter how heavy the subject is, it doesn't matter. A circus can be heavy.

Euripides Griffiths . . . The only academic studying I ever did about theatre was on the Greeks, and the pre-Greeks, and all that led into the festivals. And I don't pretend to know much. You put me down with anyone who's really studied the period and I couldn't compete. I would *feel* something, but I wouldn't *know* anything.

For me, the spiritual element of theatre is the most important part. There's always a spiritual element in my plays, including *Maggie and Pierre*. With *Maggie and Pierre*, the moment the play was produced in Edmonton during the oil crisis of the 1970s and 1980s, the spiritual side became vital. In the scene when the Trudeau character gets down on his knees and prays, I knew that I was holding that whole audience in my fist and keeping them from laughing. And nobody did. Because to laugh at a man praying is evil, even if you've decided that he is the Devil incarnate.

There's an understanding of what that spiritual moment is, an understanding between audience and actor. It also happens in *O.D. on Paradise* in the craziness of the Rastafarian stuff, when that character finally flips his lid and goes for Jah. At that moment, the audience is cheering for him, not laughing at him. They're cheering him because why shouldn't he go for Jah; he's obviously in a place where Jah is very present. That spiritual kinship is also evident in the death of Vic, and the mysticism that surrounds it.

Audiences accept the mystical because of where and when it's taking place. The Greeks had that type of belief built into their society, their culture. Today, we have to work it into our world. That's why academics will say that we can't do the Greek plays today; because they think we don't believe in spirituality any more.

JR: BUT WE DO. WE JUST EXPRESS IT DIFFERENTLY BECAUSE WE BELIEVE IN DIFFERENT GODS.

LG: I think we're no longer ashamed to admit that we believe in spiritualism. There has been virtually no spiritual element to modern play-writing for many years, except maybe during the sixties. No one was exactly *writing* that stuff, but Grotowski and others were starting to get into mythology, and the power of those stories.

It's very hard to tap into that power, because though people are feeling out some way into a spiritual sensibility, there are still no shared paths. There's not a specific moment where, for example, you can have "the witches" in the Scottish play enter and know that the entire audience will feel the same reaction.

When I began looking at the Native culture, I found that it was filled with new images for me, and not the bloody cross. We've done whatever we could with that thing as artists, and the Christian field of imagery has grown narrower and narrower. To see and hear other images and myths was amazing. Maria would say that we had to find new vision in our own culture: that we'd mined it and had to replenish it. I was jealous of the shared world that native people have.

When we auditioned people for *Jessica*, and said to the Native actors, "This character is Bear," they all used the same voice. It was shared, that spiritual sense of that character. White actors would come in to the auditions and not have a clue what I was talking about.

JR: WHAT DO YOU THINK THE SHARED MYTHS ARE NOW? YOU'VE OBVIOUSLY FOUND SOME.

LG: Actually, the shared source, the collective unconscious, is constantly growing. Now is a very fertile time because it's the only comfort in a time of global disaster. What's making people turn back to Native sources all over the world is the natives' holistic sense of the earth. Instead of being anthropological and intellectual, these people actually think of the earth as a being. Now the scientists are saying, well, actually, this is all interconnected. And the natives have always had respect for the earth: digging up plants, smoking tobacco, killing animals are all actions that are undertaken with a sense of totality and spiritual interaction.

All the New Age philosophy: I love it, I buy it all from the crystals to the astrology. In that philosophy one can find a genuine reaching out, no matter how silly it gets. But it's not shared at the moment. It's still only a portion of society that's receptive.

I like to involve myself in times and places where people are opening out and beginning to accept new ideas. Times and places where there isn't a shared mythology yet and you can't simply play directly to an audience and hit them all in the same place like in the time of the Greeks. I like the splitting out and the diversity because it's the only way we're going to come up with some spirituality which actually helps the world and allows for survival. And that is the name of the game, survival.

JR: YOU KNOW THE MAYAN CALENDAR ENDS IN THE YEAR 2010. . . .

LG: 2010 . . . not old enough, not old enough by half.

JR: DO YOU DISTINGUISH AT ALL BETWEEN MYTHOLOGICAL AND PSYCHOLOGICAL?

LG: I don't think so. I've never thought about it. I don't even distinguish between fairy tales and reality! I can barely understand the difference.

JR: WHAT ATTRACTS YOU TO FAIRY TALES?

LG: In fairy tales, whether you're a writer or an actress, there have always been good parts for women. When I was growing up, they were the only stories I read where women had adventures! In fairy tales, the females carry the burden of the story: the narrative goes through the woman. And that's so rare. I was crazy about fairy tales when I was about nineteen: it got to be overwhelming. When I started working with Maria Campbell, I realized that her myths and magic and my fairy tales were essentially the same and that I had actually been on to something back then, instead of being a teen-aged weirdo (which I thought I was).

When I was nineteen no one I knew was into fairy tales. I used to hang out at the Classics book store on Ste. Catherine St. in downtown Montreal, reading fairy tale books and looking at the illustrations. People my age were reading Ken Kesey (who was also talking about fairy tales in his own way) but I couldn't connect with that. I could only see these long-haired girls in these long dresses. . . . And they always had good parts!

When I realized that fairy tales actually came out of a spiritual tradition, a shared mythological tradition which is also a psychological tradition, I finally stopped feeling ashamed. Because I had to stop myself back then, because I really was starting to live inside one of those books. And I didn't know there was anyone else thinking about that stuff. There was no Fifth Kingdom Book Store back then, no stores that specialized in that spiritual or mystical material. Open interest in magic and spiritualism was just starting in a psychedelic sense, in the early seventies, and the druggies were starting to get into it. Today, I walk into book stores, and I see all the books that I used to read, and I think, I wasn't the only one then. I wasn't. There have always been other people wanting to walk through a mirror, to mix time periods.

When I was going through my academic vs. actress duel in college, I wrote a paper analyzing the Grimms' fairy tales in terms of the roots of Nazi Germany. The professor wanted me to publish it. But it was the same battle: I knew that if I wanted to publish it, first I had to make it more valid by using more facts and research. But then I knew I wouldn't have the time to be in the college plays. So, I didn't publish it, and then about five or six years later, a major book came out exploring folk and fairy tales and mythology as the root of nazism.

Now, I don't know what to make of the psychological side to all of this, because, in a way, many things that have happened to me have been fairy tale-ish (and nightmare-ish) in combination, sometimes in balance. I'm not always exactly sure which fairy story I'm in! I think that would be true for just about anyone who writes.

When I met up with the Native guys, my interest in fantasy was no big deal to them. Not that they were into European fairy tales, which had been all that I could find, but they assumed that those stories were just another level of reality. That's one of the reasons I love their world so much.

By being part of a tradition that evolved away from the pragmatism and materialism of my culture, they kept something very strong and very (dare I use the word) pure. Not to say that their poverty is positive: but in one sense, there has been a positive offshoot of that negative. The elemental has been preserved.

JR: IN THE NEW-AGE PHILOSOPHY OF THE EIGHTIES, WE TEND TO LOOK AT FAIRY-TALE FEMALES IN TERMS OF THE ANCIENT GODDESS MYTHS.

LG: The girl in the fairy tales is the Virgin aspect of the Goddess triad that's also made up of the Mother and the Crone. "Virgin" in that mythology simply means "untamed by men." And that freedom was what we were feeling out in the seventies, and didn't know how to articulate. It really is amazing to think that a renaissance was happening, and yet I felt utterly alone.

And amid all that spiritual growth — I had to stop. I had to touch earth and ground myself. And that's another strength in the Native world, the knowledge that grounding is a necessary part of spirituality. Our civilization has tended to make us airhead-y, full of hot air. Our primary element seems to be air, perhaps because of the emphasis in our religions on angels and heaven. That sense of god being separate from the human body or spirit. This tends to take us away from the magic realism that exists on and of the earth. That's one of the reasons I have such a strong attachment to Western Canada: to me, as an Easterner, the West always seemed to possess magic, but magic related to the land, and to the environment.

Before moving to Saskatchewan, I had stayed in my castle in the air for such a long, long time, not realizing what was missing in my life.

Trying to talk about spiritualism is very hard. I'm trying to find a vocabulary to express it in the book about the making of *Jessica*. I keep saying "earth-feelings," but as soon as I see it written down I know that's the wrong word. But what's the "right" word? Energies? We don't have words in the English language with which to talk about these things. We really don't. We have two or three words that come close. "Religious" connotes the wrong thing, even though it's probably the closest. "Spiritual"? "Mystic"? "Occult"?

Maria talks about trying to relate in English to spiritual topics and the difficulty she's had. Natives may have a zillion words for snow but they also have a zillion words for spirit. The American writer Starhawk has a good word, immanence, that she uses in *The Spiral Dance* and *Dreaming the Dark*. In using it she's trying to find a word to describe God that redefines it at the same time, that finds a new perspective on it. That's how I believe change, revolution, magic, happens. For awhile, I thought that maybe I should drop the subtitle for *Jessica*: "A Transformation." But now, it's become a buzzword, a word we use to make sense of this search we're on.

JR: WE SEEM TO BE RE-EXAMINING OUR LANGUAGE AS WELL AS OUR MYTHOLOGIES. DO YOU SEE YOURSELF RE-DEFINING OTHER COMMONLY RECOGNIZED CONCEPTS SUCH AS SAFETY, HOME, TRUTH, LIGHT, ANSWERS, SELF, KNOWLEDGE? ARE THEY ALL THE SAME THING? IS IT ALL PART OF THE SEARCH AND THE TRANSFORMATION WE'VE BEEN TALKING ABOUT?

AND YOUR CHARACTERS SEEM TO SPEND MUCH OF THEIR TIME RUNNING AWAY FROM OR TOWARDS THESE ELUSIVE STATES.

LG: I think so. I think that there's a driven nature to all of the characters in all of the plays. It's their beginning. Many of them are in a state of crisis, driven towards something that will alleviate their pain or their confusion. And they do find it. There is salvation of a sort. In *O.D. on Paradise*, each of those eight characters has his or her turnaround point.

JR: IT'S LIKE THERE'S A MISSING PIECE INSIDE OF THEM AND THEY'RE ON A JOURNEY TO FIND THAT PIECE. . . .

LG: That's right. I think that's got to be coming from me.

Though I'm sure there's no human being alive who doesn't go through that search, whether they recognize it or not.

JR: LET'S GO BACK FOR A MOMENT TO A COMMENT YOU MADE EARLIER. YOU REFERRED TO THE DIFFICULTY PEOPLE MIGHT HAVE IN GETTING HOLD OF A COPY OF *O.D. ON PARADISE.* WHY DO YOU THINK THIS DORA MAVOR MOORE AWARD-WINNING PLAY HASN'T BEEN PUBLISHED?

LG: You know, it's only been produced once since that second Passe Muraille production and that was at Edmonton's Northern Light Theatre.

JR: DO YOU THINK THE "STRAWBERRY TEA" INCIDENT HAS ANYTHING TO DO WITH EITHER SITUATION?

LG: Well, we certainly lost heart over the libel suit with the *Toronto Star.* There we were, with every indication that the show could play for a longer run when we re-mounted it, and maybe find us a new, more conservative suburban audience. Clarke Rogers spent a lot of money on the set and on seating so we could accommodate more people. We'd won the Dora Award first time out, but the re-mount was reviewed a second time.

And this time, when the *Toronto Star* review came out, the actors were accused of smoking real "ganja" on stage, which, as we all know, is a criminal offense.

I was in New York at the time and I got a phone call telling me that the police had walked into the theatre the next day because, essentially, the newspaper had said that a crime was being committed on stage every night at Theatre Passe Muraille!

JR: I REMEMBER SEEING THE SHOW AND WATCHING POLICE WATCH THE SHOW FROM THE LOBBY/BAR AREA. THERE WAS A PECULIAR TENSION AND A STRANGE SENSE OF OUTRAGE AND CAMARADERIE SUFFUSING THE AUDIENCE.

LG: There was a big hoopla, because the *Toronto Star* had absolutely no proof, and the actors were actually smoking strawberry tea on stage. The theatre slapped a lawsuit on the *Star* and the actors sued for libel. In a way, it was great: There was a Strawberry Tea Benefit to help cover the legal costs and a lot of the theatre community came and read *their* bad reviews in public: A kind of vetting of the whole business of being chained to these people, the reviewers.

But the damage had already been done. The audience we'd hoped to reach just heard or read the words "crime" or "marijuana" and that was it. The theatres that had previously expressed interest in producing *O.D. on Paradise* just didn't call back. It was quite incredible. Every time I hear about how there aren't enough Canadian comedies, I want to rant and rave and rage around the room.

JR: WHAT WAS THE AFTERMATH?

LG: Eventually, once the issue was dead, the *Star* settled out of court. Some of the money went to cover the legal costs, the eight actors each got a small amount of money and the theatre got a small amount as well. The writers didn't get a dime.

What's ironic is that the real instigator of the libel at the *Star* had understood that the play was actually dangerous and political. *O.D. on Paradise* isn't a benign comedy; it speaks of understanding anarchy and its uses. It demonstrates that anarchy can be dangerous to the people who want to box us up for all of our lives.

I know *O.D. on Paradise* could have played to general audiences. It was written for that purpose. Maybe it will be produced again. And maybe, someday, someone will publish it. I'll always know what it was like to have the police called into your play. I'll never forget that feeling.

JR: HAS YOUR WORK BEEN INFLUENCED BY GROWING UP IN AN ENGLISH SECTION OF A BILINGUAL CITY? AND THEN GOING OUT WEST, AND BEING AN EASTERNER IN SASKATOON?

LG: Yes. In Quebec, as an anglophone, you could be a *maudite anglaise*, or you could become politicized. However, there I was, someone who didn't speak French, but who hung out in the cafés, afraid to order a cup of coffee, because I'd be found out, listening to the *Independentistes* talk. Maybe it came more from a desire to join than a feeling of being separate.

I'm one of those people who just won't quit when they want in! Maria would attest to that. I've always tried to balance seeing where and how I'm different, and then figuring out whether my difference is a good thing, or whether being ignorant of the difference is more productive.

The first time western Canadian actor Bob Collins called me an uppity Easterner, I didn't know what he was talking about. I had no idea there was any problem. I knew there were a hell of a lot of problems in Quebec because this all happened just after the War Measures Crisis in the seventies. But I thought I had gone to the West where there were no problems!

But pretty soon, I also had an attitude towards Toronto. And I had cowboy boots. There's no denying that there wasn't and isn't simply an extremity to being English in Quebec. Then, you couldn't pretend you didn't know what it was to be afraid that there might be a bomb in the mailbox, and for that to be quite possible. Even so, there's an electricity about the circumstances in Quebec, the un-balanced elements; it's active and there's a constant demand for a response, an opinion.

When I lived in Montreal you *had* to have an opinion: you were involved because you were there. The uncle of my girlfriend up the street was a guy whose face was blown off by one of the bombs placed in mailboxes in English suburbs.

In Canada, it's very rare that dissent is put to you like that. And the result is an immediate politicization. I don't know if that political awareness was there for me before or not, but all of a sudden the struggle was something very close. And I was acutely aware of the contradictions on both sides. Maybe I'm always conscious of that, of both sides of the struggle, because of where and when I grew up.

JR: IS IT VERY DIFFERENT WRITING FOR A LIVE THEATRE AUDIENCE AS OPPOSED TO, SAY, WRITING FOR FILM?

LG: I think it's different, but only in the most superficial way. Essentially, you still have to do exactly the same thing, come from exactly the same source. (I'm still figuring out what is allowable in front of the camera. Doing the video of *Maggie and Pierre* was really important, because I had to throw away my tasteful film acting, because it didn't work with that material. That immediately freed me.) It's a feeling out of the moment. You feel an audience; you feel the camera; you feel the person behind the camera. They should be different, but I don't think they really are.

For example, I'm working on a film treatment of Margaret Atwood's *Life before Man*. And, in the end, my film version of *Life before Man* is about the same issues and themes that everything else I've written about deals with, even though it's Margaret Atwood's novel: what I liked about the novel is that it could be about what I wanted it to be about.

And I really don't know what the difference is between the various media, except for those surface elements, technical realities, budgets, etcetera. But those are adjustments, they're not big differences.

And because of the split and the need to balance my acting and writing, I'm too preoccupied with that duality to worry about the difference between film and stage. If I was worried about that too, I'd be paralyzed! But I do know that in film I miss the contact with the live audience.

And I really like doing writer readings. At first I thought that you shouldn't *do* anything, that I had to pretend, as the playwright, that I wasn't acting: so I came prepared to act very dry. . . .

But then I see John Gray get up, and he's got *music* with his piece! And Judith Thompson's up there, and she's acting away, and I thought, "Just a minute, now! This is silly!" Because again it's my idea of who a writer is that isn't the truth at all.

I have decided, though, that I love those staged readings. I did one recently of one of my short stories — a long short story — called *The*

Speed Christmas and Thompson directed me in it. I need to do more of those sort of readings. If I did, I think I'd complain less about the sensory deprivation of writing alone up in the attic. I miss the easy access to an audience; I miss getting out there every once in a while and hoofing it. That contact with a live audience is a very special thing, and it's something that I truly love.

I got so much of it at one point, during the two-and-a-half year run of *Maggie and Pierre*, that to cut it off completely is very odd. So I miss it. It does feel like acting when I'm acting for the camera, but unless you've got a really big part, it's not the same thing. It's not that fulfilling when you think that the hairdresser or the costume designer is building your character.

JR: DO YOU FIND THAT IT'S IMPOSSIBLE TO TAKE WHAT YOU'VE WRITTEN AND THEN GIVE IT TO SOMEONE ELSE TO PERFORM?

LG: No. Sometimes it's hard, when I've played the role in my head as part of the writing process. I was able to give *Jessica* over completely. I worried that I wouldn't be able to, but I had no problems with it, because all my energy was necessary as part of an outside perspective in order to keep it going, in order to do part of the directing, and to help in the creation of the music.

JR: BUT YOU DID ACT IN *JESSICA* WHEN IT WAS PRODUCED OUT WEST.

LG: Yes, but that was a very different script. That was what I call the improvised version.

Yes, I think I can give my work over. Every once in a while, though, I'll start playing the scenes in my head. But I'm very careful never to let that be known around actors. I'm really the Writer around actors: I get coffee, I run errands, I make sure they're having a good time, I listen to everything; it really brings out the latent mother in me, being a writer around a cast.

In the piece I'm working on now, *The Darling Family*, I definitely felt that I had to be the writer. Only the writer. And I still don't know if that's right for me, to cross to one or the other sides of the actor-writer line. But I do know that I have split my identity again because if I act in the pieces then I can't be working on re-writing while it's being rehearsed, which is a very important part of the process. And also, because I need to watch my plays in rehearsal. I need the distance.

And in previous writing situations, I also felt a real need to be respected as a writer, separately; and if I was acting too, people didn't seem to be able to distinguish between Linda Griffiths, the Actor, and Linda Griffiths, the Writer. So I just absented myself; and that's how you get to be called a playwright as opposed to a creator.

JR: THIS IS THE FIRST PLAY THAT YOU'VE WRITTEN WITHOUT A COLLABORATOR.

LG: Yes. It would be interesting to get all my collaborators in the room and see what they would say!

I am thinking of finding a collaborator, but only after I've written it. When I feel that I'm getting a little dusty up there in the attic, a little tweedy, I like the idea of at least having access to conversation about the piece. The workshop process can be a collaboration on the script, and give you the feedback you need at that stage, but then I need to know there's someone there afterwards.

JR: WHAT ABOUT A DRAMATURGE RATHER THAN A COLLABORATOR?

LG: It's not the same thing. Clarke Rogers was a dramaturge to *O.D. on Paradise*, but Patrick Brymer was the collaborator. With Patrick I had the chance to explore possibilities verbally, as opposed to getting someone's judgement call. Dramaturgy is great, but it's not the same thing.

JR: TELL ME ABOUT YOUR COLLABORATORS. DID YOU HAPPEN UPON EACH OTHER? WAS IT ACCIDENTAL? THEY'RE ALL SUCH DIFFERENT PEOPLE.

LG: Paul Thompson was actually the one who suggested doing *Maggie and Pierre*, which came out of the rehearsals for *Les maudits anglais*. I made it clear to Paul that I wanted to work *with* him: that I wanted to do the words, and the characters, and I wanted him to do the structuring. At that point, I considered myself incapable of doing such a thing. I couldn't imagine how else the play would get finished.

And Paul said, "Well, if we're going to do it that way," (he'd already worked on so many shows where he'd workshopped the entire piece and then the person had gone off with the work, and he had not been a part of the future of the piece), "then I have to be given credit, I have to be a part of it." I didn't even think twice about agreeing. And that initial collaboration was really the Sibyl and the Guide. But the Guide does more than lead: he/she also keeps the Sibyl on track. Giving feedback just doesn't express the nature of the relationship. It's more like feeding in than feeding back. The metaphor of stuffing the old goose for the paté is so important to the creative process. And how you stuff her, and with what and when. . . .

Thompson watched the Writer emerge and he helped me to do it. Collaborating with him was a natural evolution, having worked with him so many times before (as an actor in collectives), and from having him as the Guide in many of the improvisations in many shows.

With Patrick, the collaboration began when we were down in Jamaica, on a vacation. What happened to white people down there from a cold country was amazing. And I just turned to him and said, "We should do a play." I didn't think, "Aha! A collaborator." I didn't think about it in those terms. We decided to do it. That just made sense.

At one point, we were going to try to improvise it, but then that seemed like too much trouble with all those characters, so we just started writing. It took a very short period of time, and we tried maybe one improvisation with just the two of us. That just seemed silly: we just had to get it down on paper.

JR: SO THEN WHAT DID YOU DO? DID YOU GO OFF SEPARATELY TO WRITE AND THEN BRING IT TOGETHER?

LG: No. We talked it out. I would write a section, and then I would give it to Patrick, and he would critique it, and then we'd talk about it some more. He organized all the material. That was the split. I just "jammed" it out. I was still jamming it out with somebody else remembering and putting it together, and saying to me, "What about this?" and encouraging me to keep going.

If Patrick had a strong line on something, I would follow his strong line. It's just like being a sponge.

The creation of *Jessica* is so complicated that we're writing a book about that collaboration!

By the end of that writing process, I took the responsibility of the script (which had started out being words by me and structure and "feeding in" by Paul and Maria) and from the improvised, written down draft, I wrote a play on my own. I took that script and then I went back to Maria with it and said, "Talk to me about this." She did, and I responded to her.

Each collaboration has, in a way, been entirely different. In each case, I'm the words. And sometimes the structure. But there's something else to the collaborative relationship. Maybe it's partially the actor in me needing the director. Which is not to say that I always listen to the other person. I think all my collaborators would say that eventually, there's a certain point where I take the ball and run, and either they resent it or they don't.

I'm not entirely insensitive to that moment, either. It becomes a visceral need on my part to take whatever has been fed in, digest it and then spit it out.

There was a point during the writing of *Jessica* when Maria felt that I had taken everything from her, and still wanted more, and wanted more, and wanted more, more, more. And then I wanted to go off and write, when originally it was supposed to be a collaborative process. And I don't think, in the end, that I had anything to say to her in response to that except that I felt it, I felt that moment, and I didn't think there was any way it was going to get done otherwise. Which was a pretty practical attitude when she was speaking about a metaphysical process, of a kind of mind-warp.

Maria talks about artists as thieves. For years I fought against that image, until finally, with this project, I admitted to myself, "Okay, I'm a thief! I'm a thief! When it comes down to that moment, I will go off on my own and write, because I can't help it, I'm just a thief! A kleptomaniac."

That particular collaboration was as close to an alchemy as I ever want to come with another human being. I'd like to put the wires back to my own self now, and reveal the individual a bit more than I have before. And my writing, the material I've been writing more recently, is much more personal. In fact, I think it tends to lean to the other extreme.

JR: IS THERE A COLLABORATOR OR A DIRECTOR THAT YOU WOULD LIKE TO WORK WITH? SOMEONE YOU HAVEN'T YET WORKED WITH?

LG: I don't think it works that way. It has to "happen." I don't set out actively to work with people. I didn't set out to work with Maria: Paul was going out West to work with her, they needed an actor who could improvise and I was deemed the best person for the job. It's always an accident with me, so all I hope is that I keep having those fortunate accidents. Those people become magnets in the natural course of things, and I become a magnet for those people, too. We'll see what happens.

JR: DO YOU CONSIDER YOURSELF EITHER A CANADIAN PLAY-WRIGHT, OR A FEMALE PLAYWRIGHT? DO YOU SEE THAT AS BEING DIFFERENT FROM A PLAYWRIGHT?

LG: No to the first question and yes to the second. As someone very conscious of the country, I say I'm a Canadian playwright. Many of the actors involved in the film I acted in recently, *Passion and Paradise*, were British and I would identify myself to them as a *Canadian* playwright. I may be the first Canadian they've met, and that's okay. To them, I'm from this unknown place: I make it this unknown and mysterious world that one day they will know, as a nation.

On the issue of being called a "female playwright" . . . well, it's only recently I've started to hear questions like, "How many women are we doing in the season this year?" There's so much strength in the woman writers here, and as we become more and more of a group, I think it makes more sense to say "woman playwright." Titles are partly to help make definitions tidier. I'm not offended by titles, but sometimes I'm confused by the need for them.

JR: DO YOU PLACE LESS EMPHASIS ON THE DISTINCTION "FE-MALE" PLAYWRIGHT THAN "CANADIAN" PLAYWRIGHT BECAUSE YOU CAME OUT OF A HISTORY OF COLLECTIVES WHERE MEN WERE PLAYING WOMEN, AND WOMEN WERE PLAYING MEN?

LG: Yes. And I played so many men. And by the time *Maggie and Pierre* came along, that was kind of the end of a stream of male parts. I didn't even think twice about playing men. Plus, with my gang of actors at Saskatoon's Twenty-Fifth Street House Theatre (and that wasn't news on Thompson's old gang), there was usually an even number of men and women. . . . No, I lie, there were always two women: Columbine and Isabel. . . . I felt that there were an even number. In the *Paper Wheat* cast (the original *Paper Wheat* cast), there was half and half. . . . No: four women and two men. You see, you don't really know, because you're switching all the time. And if you're doing anything historical, you're *really* switching.

But there was a point, where the original Passe Muraille women had to sit down and say, "We're tired of playing men all the time just because the subjects are historical." But, it was always an option. And it's given me an odd perspective on it all. And also, because I never felt like I was working with Paul Thompson simply because I was a woman, it never occurred to me that I couldn't play a man, or that I might or might not be produced because I was a woman. It was only later that this issue came to mean anything to me. I never once considered that Clarke Rogers might be producing *O.D. on Paradise* because I was a woman playwright.

JR: I THINK WE'RE ALL VERY CONSCIOUS OF THE INSIDE AND THE OUTSIDE AGAIN. THE ANDROGYNY OF THE SIXTIES AND SEVENTIES HAS BEEN TAKEN AWAY, AND GENDER-IDENTIFICATION HAS TAKEN OVER.

LG: I guess so. And in that I might just have to be old-fashioned.

JR: DO YOU REMEMBER THE FIRST CHARACTER YOU CREATED?

LG: Apart from being given a script. . . . It wasn't exactly a character, but the first time I ever felt the Great Surge was after two weeks of doing almost nothing in Paul Thompson's rehearsals (and I can't stand to do nothing). We didn't know what the hell we were doing. As far as we were concerned, nothing was happening. Long silences.

And then, we went to a rehearsal with the "old guys" (that's an awful way to say with *The West Show* people). Layne Coleman and I went, and we just didn't know what it could be that these people did. What were they doing? And there they were: Miles Potter, David Fox, Eric Peterson, Janet Amos, Anne Anglin, Ted Johns. . . .

I just get shivers when I think of that rehearsal. And Connie Kaldor as well. She was the new guy in there; there was always one.

And we sat there watching them and laughed, and practically cried, and saw this amazing event go on. And we just kind of sat there, stunned, thinking, "Is this what this is supposed to be like?" They were just amazing. It never stopped; they just kept on going for four hours. And meanwhile, they were trying to pretend that nothing was happening.

So our group goes back into rehearsals for our show (Thompson was directing two shows at the same time: *The West Show*, and this young company, Twenty-Fifth Street House.) And he was doing our rehearsals in the evening. And he would fall asleep, lying there across these three chairs. He'd actually fall asleep during our improvs! It was just dire. We just all felt like worthless beings.

And then one night, he set up a scene with Layne and Andy Tahn going to a drive-in. He kept having us *be* things that we didn't know how to be. How do you *be* things? Layne and Andy were supposed to be two guys going out drinking beer (before Doug and Bob MacKenzie!) and they were supposed to go to a drive-in movie. And Thompson said to me, "You be the movie."

And it was like I went blind, and then I jumped up and did *Jaws*. The entire movie: the shark, Robert Shaw showing his scars, the drowning, the boat, the ending with the paddling. *The whole thing*. I didn't see or hear anything but me. Until I heard laughter. And then I looked up, and they'd given up the whole idea of the car at the drive-in because I wouldn't shut up! Apparently, they had tried to turn me off, they had driven away. I didn't hear anything, I didn't see anything. Zero sensitivity!

And after that, I started doing these bizarre riffs in rehearsal. I was able to do whole scenes, and I wrote this weird poem. I realized that I didn't have to be normal to do this. As a matter of fact, all I had to do is entertain all my bizarre thoughts, and to go with them. It's when I get away from the sense that I have to fit into something that I can work. The idea of compartments is wrong for me because I feel I always have to come in from the underground, the side door, the kitchen. I used to think that I wasn't a real actor because I'd gotten kicked out of National Theatre School. Well, that wasn't valid at all.

JR: DO YOU HAVE ANY OTHER EXTRAORDINARY MEMORIES OF MOMENTS THAT DID SOMETHING TO YOU, OR THAT SHOWED YOU SOMETHING, THAT BROUGHT YOU TO TRUTH?

LG: There have been so many things that informed me. Like being in Jamaica, and watching the guy that the character of Vic in *O.D. on Paradise* is based on be carried in from the water, and having him lie there on a bier, with us all eating dinner on the beach around him, and more and more people gradually realizing that he was dead. That's the sort of moment you recognize. And if you have the inclination at all, those are moments you have to write about.

In writing *Jessica*, there were many moments like that. I don't know what kind of moment I'm actually speaking about but there's sort of a flash, or a feeling that you get. And you know that whatever you do, if you're any kind of artist, it's going to work.

Actually, I would say that all of *Jessica* was like that for me. And it came out so badly at times, that I'd think, "What am I talking about?" But all that had to come out.

The improvisational rehearsal period was horrendous. There was once a time when Maria and Paul suggested that I do the Wolverine; I think I was appearing too soft to have done the things the character had done. And Maria "gave" me something. (She was always giving me things. When she talks about giving you things, she's really speaking about going inside you and planting images inside you. That's why I say that in terms of the collaboration, Maria is the farmer.). She really talked about the character of the Wolverine. She spoke of the unbelievable viciousness, the memory. If a Wolverine feels that a trapper has done something to him or gotten at his kill in any way, the Wolverine can remember that trapper for ten, even fifteen years, and continually go back and find that trapper's trap line, and piss on all the traps and ruin them, and then maybe go back and find the trapper's cabin and devastate it. A bear will back down from a wolverine.

I was really terrified of these images being fed in. Not just the images, but the feelings. I thought about it for a few days, and Paul would keep coming up to me, and he'd say, "Is it time to do the Wolverine?" I figured that Maria was asking him and he just assumed that as usual, I'd just jump into it. But I kept saying, "No."

And I'd go home and I'd put out my stuff: a candle, a stone or something. Some sage maybe. And I'd meditate about it and get prepared. And the next day he'd say, "Do you want to do the Wolverine?" and I'd say, "No, not yet."

And I think Paul actually gave up. So the next day, it was more of a request than a typical Thompson demand, "Are you ready to do the Wolverine?" And I just said "Yes."

It was one of those times where it had built up, and I wanted to do it so badly, I wanted to show that side of myself, and of her, of whomever. I wanted to do it so badly, and it was just a matter of time, of letting go.

It was all from the dark side: it was jealousy, and rage, and desire for revenge against petty things. I didn't know who did them or when, but I still carried them inside me. It was desire to kill. It was violence. And I just went with all of them. Unconsciously.

I finished, and stood up. And I remember . . . I looked up, and the sun was coming through window and I felt released and cleansed.

Then I looked at the people watching: dead, white faces. Absolute silence.

And I expected something. Some reaction. You don't get a lot of praise at a Thompson rehearsal, that's not what it's about, but you know if he thinks you've done good work or not. Nothing. No reaction.

And I thought, "Hey, amazing Wolverine!" And then Maria said, "I'm sorry, I should have been doing the circle at the beginning and end of each rehearsal. Let's do one right now." And I felt, (and this is partly because of the relationship between Maria and me) that I had to distinguish, from then on, when the moment is spiritual with its own dangers, or psychological with its own dangers, or when I'm just hoofing it, when it's improvisation. And that line was what we crossed constantly in writing *Jessica*. And because these were spiritual matters that we were dramatizing, I had to discover where the line was between theatre and ritual. These lines were constantly being crossed, and it was like fire every time we did it. I was ravenous and Maria felt that.

I would just take whatever the idea was and go with it, improvise. And how little I knew about any of this material didn't matter to me then. I couldn't believe anyone was pissed off; I didn't understand. I understand now. I understand that there is danger in playing with spiritual matters and I've experienced that danger to some extent. But I only know how to learn that way: I only know how to jump in knowing absolutely nothing. And see what happens.

I had the tape of that first Wolverine improvisation and I listened to it when I got back to Toronto, and it scared the shit out of me: it was a voice I had never heard.

And then I lost the tape. The Wolverine material gets lost continually. The computer will go down. I've had to have the transcripts done twice.

JR: LET'S TALK ABOUT *MAGGIE AND PIERRE* FOR A BIT. THERE'S DEFINITELY A LINE THROUGH YOUR CAREER THAT DIVIDES THE PRE-*MAGGIE-AND-PIERRE* AND POST-*MAGGIE-AND-PIERRE* PERIODS. WHAT WERE SOME OF THE EFFECTS: POSITIVE AND NEGATIVE?

LG: I think responsibility was the hardest effect of all for me to accept. There's this unconscious voice that pipes up, the one that shies away from reaping what's harvested. Sometimes I'm like a child: I think I can start a project and then not have to carry it through to the end. It was during the carrying through part of

Maggie and Pierre where I realized that I had made a pact with the Devil!

When I had talked to Paul Thompson in our initial discussions we agreed that if the play was a success then I was committed to performing it for two years. And I laughed, and agreed. I never thought of it working. I had no sense of what that could mean. I was used to a situation where you created the plays, you did them, they ran full run, you did them some place else. . . . But the idea of being on that particular roller-coaster by myself (as opposed to with the gang at the circus), well, that just never occurred to me as a possibility.

And not only did *Maggie and Pierre* turn me into a writer, it turned me into a writer that had notes ahead of time, who researched on my own. I knew what I was going to do when I went in to a rehearsal. I knew that I wanted the play to have only three characters. I knew that I didn't want to do a one-person show with a lot of characters, and that, in my mind, I wanted it to be like a "real play." I had a hunger for it to be a piece very different from other one-person shows that I had seen, those with either single performers doing one character, directly addressing the audience, or nine million characters, and the whole fun of the piece is surprising the audience with how many different characters you can do.

With *Maggie and Pierre*, I wanted a plot, I wanted scenes that connected, and I wanted to avoid a narrator. I did end up with a sort of narrator, Henry, but that's okay. I remember saying to Paul, "I want a real set, I want real costumes, and I want it to be pretty. I'm tired of being on ugly sets. No more brown and grey." And Paul agreed! And then I was stuck with "pretty," which I wasn't really prepared for at all. It was incredible, having the power to say, "I want this, I want that" (not that there was lots of money, but whatever there was, I could spend) and getting it!

And I got real costumes. We'd never had designed costumes before: I was always going to the Sally Ann and "getting" costumes. And because I got costumes, I got costume changes!

And then, success. And it was, "Okay kid, it worked," and that meant responsibility. And the run was longer than two years: it was two and a half years, and then the video.

I have the same extraordinary feelings with *Jessica*, with all my writing projects. There is a part of me that doesn't want the responsibility. I want to start the ball rolling and I want to get everybody excited, *I* want to get excited. And then I think, "Okay, to write a play, jamming, thinking about it, well, for *Maggie and Pierre* that took a good year-and-a-half." I just want to get out there and do the plays. . . . And then there's the production, which you have to be involved in as the writer. At the same time, if you want to keep acting, then you have to take on other projects. The juggling that I do with my time and my energies is outrageous. That's the responsibility of following through. I hated it then and I hate it now.

There I am, these days, in an attic by myself, picking out those commas and editing and structuring. I used to do the structuring automatically, on my feet. I would jam through the whole play, sometimes in an afternoon. That was a Thompson technique: you get all the material and you just jam it through. Well, that takes an afternoon! This takes. . . .

I remember when we were in Vancouver performing at the Vancouver East Cultural Centre, and I was completely exhausted. It wasn't just the performing that exhausted me (though Vancouver was the end of the first long cross-Canada tour), it was also the fact that I'd gone from the research to the writing to the production with virtually no time off. And it seemed as if the interviews were all scheduled at nine o'clock in the morning. It often took me till three AM to get to sleep, and though I would try to sleep in the afternoon, I couldn't.

I was so tired, and I started thinking: I'm in jail. I'm in jail, and I'm being made to do this thing, and this is punishment. And I thought, I'll get on a plane; I've got enough money, so I'll get on a plane and I'll just go. I really did begin to think like that: it was madness, it was like being trapped.

Then one night, I started to cry in the second act (and that was okay because the second act was heavy and crying made sense). The next night, I started to cry in the first act and at the intermission I went down to my dressing room and I looked at myself in the mirror, and I said, "You can do this technically. You know what the moves are. You have to absent yourself. You can't perform this show on the raw, gut level that you've been using."

And it was amazing: I went out there in the second act and people didn't even seem to notice a difference. Maybe there was no difference. But I learned from that experience. I still play back and forth with that particular duality: with needing to work and pull it through with all my energy, and then burning out and not being able to do it except by stepping away a bit.

I had to remember why I had started the project in the first place. I had wanted to play to these people, the audience. I had wanted them to see this play, to hear what I had to say. And I'd done it: I'd made people want to see the play. And now I had to fulfil my responsibility to them.

It's not just the acting energy that drains me, it's the sense of being alone. I like gangs, I like the group, I like touring. It was only because of *Maggie and Pierre* and learning from being alone that I could write *O.D. on Paradise* and *Jessica*. And that I can write now.

Because I didn't like that aloneness, but I accepted that it was a necessary part of what I wanted to do.

Some people have always wanted to be writers, and always knew that writing was part of who and what they were. Not I. I always had flashes of mad things, and all of a sudden I would write something. But that isn't that "thing" that I am still teaching myself to do, the "thing" that's so hard. It's partly discipline, and it's partly technique, and it's partly, I think, a very serious responsibility to the creative idea and its actualization.

But I'm like a dog with a bone about *Jessica*. *Jessica* could have died a million times. And now what I'm working on is losing the gritted teeth about the responsibility. I have to find the fun in it.

JR: WHAT'S FIRST IN YOUR HEART NOW? ACTING OR WRITING?

LG: Writing. There's no question. I've done almost everything I could to kill my acting career! My poor agent. I'll phone him up, and I'll say, "Don't send me on any auditions, I'm writing!" I haven't given the attention or spent the time on my acting career that I should have: I'm just lucky that CBC still calls me and I'm really happy to be able to get out and do television and film.

I'm hoping to act in my film version of Atwood's *Life before Man*. I want to try and start to weave acting and writing back together and see where that leads me.

But there's no question, when I'm looking out at the ocean, and all the stars are above, I start thinking of writing a new show, of acting. I think of doing another one-person show (I can't believe I said that out loud). I think of directing a collective, and I think of all the writing projects that I still want to do.

2. Playwright Wendy Lill

Joseph Robichaud

Wendy Lill was born in Vancouver in 1950 and currently resides in Dartmouth, Nova Scotia. Originally a freelance journalist and broadcaster, she has written for radio and film, including the ACTRA-award-winning radio documentary *Who Is Georges Forest?* (1981). She was nominated for the 1987 Governor General's Award for Drama for *The Occupation of Heather Rose*, which has been translated into Danish and produced at Copenhagen's Tukat Teatret.

Sometimes, during the winter, my fantasies weren't much different than my reality. I'd see a raven or I'd dream a raven . . . and each evoked the same aloneness, the same gaping separateness.

Heather Rose in *The Occupation of Heather Rose*

Well, I am a dreamer! And I believe there are changes coming. Wonderful changes . . . that will allow everyone to live in freedom. Those days are coming but we have to fight for them.

Francis Beynon in *The Fighting Days*

Produced and Published plays:

The Fighting Days. Vancouver: Talonbooks, 1985.

The Occupation of Heather Rose. In *NeWest Plays by Women*, Edmonton: NeWest, 1987.

My Memories of You. Toronto: Summerhill, 1989.

Produced plays:

On the Line. Premiere at Agassiz Productions, Winnipeg, Manitoba, 1982.

Sisters. Premiere at Ships Company Theatre, Parrsboro, Nova Scotia, 1989.

Wendy Lill Interview

by Judith Rudakoff

JR: YOU WERE BORN IN VANCOUVER, GREW UP IN ONTARIO, AND HAVE LIVED AND WORKED IN WINNIPEG AND IN THE MARITIMES. HOW HAS THIS INFLUENCED YOUR WORK?

WL: I met my husband, Richard Starr, in Winnipeg. He was a transplanted Maritimer, nostalgic for home. Moving around, never getting too comfortable and using the perspective of the Outsider seemed to me at that time to be a very useful state in terms of my work, so I agreed to move East.

We had a couple of lonely and frustrating years trying to fit in and also make a living, and I found myself continuing to do work for theatres in the West as well as for the CBC and the National Film Board.

During those years, we also had two children: I wrote *The Occupation of Heather Rose* while pregnant with Samuel and *Memories of You* while pregnant with Joseph. There was quite a wonderful urgency with *The Occupation of Heather Rose* that came with the creative burst of energy of a first pregnancy. I must admit that the second time around that energy was a lot harder to call up. But the new emotions which I now had inside because of mothering Sam (and they ran the gamut from rage to helplessness to giddy delight . . .) were essential to my understanding of *Memories of You*. I wanted to examine the incredible state of being a mother and a lover and a writer and I felt pretty much in the middle of it all during the process.

I would like to do more thinking and writing about women in their various stages of life. It is all so incredibly profound in the grand scheme of things: what women endure and uphold and support. I don't think I ever understood that fully until I became a mother. Not only did I become a mother, but I became the mother of a mentally handicapped child. And that has changed the world for me forever.

Although I have always written and been committed to telling the stories of people who are vulnerable or at risk, I suddenly found myself committed on a personal level to another person with built-in problems (as opposed to the problems we begin to program into children from the day they are born). And as a direct result of that commitment, I am no longer an Outsider. Children make that impossible. I am attached. Engaged.

I've never worked in Vancouver, but there's a great difference between working in the Maritimes and in Winnipeg, the prairies. It's an interesting phenomenon. The people in Winnipeg take their culture extremely seriously: they're eager to mythologize their stories, to embellish them and even to analyze them. The Winnipeg Strike was a constant topic of interest when I lived there. People were always trying to get films or stories or plays written about it. Westerners seem to be quite proud of their history and are quite willing to discuss it openly.

In the East, I find, as with everything else, a sense of reticence. It's not insecurity, because there's certainly a great deal of pride here: people who are here want to be here. It's more a feeling that's been drummed into Easterners for decades that historically "East is Least" and that their stories aren't as interesting as those from the West. At least not to anyone who isn't an Easterner.

JR: HAVE YOU TOLD ANY OF THOSE EASTERN STORIES YET?

WL: Yes, in my most recent play, *Sisters*. The piece was commissioned by the Ships Company in Parrsboro, Nova Scotia. They wanted a play about the native residential schools at Subencadie. I'm quite hard on my plays, especially when I see them in production and I think that this production, directed by Mary Vingoe, is the one I'm most pleased with. Mary totally understood the piece and she took it further then I could ever have explained it.

The plot layering in itself is complex. The primary character is a young girl who ends up being a nun and working in a residential school for natives. She becomes disillusioned by what she sees and experiences and finally, she burns down the school.

I had a lot of difficulty writing this play. The story is so complex that I felt it called for a structure that wasn't straight ahead or linear. I move the action forwards and backwards in time from the young girl's experiences up to the time of the play's present action.

I also had a crisis of confidence about being able to write about nuns and that level of belief and faith. I'm just not that comfortable with it.

JR: IS THE SOURCE FOR THE PLOT A REAL PERSON OR A REAL EVENT?

WL: Well, my story is based on my research about the school and on what natives have told me about their experiences in residential schools across the country. They're very unfortunate places.

I was asked by the Ships Company to write a play that would go past the stereotype of the "nasty nun" and the victimized Indian children. I wanted to get past those images, get underneath them.

JR: WHAT DO YOU DEAL WITH THAT GETS UNDERNEATH THE STEREOTYPES?

WL: I'm trying to illustrate that the nuns in the residential schools were suffering from their own level of oppression. They were certainly oppressed by the Catholic church: they were the workhorses! They were doing the bidding of the government too. They were stultified by the set of rules imposed upon them. They had to turn away from the compassion that they knew was needed by those kids in the schools.

I hold a feminist position on nuns. After Vatican Two, the doors were opened for nuns: the male power structure allowed them to relax their rigid rules. They were permitted to stop wearing the long habits. They could let air swish around their necks. Around their legs. They could take back their names. They could start acting human again. Now, I'm not Catholic and I'm not sure why or where Vatican Two originated except for the fact that obviously the Church recognized that it had to become more relevant.

In the same way, the federal government closure of all those schools in the sixties wasn't necessarily motivated by any great recognition that it was time to do the "right" and decent thing. I don't think anyone "saw the light": there wasn't any great centre of good operating. I think it was simply an almost arbitrary useful decision on the part of the powers that be.

JR: SO YOU'RE WRITING AGAIN ABOUT A CLOISTERED PERSON WHO FINDS HERSELF IN A POSITION WHERE SHE IS EMPOWERED TO ACT OR IS STILL LIMITED AND TRYING TO ACT REGARDLESS, AND IS MOVED, ULTIMATELY, TO LOOK AT HERSELF AND SAY, "WHAT ABOUT ME?"

WL: Yes, that's right. Now where else have I done that?

JR: IN ALL OF YOUR PLAYS!

WL: In all of them . . . I guess it's an ongoing rant of mine.

JR: AN ONGOING THEME, IN ANY EVENT. HAVE ALL YOUR PLAYS BEEN AS DIFFICULT TO WRITE AS *SISTERS*?

WL: No. *Memories of You* was extremely easy. It was initially hard to figure out what the actual story was going to be, and how I was going to tell it. But once I had thrashed it out, it took me about three months to write the play.

I'm not even sure why that was. I had no problem creating and writing the character of Rose, the daughter. I had spent so much time poring over the Elizabeth Smart material that I ended up feeling very strongly about the mother/lover conflict that Elizabeth felt. In a sense, at the time I was researching and writing I was living that conflict: I already had one small child and was pregnant with my second. I simply couldn't have written that play without having had children. I'm sure of that.

Oh, I suppose I could have written it (after all, I've never been a nun!) but it just wouldn't have meant as much to me.

JR: YOUR STYLE HAS UNDERGONE MANY CHANGES SINCE YOUR FIRST PLAY, *ON THE LINE.* YOU'VE MOVED FROM REALISM TO MONO-DRAMA (*HEATHER ROSE*) TO REALISM INTERSPERSED WITH POCKETS OF THEATRICALITY (*THE FIGHTING DAYS*) TO TIME SHIFTING AND MEMORY PLAY (*MEMORIES OF YOU*). IS THIS A NATURAL PROGRES-SION OR IS IT SIMPLY THAT THE NATURE OF THE MATERIAL IMPLIES A CERTAIN STYLE TO YOU?

WL: I think the style comes organically out of the material.

JR: IS THE EAST-WEST DIFFERENCE IN ATTITUDE REFLECTED IN THE AUDIENCES YOU'VE ENCOUNTERED?

WL: I don't know. *Sisters* is the first production I had in the East and audiences seem delighted by it. Critics have loved it. It's so gratifying to feel like you're coming home and people are supporting you, your work.

JR: SO HERE YOU ARE, WITH A HIT AT THE END OF THE SUM-MER. THE SEASONS ACROSS THE COUNTRY ARE ALREADY SET FOR 1989-90. THERE'S NOT MUCH CHANCE OF THEATRE-GOERS SEEING *SISTERS* MUCH BEFORE THE 1990-91 SEASON. DO YOU THINK PRINTED PLAY-TEXTS ARE ONE WAY OF MAKING YOUR WORK KNOWN COAST TO COAST, QUICKLY?

WL: I don't know. It's certainly nice, when people call me up to request a copy of one of my scripts, to be able to say, "Well, it's published and you can buy it," instead of printing a copy each time there's a request.

But do you know what my royalties are for, say, *The Fighting Days* in any given year? About twenty dollars.

I certainly love reading play scripts. In fact, when I was work-ing on *Memories of You*, one script I read and re-read was Sharon Pollock's *Doc.* I did that for several reasons. I was living in New Brunswick at the time and I saw the play at Theatre New Bruns-wick in Fredericton. It was wonderful for me to see it in the city where Sharon's from and to be able to contemplate all the different layers. I was consciously looking for a style for my piece, for a way to get my story across and this was one of the pieces, stylisti-cally, that influenced me in its use of time-shifting and fluidity.

And Sharon is going to be directing *Memories of You* next season in a co-production of Theatre New Brunswick and Ottawa's National Arts Centre!

JR: ARE THERE ANY DIRECTORS WHO HAVE BEEN PARTICULARLY IMPORTANT TO THE DEVELOPMENT OF YOUR WORK?

WL: There are definitely people out there, in this business, who can take the words, my words, and move them further. Mary Vingoe has been one of those people. And Kim McCaw at Prairie Theatre Exchange. When I moved east, I didn't want to leave him! I was quite nervous about working with another director.

JR: YOU'VE WON AN ACTRA AWARD FOR A RADIO PLAY AND YOU'VE ADAPTED *THE FIGHTING DAYS* FOR TELEVISION. IN ADDITION, YOU HAVE A WIDE RANGE OF RADIO DOCUMENTARY CREDITS. IS IT DIFFERENT FOR YOU WHEN YOU WRITE FOR THAT INVISIBLE, ANONYMOUS AUDIENCE?

WL: In terms of radio, I do think about those people who are out there listening. But, actually . . . I just think of myself. I never think of anybody else when I'm writing. Because, when I'm writing, that's all I really can think about. I ask myself, "Would *I* find this interesting?" and obviously I do find the pieces I write interesting. If I find myself on the wrong track, if I see it's getting boring or trite, then I get outraged and change it. It doesn't take long to see when or if that's happening.

Where I fall apart or get muddled is when I bring in too many elements. But I don't think I ever fall into the trap of writing superficial material.

In *Sisters* the loose ends were trimmed and I was kept on track by Mary Vingoe and by the cast.

JR: WHAT ABOUT *ON THE LINE*?

WL: That's a good example. It's about a garment workers' strike, and I clearly didn't care at all about the Bosses. My play was a rhetorical tract. Now I have no trouble with that, *per se* but I know that I lost a lot of audience members because I didn't give any credence to the other side of the story, management.

JR: NEITHER DID DAVID FENNARIO IN HIS FIRST PLAY, *ON THE JOB*.

WL: Yes. You have to learn from that first play, when people walk up to you and say, "Well, what about the other side?" My father, for example, who has always been extremely supportive of my work, wasn't as affected by *On the Line* as say, *The Fighting Days*. He's a conservative man and he needed the conservative elements of the play fleshed out, given their due. The characters I had written in a two-dimensional way, "the other side," had to have heart too. I've learned that that tender side has to be there.

JR: WHEN YOU GO BACK TO ONE OF YOUR PLAYS, IS YOUR IMPULSE TO CHANGE, TO REVISE? OR ARE YOU COMPLETELY SATISFIED WITH THEM AS THEY ARE?

WL: There was a reading here in Nova Scotia recently of parts of *The Fighting Days* and I found it oddly out of context. Many of Francis Beynon's speeches seemed . . . "speechy." Now in that particular reading, most of Francis' speeches were hauled out and they cut out a lot of the parts that created the balance.

It did cross my mind that what I'm calling "speechy" is more acceptable in the West. . . .

The Fighting Days is being produced this year in Regina at the Globe Theatre and I'd like to see it, particularly after the experience of the reading in the East. I mean, Francis almost seemed to me to be a windbag and I wonder now if she was. Is. . . .

I was watching the audience during the reading, and the material was just so foreign to them. Those poignant letters in the play from Prairie women who sat out there for ten years by themselves, having one baby after another and watching the dust collect on their noses is not a part of the Eastern Canadian experience. The experience in the East is equally rugged, but it's filled with many different images. And I just don't know if the Prairie images caught fire in their hearts.

JR: IS THERE ANYONE ELSE IN THEATRE WHO HAS INFLUENCED YOUR WORK?

WL: Caryl Churchill. I like the way in which she works collectively with a group and then takes the material and shapes it into a whole idea. That appeals to me.

I might be on the verge of doing that myself. I've been asked to join a project that's in process about prostitution. It involves Mary Vingoe, Nikki Lipman, Marsha Coffey and Carol Sinclair and they've asked me to be the writer. They've been working for quite a while and they've kind of paralysed themselves with the wealth of material they've found and created. I don't want to be the fifth person who gets paralysed.

JR: HOW WILL THE PIECE YOU'RE CONSIDERING WORKING ON ABOUT PROSTITUTES SHED LIGHT ON THE STEREOTYPE?

WL: My early thoughts on it are leading me to discover what the stereotypes are, and then I'll examine the types and take them in different and unexpected directions.

I don't believe the concept that prostitutes are really strong and in control, so I think I'll be working to dispel that myth.

I'll start by reviewing the literature and what's available to me and use that as my beginning point. That's always where I begin. With *Sisters* and the nuns, with *The Fighting Days* and the suffragettes in Western Canada, with what are we being told about them and with what are we being soothed to sleep at night. And then I try to really shake people up. And then re-arrange the material and try to shape it in new ways, so it's perceived in new ways. Ways that I feel are *true*, of course, not just for the hell of it. I find something that I believe and then I put it together in an interesting way that will make people look at it.

JR: WHAT IS YOUR METHOD OF RESEARCH?

WL: With *The Fighting Days*, I was commissioned to write a play about "Women in Manitoba History"! Can you believe it? I was so new at theatre, that I thought that was great. And I marched off and started doing all this reading about feminists and I began to think I had to do a revue: all these women marching through history, across the stage. That's where I was in terms of style at the time. But I didn't really want to do that.

And then I came upon this person, Francis Beynon. In my efforts to impose order, I literally *found* this person, this character, who turned lights on for me. The reading I'd been doing was extremely boring to me, and I couldn't conceive of how boring it was going to be for an audience after I'd regurgitated it. And then I found this character who really fired me up.

I knew instinctively that when I found a character who really fired me up, then that was where the piece had to go, it had to follow her.

And I knew immediately, as soon as I'd read a short piece by Ramsay Cook, an academic, called "Francis Beynon and the Rise of Christian Reformism." It was pivotal for me: it gave me a context for the character and I understood her in her own time and as she relates to issues today. I've credited Ramsay Cook throughout the history of the play being written and produced for helping me write the piece. I wrote to him too, and thanked him profusely for the lucidity he brought to that topic.

The Fighting Days was a play that could just as easily have turned into an uncritical celebration of the great old dolls in the Canadian suffragette movement if I hadn't had a certain built-in suspicion of sacred cows.

JR: WHAT'S THE DIFFERENCE FOR YOU BETWEEN WRITING DOCU-MENTARIES AND WRITING DRAMATIZED VERSIONS OF HISTORY? CON-TEXT?

WL: Well, in documentary writing you still have to have an idea that . . .

JR: KICK-STARTS YOU?

WL: Yes. Very much so. And an image. It's harder to write a documentary. You're often frustrated by the reality of it and it rarely meets your needs. So many documentary writers move to fiction. They couldn't say what they wanted in documentaries.

JR: WHEN YOU MADE THAT MOVE, WHY DID YOU CHOOSE THEATRE AS OPPOSED TO, SAY, SHORT-STORY WRITING?

WL: I've never considered short-story writing and I've never thought of writing books. And I was doing extensive radio writing when I began writing theatre pieces. I would write half-hour or hour-long stories, historical pieces for Manitoba School Broadcasts on the CBC and then the garment-worker strike idea came along. I tried to sell the CBC on the piece, but they weren't interested because it wasn't radiophonic enough! The piece was filled with immigrant characters who couldn't speak English very well and it just didn't make for good radio. People lose interest when they can't understand what they're hearing.

There were also problems when I tried to sell the idea to CBC as a radio drama: for example, they thought there weren't any "immigrant actors" in Winnipeg who could play the roles!

I ended up working with a gutsy little theatre company called Agassiz Theatre, who produced *On the Line.* I spent lots of time talking to the women on that picket line and in their kitchens. And they were often hard to understand and the tapes were hard to hear, but finally I did understand. And we found the immigrant actors, who were non-professional. And it all worked.

JR: YOUR CENTRAL CHARACTERS SUFFER GREAT ANGUISH AS A RESULT OF THEIR DARING. THEY SEEM TO BE IDEALISTS IN AN IMPERFECT REALITY WHO WON'T GIVE UP THEIR GOALS. ELIZABETH SMART SAYS, "I'VE DONE IT TO MYSELF. I WAS NO VICTIM. I WAS AN EXPLORER."

WL: In a sense, even though Elizabeth says that, it's both true and untrue. She is a victim of a state of being, yet she makes choices, she acts and decides what to do. At the same time, I don't know how much I believe in free choice. I think that people do make individual choices, but always influenced by a combination of emotions and personal characteristics that make them head unerringly towards things.

The question of choice is certainly an important one. And all the plays I write are about choice. My characters are all faced with that fork in the road: they have to make a choice and they do choose one direction. And usually, horrendous events befall them as a result. But I don't know what alternatives there are to making those choices.

JR: DO YOU THINK THAT ONCE A PATH IS CHOSEN, ONE CAN GO BACK?

WL: No. I don't think so.

JR: FORWARD IS A POSITIVE DIRECTION, I SUPPOSE, NO MATTER WHAT THE REPERCUSSIONS ARE.

WL: Any direction that you take changes you. You take an action and then the world reacts in a certain way because of the action that you've taken. People respond to you because of what you've done.

JR: SO RATHER THAN CALL THESE PROTAGONISTS VICTIMS, YOU COULD CALL THEM CHOICE-MAKERS, CHANCE-TAKERS, EVEN SUF-FERERS. THEY ARE EITHER SURVIVORS OR NOT. PARTS OF THEM BREAK UP, DISINTEGRATE, AND AS A RESULT THEY CAN GAIN A NEW PERSPECTIVE AND STRENGTH. HEATHER ROSE, IN *THE OCCUPATION OF HEATHER ROSE*; IS THAT WHAT HAPPENS?

WL: I think it's possible that Heather Rose gets stronger after her experiences in the North. She did come out of it. Her experiences were pivotal to her future. What she did to the native people is another issue!

There's this cycle of white helpers going through the North, having personal revelations but also having a somewhat sinister cumulative effect on native culture.

JR: YOU ARE CLEARLY VERY CONCERNED ABOUT THE NATIVE CULTURE AND THE NORTH. WHEN DID THIS INTEREST BEGIN?

WL: I was living in Toronto and I wanted to get away. I moved north and had a job there as a mental health consultant. That was a silly job for me because I had no experience and I wasn't that type of person. But I did it for six months, basically trying to ascertain whether a Canadian Mental Health Association would be useful in Northern Ontario. Well, that's sort of like saying, "Would an aspirin be helpful in the middle of Bangladesh?"

I concluded that there were already forty-four associations in Kenora trying to work with alcoholics and violence, none of them making much of a dent or doing much good in terms of the basic socio-economic problems. I didn't leave the organization in much glory.

I didn't actually work with natives then. After I left the Canadian Mental Health Association, I began doing work for a native newspaper, flying around to reserves and doing little stories about sawmills and whatever. I spent a lot of time sleeping on floors in nursing stations, and I was surprised at how much people wanted to talk about what they were doing.

I started writing seriously when I lived in Northern Ontario at the age of twenty-six. It was the first time I'd witnessed and experienced events which moved me so deeply that I needed to examine them carefully for myself *and* for others. I began writing a journal there which later became *The Occupation of Heather Rose*.

I had a friend who was a geologist, who was up in one of the reserves, and every week he'd write me reams of material about how he was feeling and where he belonged and trying to understand it all.

And I became very interested in the concept of people feeling like outsiders. It certainly struck a chord, because I felt that way, like an outsider.

JR: WHAT ABOUT THE IMAGE, IN *THE OCCUPATION OF HEATHER ROSE*, OF THE RAVEN, AND THE CHARACTER OF NAOMI AS THE RAVEN, THE TRICKSTER?

WL: It's very important. The trickster, laughing at the outsider, is mocking her efforts.

JR: IN THE PUBLISHED VERSION OF THE PLAY, NAOMI DIES. HOW DO YOU RECONCILE THAT WITH THE IMAGE OF THE TRICKSTER GETTING THE "LAST LAUGH" AND SURVIVING?

WL: I did another version of the play and Naomi the Raven doesn't die at the end. I'd copped out with that ending. I'd taken the spotlight off Heather Rose, who was the main character and placed it on the native character. The last image you were left with was a native person self-destructing. It was vital to keep the spotlight on Heather Rose at the end, because it's she who's self-destructing. She's the one who falls apart. She's the one who spirals down inside herself, not Naomi.

The other difference is that there's no "coming out," Heather Rose isn't talking in hindsight. She's sitting in her nursing station with its four white walls and the old native woman is right outside the door, chanting. She is, literally, being occupied. It's simply much stronger. I just didn't get it out the first time.

The Occupation of Heather Rose was a very important story for me to tell. I don't know how people hear it, what they hear when they see the play. I don't know whether they see it as totally dark or whether they understand that Heather's actually gone on a journey that's essential to everyone. It's a journey that has to happen.

JR: LIKE A VISION QUEST?

WL: Yes. There aren't many opportunities for it to happen. Heather Rose threw herself away. She went up North and she just threw herself away and came back in pieces. But she could then put those pieces back together. Most people never bother.

It's certainly the same situation with *Memories of You*. Elizabeth also threw herself away and came back in pieces. But that's marvellous. Elizabeth wasn't a hopeless character at all.

JR: WHAT'S HER GREATEST STRENGTH?

WL: Oh, her passion. Definitely her passion. She also had a great deal of courage and strength. To be passionate you *have* to have a great deal of both.

JR: AND YOU HAVE TO BE AN INDIVIDUAL.

WL: I spoke with her brother at length. And he told me that Elizabeth was a scientist of human emotions. And that she would always put herself in situations which could bring about heightened human emotions. She would put together strange people, simply to make a new potion and see what would come about and then she would study the effects. That's what writers and theatre people do: she did it, literally, in her life too.

JR: WHAT KIND OF A MOTHER DO YOU THINK SHE WAS?

WL: She probably had a terrible time. It sounds like she was very, very torn between George and her children. And he was extremely needy. As were her four children.

JR: AND THROUGHOUT ALL HER DIFFICULTIES, SHE SEEMED TO MAINTAIN A PIECE OF HERSELF.

WL: No, she didn't lose herself. But she did disappear (as a writer) for twenty years. . . .
She was an editor in London, but it wasn't her own personal writing.

JR: WHAT'S MORE IMPORTANT TO YOUR PROTAGONISTS, FREEDOM OR IDEALS?

WL: For Francis Beynon, the ideal was freedom and she was totally singular about that. It never varied. That was the one truth through which she distilled all else.
People like that are often tedious. They are extremely important and they're like beacons. But even so, if Francis were alive today, she'd likely be one of the women at Greenham Common. People would've turned off the television and thought, "Well, that's a boring bunch of broads. . . ."
So the challenge was to put Francis into a context that an audience could understand: children, family loyalties, career aspirations, love affairs. It sort of sounds like the ingredients in a soup. But as with soup, there are a limited number of ingredients available and it all has to do with what you do with them.

3. Playwright Banuta Rubess

Michael Cooper

Born in Toronto in 1956, Ms. Rubess won a Rhodes Scholarship to Oxford in 1978, where she completed a doctorate in history. In 1982 she co-founded the 1982 Theatre Company, which was based in London, England, and in the 1980s she became a major force in the feminist theatre movement in Toronto, where she currently resides.

I didn't want to talk to anyone. Then the interviews started and they offered me the cover of Stern *magazine. I thought, it's the least I can do for Anna. I thought, I want the whole world to know about this.*

Marianne 3 in *This is for you, Anna*

. . . will you put that thing DOWN
lady, what the heck
I live the life that Jack Kerouac imagines he lived
heck
it's a drag to be an artist in this day and age but
we shrug as we look at our TV dinners and

Jekyll in *Boom, Baby, Boom!*

Produced and published plays:

Heroica (in Latvian). Place des Arts, Montreal: Fourth Latvian Youth Arts Festival, 1979.

Smoke Damage. Toronto: Playwrights Canada, 1985.

This is for you, Anna (collective creation). In *Canadian Theatre Review*, 43 (Summer 1985).

Pope Joan. Toronto: Playwrights Canada, 1986.

Boom, Baby, Boom! In *Canadian Theatre Review*, 58 (Spring 1989).

Tango Lugano (in Latvian). In *Avots*. Riga, Latvia (February-March 1989).

Produced plays:

The Last Latvians (in Latvian). Presented at the Sixth World Latvian Youth Congress, Melbourne, Australia, in 1983.

Thin Ice. Produced by Theatre Direct at high schools throughout Ontario between 1986-89, as well as the Edmonton Fringe Festival, 1988, and for a national tour, 1988-89.

The Last Will and Testament of Lolita (collective creation). Premiered in Toronto at Theatre Passe Muraille on June 2, 1987. Produced by the Humbert Humbert Project (Project) with Nightwood Theatre.

Horror High. Premiered in Toronto at Factory Theatre, 1989. Produced by Theatre Direct.

Bonnie and Clyde Are Dead. Produced by Theatre Smith-Gilmour at the Poor Alex Theatre, Toronto, 1989.

Banuta Rubess Interview
by Rita Much

RM: LET'S START WITH YOUR BACKGROUND. I UNDERSTAND THAT YOUR ROOTS ARE LATVIAN.

BR: My parents originally came from Latvia though they met in Europe. My father was in a D.P. camp in Germany, and my mother was working in a factory in France. They came to Toronto in the fifties so I was born here.

RM: HAVE YOU EVER LIVED IN LATVIA?

BR: No. I have visited several times and I speak the language. Latvian is actually my first language. I didn't speak English until I went to kindergarten. I suppose mine is a very common East European immigrant story.

RM: HOW DO YOU THINK THAT THIS BACKGROUND, WHICH IS RATHER EXOTIC, HAS INFLUENCED YOUR CAREER AS A WRITER?

BR: I think my writing has been influenced, not only by my Latvian background, but also by the six years I spent in Germany as a kid. My point is that my perspective is cross-cultural, international, if you like. When I write I am conscious of many cultures being present, cultures not much represented in this country. I also think my European experience has given me a heightened sense of politics which I might not have if I had grown up here. For one thing, the classics came naturally. Hermann Hesse, for example, was someone who was talked about around the dinner table. His work wasn't something I had to learn later on at university.

RM: CAN YOU DESCRIBE YOUR INVOLVEMENT IN THEATRE IN LATVIA AND IN THE LATVIAN COMMUNITY HERE?

BR: I have worked in the Latvian community, in the diaspora, as you would call it, since I was a teenager as a theatre artist creating pieces that were satirical and very controversial, and which related to the exile experience. Eight years ago I wrote and directed a musical called *Heroica* which is steeped in Latvian mythology. In September of 1979 it premiered in Place des Arts in Montreal. Then in 1980 it played to nine hundred people at Ryerson Theatre in Toronto and it was also performed in New York at the Fashion Institute. It was so controversial that full page ads were taken out in Latvian newspapers saying, "Banuta Rubess destroys the moral fabric of our youth." Of course, the play sold out and I think it immediately put me on the map in Latvian letters because all of a sudden I was such a notorious personality. I don't consider the play dangerous, but it became scandalous because I was touching on sacred cows which I didn't realize were so sacred. It's hard for Canadians or Anglo-Saxons to understand this because there's not a lot that's sacred in our society.

RM: OUR TRADITIONS ARE FEW?

BR: Yes. Doing *Heroica* was a bit like doing *The Last Temptation of Christ* or *Jesus Christ Superstar*. People over a very large segment of society got very upset — not just the fervent religious types.

During my last trip to Latvia this past May (1989) my second Latvian musical, *Tango Lugano*, was performed. In general, it's about lack of communication. It's a story about two famous Latvian writers and revolutionary political figures, Aspazija and Janis Rainis, whose major influence lasted from the 1890s to the 1930s, and who also happened to be a romantic, in fact, married, couple. After the 1905 revolution, they spent fifteen years of exile in Switzerland. The concept of the story is that they secretly returned to Lugano, Switzerland, in 1929, and are still alive today at the approximate age of 124. They have had a huge quarrel, so they've locked themselves in their rooms where they write letters to each other. They each throw letters out the door, thinking that the other is running around all over the house and stubbornly refusing to respond. Then two delegations appear, one from Soviet Latvia, and one from the States, both of which want to create a museum in the house in honour of the writers. Nobody realizes that the poets are alive and when they discover the letters they fail to look at the dates. An ideological quarrel ensues between the older and younger representatives of both countries. The older ones demonstrate their political intransigence and the story takes off from there. Basically, it's a clash of the Soviet Latvians and the Latvians of the diaspora, the North Americanized Latvians.

The piece is controversial on two scores. One, venerable writers are shown shouting and quarrelling with one another in the form of operatic arias, a stylistic device considered outrageous by the older generation of Latvians. Two, *glasnost* has brought to the forefront what might be called the Latvian identity crisis. Latvians are barely fifty percent of Latvia because they have a very low birth rate and there has been such a huge influx, an organized influx, of immigrants from the rest of the Soviet Union to Latvia. As a result, they have this "Last of the Mohican" mentality. They often asked me whether I was coming home. I said to them, "Home, where's home? This isn't home." They are waiting for the one hundred and fifty thousand Latvians who left during the Second World War to return and they don't realize why this is impossible.

The production in May was sold out before we even arrived, six shows in a thousand-seat theatre. We also performed the piece in the countryside, where we had an audience of nine hundred people for one night. The performances were regularly received with standing ovations and the present "head of state," Anatolijs Gorbunovs, attended. It was an incredible audience, one that was always applauding lines and always looking for sub-text and innuendo. Many tears were shed. The reviews were uniformly positive and written with a depth lacking in our Western reviews. At present, I have no future plans for the work, although the technical staff at the Daile Theatre in Riga decided to keep the set in storage, since they hope the piece will be produced again in Latvia.

RM: IS THE CULTURAL LIFE RICHER THERE THAN HERE?

BR: Yes. You can't get tickets to the theatre there. They are always sold out, and what the theatre says has major repercussions. There, poets are politicians, very involved with society. In general, the value of the artist there is very different from the value of the artist here.

RM: ARE YOU TEMPTED TO EMIGRATE?

BR: There is a temptation to live there. At the same time I am very, very glad that I have lived here because of the serious lack of information there.

RM: YOU STARTED WRITING WHEN YOU WERE A YOUNG GIRL BUT AT UNIVERSITY HISTORY BECAME A RIVAL INTEREST, DID IT NOT?

BR: I started out at Queen's as a drama major, but became disaffected by the drama department and became a history major. Then in 1978 I won a Rhodes scholarship to Oxford — I was the second woman in Ontario to win it — where I did a Ph.D. in history. My thesis was on the poet-playwright and political figure I've just talked about, Janis Rainis, and the problem of nationalism. I was very much an intellectual historian. I have always been interested in the impact of ideas and the development of ideas and so I was able to combine that central interest with a thesis and, at the same time, my theatrical interests. I knew that history and theatre were a matter of presentation, of story-telling. Who is telling the story is the crucial question.

RM: WHAT KIND OF THEATRE DID YOU BECOME INVOLVED WITH?

BR: One of the great things about Oxford's doctorate program is that you don't have any exams, you don't have any lectures, you don't have any essays. You do what you like and so in my first year I worked very little on my thesis. Soon after I arrived I saw a little sign, a little ad in one of the university papers announcing that someone was trying to create a company that was interested in process as much as product. That was it. The ad was written by a man called Neil Bartlett who was very young at the time. He must have been twenty-one. Apparently he auditioned some 125 people and I was the only one he chose. Everybody else was invited. We formed a group called A Company, which was devoted to, first of all, working as a radical collective. In other words, everyone directed, performed, administered and wrote together to create pieces that were not in traditional theatrical spaces. Neil had associations with the Richard DeMarco Gallery and was influenced by the work of Kantor. All of us were quite steeped in Brecht and Artaud and knew everything that we were supposed to know. We were particularly interested in the relationship between performer and audience and we were constantly testing out the boundaries in different ways. For example, our first piece, *Feasting*, was performed on a giant dinner table. It was very much a matter of the forced participation of the audience. Eighteen people were invited and coerced, practically, to sit around this giant dinner table where they had bibs tied around them. It was quite a black piece. The dinner table was destroyed at the end of the play, an act which appalled the audience.

RM: HOW MANY PERFORMANCES WERE THERE?

BR: There were three. We had to put the table back together again each time. That show was so violent in its essence that the audience was quite alienated by it and very angry with us at the end. Consequently, in *Very Moving*, the next work, we thought we would try to be very gentle. The audience had to move with us from room to room, building to building, through streets and cloisters. In one case, where the main character changed sex, magically, the audience was told beforehand that there would now be a very scary scene and a very funny scene. Only eight people could fit into the room with the very funny scene. Of course, the same scene, the sex change, was played simultaneously in both rooms. The people who laughed hardest were in the "scary" scene.

In the third production, *Not Heartbreak House*, the audience participation was more extreme. The audience entered a tiny chamber until a spectator spotted a note, left on a chair, asking him or her to begin the play by removing the dust cloths. There were times when the audience was asked to move around and look in the space, and there was a game in which the audience could choose to participate or not. At the end the audience was asked to view the last bit according to whom they had voted for in the last election. In other words, they were asked to stand on different sides of the room according to whom they had supported. So, we had a few Thatcherites standing on one side with their arms crossed, the Labourites on the other, and the Americans in the middle because they hadn't voted. It was very interesting because what we then performed was the last scene of Shaw's *Heartbreak House* in order to show that politics is largely a matter of perception. The play was ultimately about how one is a political animal. There were several pieces after that but those are the ones that stand out in my mind and those were the ones that, apart from some excellent theatre courses in high school and excellent training at Queen's, developed my theatrical skills and interests.

RM: DID YOU HAVE ANY FORMAL TRAINING AS A WRITER?

BR: No, I don't really understand how that works. I understand studying acting or performance, but I don't understand studying writing. Writing courses for T.V. makes sense because it's a matter of learning a formula.

RM: DID YOU ALWAYS REGARD YOURSELF AS A WRITER?

BR: Not at all. I had no idea what I wanted to do. I started out as an actor — so many of us do — but then I discovered that there were no scripts or roles I wanted to play. Eventually the acting choice became the least attractive, compared to writing and directing, because any actor is very vulnerable to another's will. I suppose I've been lucky in that I've almost only acted within collective creations; in other words, I've had an input and I've retained all my dignity and independence. I've never felt like just a puppet.

RM: WHILE IN ENGLAND DURING THE LATE SEVENTIES AND EARLY EIGHTIES YOU MUST HAVE BEEN INFLUENCED BY THE FEMINIST THEATRE WHICH WAS BURGEONING AT THAT TIME.

BR: Absolutely.

RM: DO YOU RECALL WHICH PARTICULAR COMPANIES OR WHICH WOMAN PLAYWRIGHTS IMPRESSED YOU AT THAT TIME?

BR: That's a good question. I was at the time a card-carrying feminist, i.e. I had read all the literature, worked in women's centres, and was ready to join any demonstration at the drop of a hat. I spent many long hours discussing female sexuality and feminist aesthetics and imagining the feminist counterpart to Brecht. In England, at least in Oxford and London, these questions were often taken to their extreme, and I knew several women who chose to become "separatists," refusing all contact with men, including their brothers. I was very impressed with the commitment, but alienated by the extremism. As far as theatre is concerned, the feminist pieces I saw tended to be too agitprop for my taste, and the popular writers like Caryl Churchill and Pam Gems didn't have much influence on me. The shows I most enjoyed were by a group called "Hesitate and Demonstrate," who created a kind of performance art: image theatre, if you like. Image theatre in general was a much greater influence during my years in England than "feminist" theatre. There was a piece at the Almeida — I can't remember the name of the company — in which the actors performed all around the outside of a house. A black, beat-up car arrived and disgorged a gang of man-size, rowdy bees. A man fell asleep in the upper storey and his bed was made to literally fly through the air (with the help of some industrial machinery).

Germany's Pina Bausch also left an impression on me at the time and for the same reason. The images she creates in her work are very, very powerful. Her works are large and exciting, usually without a straight-forward narrative and inspired by improvisations. She uses non-traditional performers, from very beautiful ballet dancers to fat, middle-aged gymnastics teachers. In the piece *1980*, which I have seen about three times over the years, she manages to talk about the year in which, I believe, her lover died in both an intensely personal and intensely impersonal way. She is able to move people with barely any text and what text there is seems to come out of nowhere. There's one section where all her dancers come up and identify where they came from in three words, and in another they show the scars they got from operations. In *Kontakhof* she explores male-female relationships by, in part, having women do impossible things in high heels. It's very violent and sexual at the same time and, once again, there are no words.

At that time in my life I definitely identified with processes, such as the collective process, and I identified with performances which were very visual as opposed to verbal, "languagey." I think I am starting to appreciate literary works of the theatre as I grow older.

RM: IS FORM MORE IMPORTANT THAN POLITICS IN YOUR THEATRICAL WORK?

BR: No, I can't really say that. They are of equal value. I have always been interested in "revisioning" history, in showing history from a new perspective in order to uncover truth, and form is the means. I should add that I also feel the product should be entertaining. I was strongly impressed by Brecht's insistence that we must have fun (*spass*) in the theatre. After all, if I can't present the politics in a theatrically exciting manner I might as well run for office or participate in a political campaign.

RM: CAN YOU DESCRIBE YOUR PARTICIPATION IN THE 1982 THEATRE COMPANY, WHICH WAS AN INTERNATIONAL THEATRE ENSEMBLE BASED IN LONDON?

BR: This is a company that grew right out of the first company, A Company. I co-founded it with Neil Bartlett. We invited six other people to come and work with us for nothing for only a year. We did not want to create an on-going theatre company. The goal was to collectively produce one play by a woman and one play by a man in an exciting style which had a sexual politic at all times. All of the eight members of the company were also the directors, the actors, the designers, the administrators and the producers. We were always very, very tired. We toured one piece by Brecht, *In the Jungle of Cities*, which is about economics and power but you could interpret it as a homosexual love story or love-hate story, which is what we did. The other work was a play by the other Latvian writer in *Tango Lugano*, Aspazija, called *The Silver Veil*.

Aspazija is a female writer who has influenced me a great deal. I find it fascinating that Latvian literature doesn't really begin until the 1860s (the populace consisted mainly of serfs and peasants whose culture was chiefly codified in folk songs), and yet by the 1890s a woman managed to be one of the major writers. There is no parallel for that in European history; there is no other woman whom everybody knew, everyone admired, whose poetry everyone bought and knew by heart. She called herself "the sunset of the last century," which one can understand when one considers her old-fashioned views about sexual relations and how men treat women. At the same time her writing possessed some very twentieth-century sensibilities in its references to the suffragette movement and in its erotic elements.

Our production of *The Silver Veil* was an interesting experience. The play is about a woman soothsayer who refuses her king's request to use her gift to his advantage. He wants her to say that the source of all evil is the enemy but instead she turns and points at the king. She is condemned to be burned but at the end she burns down the whole castle along with herself. The piece is also a very erotic love story — the soothsayer talks about herself as the "burning earth," for example.

Our company presented this work in a very modern fashion, a de-constructive fashion. The main character, Guna, was played by every woman in the company, but at a different point. Guna develops from an innocent soothsayer in the woods, to a woman in love with the prince, to a defiant rebel at the king's court, to a terrorist, essentially, who burns down the castle of oppression. At different points in the play, different psychological turning points, "Guna" was passed from actor to actor by the handing on of her ornamented vest in a ritual fashion. One of the most amazing facts about *The Silver Veil* was that this intensely romantic play was also highly political. During the 1905 revolution, the production was a rallying ground for the population in general and Aspazija was considered a spiritual leader of the revolution. We tried to construct the piece in a way which would inform the audience of these political overtones with a variety of devices. One was to boldly interrupt the play at a crucial point, and pass out leaflets with poems from 1905 to the audience to impart selective information to them regarding the revolution. Then, gently, evocatively, sensitively, we answered the question "How far away is 1905?" by counting back from 1982 to 1905 with each group member aligning himself or herself with particular years like 1968 in Paris and the 1914. The audience was invariably mesmerized at this point, silently marking their own socio-political graph as we mentioned each year.

The Silver Veil and *In the Jungle of Cities* toured throughout Britain, Germany and Sweden. We played both pieces twice in Toronto and we performed in New York and Chicago as well.

RM: WHO CAME TO SEE THE PLAYS?

BR: General audiences. In England there's a very good system of touring, organized by the arts councils so we had a general audience from fringe theatre-goers to members of the Latvian community. It was amusing to see the older segment of the Latvian community all dressed up for the theatre and expecting plush seats!

RM: WHEN YOU RETURNED TO CANADA AT THE END OF THAT YEAR YOU FORMED A LONG AND FRUITFUL ASSOCIATION WITH TORONTO'S NIGHTWOOD THEATRE. HOW DID THIS COME ABOUT?

BR: What happened was that I returned to Toronto at a good time because I ran smack into two major women's festivals. One was organized by the Women's Cultural Building and one by the Women's Perspective Series. The result was that I got an overview of the feminist culture here and met a lot of people — I made a lot of contacts. To my surprise, since I'd been back only a month, the Women's Perspective invited me to do a show, a short, twenty-minute piece, for their festival. At the time I was very interested in the taboos of feminist art, particularly the violence in women. I had had long discussions with another member of the 1982 Theatre Company, Suzanne Khuri, who was very much taken with Aspazija's early plays, which are full of revenge. We had talked about putting these plays about female avengers together and creating a Grand Guignol piece with a guillotine at the front door and so on. Then I saw a newspaper clipping about Marianne Bachmeier, a West German woman who shot the man who killed her seven-year-old daughter. The article led me to put a group together to do a twenty-minute piece called *This is for you, Anna*. Nightwood's involvement at this point was quite arm's length. They gave us a very small bit of money with the agreement that I use one of the Nightwood members for the show. It happened that Cynthia Grant was too busy and Mary Vingoe was out east, so it was really between Kim Renders and Maureen White. A first impression of sympathy led me to ask Maureen. I then invited Ann-Marie MacDonald to join the group. I had met her at various arts events and knew that she was interested in trying something new. She had come to *The Silver Veil* and had been very impressed. Aida Jordâo was also in the first production, after which she went off to Portugal and disappeared from our lives.

This twenty-minute version was very important for me because it was the first thing I had done in five years, apart from my Latvian work, without Neil Bartlett. I so admired his talent that I always wondered whether I would be able to do something on my own. Not surprisingly, I was very gratified by the tremendous success of the work, which led to other work. Ann-Marie MacDonald had a friend who wanted to find a collective to write a piece about the witch hunts and I was invited in on that project, which turned into *Smoke Damage*.

So, in my first year back I established personal connections that were linked to Nightwood though the association was at arm's length until quite recently. What Nightwood offered me was support, encouragement, freedom. They sought me out. After *Smoke Damage* they commissioned me to write a play about Pope Joan. I could go to Nightwood for money for a tour of *This is for you, Anna*, and they would give us a large sum when the larger theatres refused to give us even a hundred dollars. Of course, Nightwood was a natural association because they were very interested in women's work, they were interested in collective work, and, as a women's company, they could accept that I would want carte blanche, that I could say, "I want to direct a play by Ann-Marie MacDonald called *GOOD NIGHT DESDEMONA (Good Morning Juliet)*." They just included it in their season without any doubts or worries about my ability. I would like to point out, however, that there have been other supporters along the way. Theatre Direct with Susan Serran at the helm has been a major support. I was a playwright-in-residence for Mixed Company, a political company, and I've been supported with playwrights' grants by the Canadian Stage Company and Theatre Smith-Gilmour. Men like Bob Wallace, Stephen Bush and Andrey Tarasiuk have also been extremely supportive over the years. But it's Nightwood that gave me the biggest boost.

RM: WILL NIGHTWOOD FORM PART OF YOUR FUTURE?

BR: I don't know. It depends on how Nightwood changes in the next while. Toronto has become an increasingly expensive place to live in the last few years and this is having a major effect on artists across the board, because just making a living is almost as hard as it was when I was twenty-five, since I want more, or I want an easier time of it. I also want larger audiences. I want to create larger pieces. And I want to avoid being part of the whole ghetto-ization of my generation, the generation of artist-companies, who have got to a certain point where their companies can barely grow any more and who cannot get access to theatre real estate.

RM: DO YOU HAVE A VISION OF THE DIRECTION FEMINIST THEATRE IN CANADA IS GOING IN?

BR: I don't know if I can talk about it. When I think about feminist theatre in Canada I think about very specific companies and individuals. I think I am too immersed in it to have a valuable perspective on the movement as a whole.

Interestingly, this is the first year that I have been tired of feminist issues. I don't seem to want to write about them. The three plays that I have been working on this past year are about other problems. *Tango Lugano* is highly political, *Horror High* is about the obsession of teenagers with horror films and death, and *Boom, Baby, Boom!*, though feminist, is also about jazz and the experience of immigrants in this country. In *Boom!*, Austra's story is very much taken from my parent's world. The character of Austra is what my mother might have been had she run away from home. I wonder if other writers who were influenced by the women's movement feel as I do. There is a lot of work to do in the world for women. There's a lot of things that have not been said about every aspect of society, not just the "obvious" things like violence against women, date rape, witch hunts. The anger that I felt when working on *Anna* and *Smoke Damage* has been exorcised. I suppose the issues are too familiar to me now and that is why I am tired of them. Now I am much more interested in female characters throughout history and in "revisioning" history. I am interested in having good roles for women and letting them speak on stage.

RM: DO YOU THINK THAT MORE FEMALE ARTISTIC DIRECTORS ARE NEEDED IN MAJOR THEATRES IN THIS COUNTRY?

BR: Yes, yes, yes! I think that the writers are there but there aren't many second productions. There aren't a lot of risks taken with young woman writers, and I think that the reason is the old boys' network. I think it's quite logical that a sports-oriented male artistic director feels much more comfortable talking to a sports-oriented male writer than a singularly unathletic female writer like me.

We also need more female directors. The problem is that women are not encouraged to think of positions of power as appropriate for themselves. And neither did I when I started and neither do my students. This isn't surprising given that men tend to hog the positions of power and that there are few female role models. There's really nothing to encourage a woman to be a director. It's very easy to be an actor, at least for a while, or to imagine being an actor. It's a pretty straightforward process, as is becoming a playwright. You start with a few drafts and then you get to a festival and then you get a playwright's grant. But there is no system for woman directors. Where do you apprentice within the old boys' network and how can you prove yourself unless you are given a chance? There is the option of creating your own company, but I think that is a waste of talent and time. It's not a choice as far as I'm concerned.

I think that it's too bad that we have so many theatres that are devoted to nurturing young or new Canadian playwrights but none whose whole mandate is to nurture Canadian directors. One result is that actors develop the habit of expecting authority to be male. I recall once directing a show where certain members of the cast did not understand my democracy. They interpreted the democracy to be weakness which very much offended me. It was quite a shock. I tend to assume that my authority is just there, that it is established from the start. I'm not afraid of shouting at somebody and I'm not afraid of firing somebody. I've done all those things. But, maybe because of my collective training, I'm interested in everybody's opinion and I assume that everybody is interested in an ensemble experience. I assume that everyone understands that directing is a series of questions that are being answered on the spot.

RM: YOU TALK A LOT ABOUT COLLECTIVE CREATION AND A NUMBER OF YOUR WORKS ARE A PRODUCT OF IT. DO YOU THINK THAT IT IS IN ANY WAY A COMPROMISED VISION?

BR: I don't think so, because any piece of writing is as good as the person, or people, writing it. If you have a collective of over-large egos you might have a bad collective creation. If you have members of a collective who work together well and who can challenge one another, whatever ideas you have will be enhanced by the input of the others. I definitely feel that a collective creation can be an enormous artistic achievement if the standards are high and there is consensus about the goals. The only collective creation that I've worked on that really didn't achieve its potential was *The Last Will and Testament of Lolita*, a work I frequently forget is a part of my career. The circumstances surrounding it weren't the most favourable. I think we were collectively under an emotional dark cloud. When I watch the videotape of the production, I feel quite regretful, because it's so clear where the piece is strong and where it suddenly comes apart. We were trying to wed madcap humour with strong image work, and thereby alienated some part of the audience most of the time. Either they just wanted to laugh, or they just wanted to be mesmerized. I do want to say that there was a substantial part of the audience which accepted and appreciated the thing as a whole. But we knew we could have done better. It was a heartache.

My friend Neil Bartlett wrote me a lovely letter around that time in which he forbade me, us, any artist, to reject anything as a failure. He made the significant point that all of our work is a re-working, a polishing, an exploration of ideas raised by other pieces. The main thing is to be able to go back to the piece and work on it again.

RM: ON THE BACK COVER OF THE PLAYWRIGHTS UNION OF CANADA EDITION OF *SMOKE DAMAGE* YOU ARE DESCRIBED AS THE "MAIN WRITER" WHO GAVE THE PLAY ITS "FINAL SHAPE." CAN YOU DESCRIBE THE DEVELOPMENT OF THAT SCRIPT AND EXACTLY WHAT YOUR ROLE WAS?

BR: I was invited by Mary Anne Lambooy to work on a collective creation called *Burning Times*, which we were going to workshop. We did two weeks of improvisations in a search for characters for the five women in the company, gestural texts, story lines, etc. After these two weeks I took the loads and loads of notes that had accumulated and went off for about three weeks to write a first draft. We then got together and workshopped the script. So I developed the whole story of the tourists who turn into terrorists, I developed their characters, and I made the decision that we would travel among several worlds: the Renaissance, the seventeenth century and the modern world. *Smoke Damage* marked the first time I began to think of myself as a real writer even though I had written a musical and contributed a great deal to so many other pieces. Of course, the actors also contributed a great deal. Kim Renders, for example, created the story of "Lopsy Oppsy." Ann-Marie MacDonald wrote a song and a poem and Peg Christopherson basically created the Anna Käser monologue which I placed in the text and polished. In my contract with the writers of *Smoke Damage* I own fifty-one percent and the group of them own forty-nine percent.

RM: IS *SMOKE DAMAGE* IN ANY WAY INSPIRED BY CARYL CHURCHILL'S *VINEGAR TOM*?

BR: No. I read *Vinegar Tom* but it didn't influence me. Frankly, I didn't much care for Churchill's play and others like it. They are too serious. *Vinegar Tom* tries to make a connection to the present but doesn't quite succeed. In *Smoke Damage* I think we made very clear how much we could all be considered witches today. The work revealed clearly the shocking level of carnage, how many women were killed, which most people know nothing about. We don't read about it in our history texts. We aren't taught that the whole era of witch-hunting was comparable to the Holocaust.

RM: YOU HAVE ALSO CO-WRITTEN SCRIPTS. *THIN ICE*, WHICH WENT ON A NATIONAL TOUR WITH THEATRE DIRECT, WAS CO-WRITTEN WITH BEVERLEY COOPER AND I BELIEVE YOUR NEW PLAY, *HORROR HIGH*, WAS ALSO A COLLABORATION. WHAT ARE THE ADVANTAGES AND DISADVANTAGES OF WORKING CLOSELY WITH ANOTHER WRITER?

BR: *Horror High* is my play but it is a collaboration to the extent that it is a multi-media collaboration. I'm not writing the music, for example, or shooting the film.

The advantages of co-writing is that it's a lot more fun than writing by yourself and it goes a lot faster, at least in the first creative stages. Later you can get bogged down by too much discussion, I suppose, though I doubt that would ever happen with Bev. We have a very good relationship and she's very used to working with a partner, having co-written with Ann-Marie MacDonald on the Nancy Drew parody.

What happened with *Thin Ice* is that the topic of date rape was proposed to me while we were on tour with *Anna*. I received some Canada Council money to work on it and at the time I was tired of the issue — I was tired of issues in general. I thought it would make it interesting for me if I involved Bev, and if I also involved Maureen White at an early stage, thereby creating an opportunity for her to direct. (This, of course, is an example of how women have to give other women the chance to use and develop their talents.)

The obvious drawback to co-writing is that if you have a strong idea you may not get a chance to explore it fully.

RM: DO YOU THINK YOU WILL CO-WRITE ON ANOTHER PROJECT?

BR: Oh yes. Bev and I are proposing a piece to the CBC together. Otherwise it depends on how much form is involved. Maybe it's no coincidence that I was encouraged by Theatre Direct to write *Horror High* on my own rather than as a partnership. It's a piece that involves music, film and movement and when I am involved in an exploration of form, either I want to work with a whole collective or I want to go it alone in order to have more control over choices.

RM: *THIN ICE,* WHICH WON A DORA MAVOR MOORE AWARD IN 1987 AND THE 1987 CHALMERS AWARD FOR BEST CHILDREN'S PLAY, WAS INSPIRED BY RESEARCH CONDUCTED AMONG HIGH SCHOOL STUDENTS WHICH DISCLOSED THAT DATE RAPE IS REGARDED AS ACCEPTABLE BY A LARGE PERCENTAGE OF STUDENTS. CAN YOU DESCRIBE HOW THE MATERIAL FOR THE PLAY WAS DEVELOPED? I UNDERSTAND THAT YOU AND BEVERLEY COOPER CONDUCTED WORKSHOPS WITH TEENAGERS.

BR: A woman who worked in a rape crisis centre did the actual research. She approached me during *Anna* and told me that over fifty percent of women assaulted were between the ages of fifteen and nineteen and that over fifty percent of men assaulting women were between the ages of nineteen and twenty-four. These seemed to me to be statistics of major importance. So Bev Cooper, Maureen White and I held workshops with high school students recruited by teachers and through a newspaper ad. We never actually raised the issue of date rape; instead, as subjects for improvisations we dealt with dating, role-switching (what happens when a girl pretends she is a guy, for example), and "coming on" to a girl or guy you liked. We researched the attitudes and the language of teenagers.

When you create plays in this process you quickly realize that you can't ask the participants to solve the problem or issue you are researching. That is the writer's concern. In addition, I had seen so many bad films and pieces on date rape that wanted to eschew the standard choice of showing the girl in a "sitting duck" position and the boy as a monster. In *Thin Ice* we deliberately don't show an actual date rape: it's an off-stage event that involves someone only talked about in the play. And we deliberately show the girl in danger of being date-raped escaping from the situation by using useful tactics like making a loud noise. We didn't ignore the girl's complicity in the near-rape. We don't mean to imply that she is to blame for the assault, but we show that certain sexual attitudes (the whole business of clothing or dress, for example) place the girl in a certain way in the position of colluding with the boy. We wanted to be as sympathetic as we could to the boy's dilemma. So in *Thin Ice* the young guy is as shocked as the girl by what he nearly does, by his potential for violence. I was amazed at the discussions that the portrayal of the boy elicited. A number of young men in the audiences revealed the anguish they obviously felt by the teasing their girlfriends engaged in — the "Yes. No. Maybe." form of teasing.

Part of the success of the play — it recently played to a thousand-seat audience in Newfoundland and got a standing ovation — is due to the fact that we were sympathetic to teenagers. We took them seriously and didn't "write down" to them. The humour also helped. Some male teachers objected strongly to the comedy. They felt it was out of place in a play about such a serious subject. Then the kids stood up in the discussions to defend it as a legitimate expression of their lives.

I consciously use humour as a means of relaxing my audience, of creating a sympathetic bond with them. I would have just alienated them if I had come on very serious. *Horror High* is equally funny and for the same reason. Even *Anna*, which is a very dark piece, has funny moments in it. One character says, "My husband, he's so funny, he calls me the mattress." That was inspired by a woman we met at a Battered Women's Shelter. Obviously, all these women could do to transcend their agony was to laugh at their predicament, and at themselves.

RM: WHY DO SO MANY WOMAN PLAYWRIGHTS WRITE FOR CHILDREN'S THEATRE OR YOUNG AUDIENCES?

BR: Supposedly women are naturally suited to write for young people because their lives are more involved with them than men's lives are. Well, I don't have any children. Perhaps many woman playwrights have a better chance of getting their work put on at "children's theatres" than anywhere else. I get bitterly angry when I think about this. It's quite amazing to me that *Thin Ice* is the "big successful play." Compared to all my other work it's not very artistically innovative. It's not where I took the biggest risks. So I found it very ironic that people think this is what I'm good for, this is the "big show."

Look at *Anna*. We toured it for three years, it won all kinds of critical accolades, and yet none of the larger theatres picked it up. Each time we revived it we produced it ourselves with the help of Nightwood. I can't help but feel that if a man had written it, it would have been picked up by a major theatre. I think the fact that it wasn't picked up had everything to do with the topic and everything to do with the fact we were four women, four women who were not actively pressing to be accepted by establishment theatre.

In Ottawa *Anna* was not advertised as a feminist play but as a play about the woman who killed the man who killed her child. We sold out. After one performance a woman talked to the audience about being a battered woman and what she should do. That was one of the most moving experiences for us. To our surprise women in the audience spoke up, saying things like, "Well, I went through this," and "You should do that." People told us afterwards, "I thought I was going to see a play about this crime and instead I saw a play about me." This made us aware, yet again, that "feminist" theatre, which is often so ghetto-ized, considered interesting only for women and only for a certain bunch of women, is actually as universal as *Hamlet* or any of the male plays we see. I think Ann-Marie MacDonald's *GOOD NIGHT DESDEMONA (Good Morning Juliet)* is one of the first Canadian feminist plays that has elicited interest from the big boy theatres and I think that it's because it's largely based on Shakespeare.

RM: GREATNESS BY ASSOCIATION, YOU MEAN?

BR: Exactly. I don't even have to go as far back as *Anna* to illustrate the sexism. At the recent World Stage Festival I was the only woman writer represented (by *Boom, Baby, Boom!*), and no one screamed about it. Not even *Now* magazine, the city's most leftist organ. In England people would have been shouting themselves hoarse over something like that. What's worse, a woman organized the festival.

But to return to your question, I enjoy writing for teenage audiences. The experience of *Thin Ice* showed me they are extremely passionate and very un-self-conscious about responding to a performance. If you can capture their interest they respond directly to the work without any politeness and so on. And they are an audience that is very open to influence. They haven't formed all their ideas and they will want to participate in a discussion. If there is a thread running through all of my work it is my concern for the audience, the need for a dialogue with the audience. I am always asking myself, "Who am I talking to and why, and how can I talk differently to them?"

RM: YOU HAVE CONSIDERABLE EXPERIENCE AS A DIRECTOR: PETER ELIOT WEISS'S *GOING DOWN FOR THE COUNT* AT GLENDON COLLEGE IN TORONTO, ANN-MARIE MACDONALD'S *GOOD NIGHT, DESDEMONA (GOOD MORNING JULIET)* FOR NIGHTWOOD, AND YOUR OWN WORK, LIKE *BOOM, BABY, BOOM!* AT THE DU MAURIER WORLD STAGE FESTIVAL. HOW DOES YOUR CAREER AS A DIRECTOR INFLUENCE YOUR WRITING?

BR: When I start to work on a play it's rare that I don't think in terms of directing the work for the main reason of being able to control all of the various elements. As I was writing *Boom, Baby, Boom!* I didn't even include in the text itself the themes for many of the scenes because I knew what they were and I wanted to work them out with the actors, the designers, and the musicians. I wanted to discover the theatrical style from actual workshops and rehearsals.

Consequently, I almost had to direct the play myself. As it happened, the acting styles of Ann-Marie MacDonald and Martin Julien directly contributed to the ultimate style of the work which started out as naturalism but became something very stylized and much more kinetic. Throughout my career, beginning with A Company, I have always wanted to find other forms of theatrical language and that requires the workshop and the directing process. So unless I'm not making great demands on myself in terms of exploring form, I tend to want to direct my own pieces.

However, at this point in my career I feel a desire to direct a series of plays by other people because the problem of directing itself interests me: how you get from point A to point B. It's a marvellous and mysterious process. I think I want to direct Caryl Churchill's *Cloud 9* even though — or perhaps because — the second act is a problem. And there's a play, *Portrait of Dora* by the French feminist, Hélène Cixous, which I've wanted to do for some time. And I would love to work in opera, to de-construct *Cosi fan tutti*, for example. In the near future I hope to spend a few months in Latvia observing the work of two renowned Latvian directors, Peteris Petersons and Adolfs Sapiro, who may have an old-fashioned style and a very serious directing style but who are regarded as masters. Is there anyone in Canada one could regard in the same light? How can we have masters? For one thing, our rehearsal period is too short. We don't have the privilege of working properly.

RM: YOU MENTIONED THAT ACTING ISN'T AS ATTRACTIVE TO YOU AS DIRECTING OR WRITING. WILL YOU DO ANY MORE ACTING? ARE THERE ANY ROLES YOU WANT TO PLAY?

BR: It would be wonderful to play Lady Macbeth, or Medea, from a modern perspective. However, I would be very surprised if I act in the future, which is why I wish more people had seen me in *The Last Testament of Lolita*. I think I did my best work as an actress there. I was very, very funny. My clown was the vengeful wallflower and I was able to do very erotic things on stage like squeezing bread between my thighs. I had a great time flirting with the audience who were in stitches. I don't think it likely I'll do much acting any more because I won't audition, I don't have an agent and I'm probably very "difficult." I won't do things on stage that I consider offensive. I'm not an obedient actor. How many male directors do you know who want to deal with someone like me? So I can't imagine who would call me up to hire me as an actress.

RM: MANY CONTEMPORARY PLAYS BY WOMEN EITHER REWRITE HISTORY OR RECOVER LOST HEROINES, WHICH IS WHAT YOU DO IN *SMOKE DAMAGE*, WHICH REVEALS HOW MILLIONS OF WOMEN WERE SACRIFICED TO MEN'S FEAR OF FEMALE SEXUALITY, IN *POPE JOAN*, WHICH IS BASED ON FACTUAL ACCOUNTS OF A WOMAN WHO BECAME

POPE IN 853, AND IN *THE SEARCH FOR OBLIVION*, YOUR RADIO PLAY ABOUT ADVENTURER ISABELLE EBERHARDT. CAN YOU DESCRIBE MORE PRECISELY YOUR EFFORT TO "REVISION" HISTORY, AS YOU PUT IT EARLIER?

BR: Let me use Eberhardt to explain. She led an extraordinary life. She lived at the turn of the century and dressed like an Arab sheik. She slept around, and only with Arab men. She smoked hashish and lost all of her teeth. She was a great friend of a famous French colonel and the beloved of the French Legionnaires. She was accepted into elitist Sufi sects and she spoke several Sufi dialects. She died in a freak flood in the desert. The Legionnaires picked her writings out of the mud and sent them to Paris where a man published them under *his* name. Her writings were, like those of Rimbaud, of the fatalistic vagrant: "I own the world because I own nothing." And yet who knows about her? When I discovered her work I couldn't help thinking that if she had been a man everyone would know about her. Apparently the American actress Debra Winger has the rights to her story. I hope a film will be made. It's the kind of thing we all needed to see when we were teenagers. I grew up on a diet of male heroes: Indians, sheiks, cowboys, etc. I would always fantasize that I was the heroine, which didn't make much sense but which reveals how much I missed a female role model.

So "revisioning" history to me means disclosing information — don't forget my Latvian roots, which to me has meant an absence of information — and it means telling the story from a new perspective, often the perspective of women, or a woman. Kids in schools today are still taught that "women never did anything" and that's just not true. *Pope Joan* was written, in part, to educate and inform. The information available indicates that a woman actually became a pope in the ninth century. I didn't romanticize Joan, however. I couldn't. After all, she didn't change things much. Christendom remained a corrupt patriarchy even though she was at the helm. Although she was a woman in power she had to play by the old — the boys' — rules. The piece is ultimately a comment on female world leaders today, such as Thatcher. The point of the play is not to trust women just because they are female.

In many ways "revisioning" history is something of a mission for me. Practically speaking, though, I also just want to create good stage roles for women. This is why in *Boom, Baby, Boom!* I lied: Austra never existed. Some women ran away but no one was as wild as she was. I consciously created a fiction, a role model for women in today's audiences. When I did research on the Toronto jazz clubs of the fifties I was told that there weren't any women involved. There were, of course. There were waitresses and cleaners and girlfriends and so on, but most people I talked to had a *picture* of a group of guys on the stage with more men at small tables swilling Scotch and smoking. Changing the picture has always been my interest.

RM: HOW DO YOU RESPOND TO THE COMMON CRITICISM THAT WOMAN WRITERS DON'T CREATE CONVINCING MALE CHARACTERS?

BR: I don't think it's true. Perhaps the problem is that there are too many male reviewers. I'm always surprised when male critics talk about the occasional weak or not fully fleshed out male character in a play written by a woman. I've seen countless plays by men in which the female characters are there just to reflect or react to the male characters. The criticism is certainly not true of my own work. Leo and Frumentius in *Pope Joan*, for example, are wildly popular with audiences, great comic roles that pack a terrific punch. Of course, the absence of male characters in *Anna* has always presented a problem for reviewers. They never seem to query plays by men that have no women in them.

RM: THE CHIEF CRITICISM OF *BOOM, BABY, BOOM!* IS THAT IT IS TOO LONG AND TRIES TO DO TOO MUCH. DOES THE STORY OF CLEM HAMBOURG'S JAZZ CLUB AND AUSTRA'S FAMILY FAIL TO COME TO-GETHER AT THE END? IS THERE A STRUCTURAL WEAKNESS AT THE HEART OF THE PLAY? OR IS THIS CRITICISM A MATTER OF THE FAIL-URE TO UNDERSTAND A DIFFERENT, FEMALE AESTHETIC?

BR: I think it's true that there is a feminist dramaturgical aesthetic which spurns the structure based on conflict and resolution. The one where everything gets built up to one screaming point and then everything is suddenly released. Women often write in waves, repeated climaxes, collages. It's true that often male critics will then complain about a lack of build or something. I hate to single out male critics, but the consistency is uncanny. I think my work, collective or solitary, has almost only received raves by women — understanding, perceptive assessments. Male critics have also liked my work at times — Henry Mietkiewicz of the *Toronto Star* loved *Boom!*, for example. But it's the consistent understanding on the part of female reviewers that makes me believe there really is a difference.

What I resent about much male criticism of writing by women is the grudging tone. For example, *Lolita* got "terrible with flashes of brilliance," which makes no sense to me. It should have read, "brilliant with some major flaws." In general, our critics are terrible. Most aren't at all versed in theatre language and they look for failure. Their focus is on why things fail and not why they succeed.

Now, regarding those criticisms of *Boom!*, I agree that the production at the World Stage was too long because it didn't hold you in all the right places, but not because it was a certain number of minutes. I think it's cretinous for a critic to comment on length. Robert Lepage's *Dragon Trilogy* is six hours long and it has its ups and downs. I think that particular criticism shows how provincial our critics are. I think some reviewers of *Boom!* just couldn't handle the combination of facts or elements in the play. People like Henry Miet-kiewicz had no trouble seeing a relationship between the club and the immigrant story, but then he *is* Polish *and* a jazz fan. He brought a different cultural perspective to bear on the play. My point is that sexism is not necessarily the root of all criticism of plays by women. I certainly think that the stories "come together." I have no trouble understanding how Latvian refugees and beatniks come together. I've read Latvian émigré beat poetry. I know there were Latvian artists hanging out at Clement Hambourg's jazz club. What's the big deal? You have to be culturally insular, perhaps too *anglais*, to not understand the dovetailing. The form of *Boom!* was pretty unusual — instrumental music and abstract movement often carried the same weight as words — and if you couldn't follow it, well, then, I guess you would get bored. Too bad for you.

RM: LET'S TURN TO THE SUBJECT OF COMEDY. *POPE JOAN* IS TITLED A NON-HISTORICAL COMEDY AND *LOLITA*, *BOOM*, *BABY*, *BOOM!* AND *SMOKE DAMAGE* ALL HAVE A REALLY RICH VEIN OF HUMOUR. EVEN *ANNA* HAS VERY COMICAL MOMENTS IN IT. WHY DO YOU WRITE COMEDY RATHER THAN TRAGEDY?

BR: That's a very interesting question. I don't think it's a deliber-ate choice on my part and now that I think about it even *Tango Lugano*, which has a very sad, pessimistic under-current, contains parts that are funny. The work is really a combination of comedy and drama. I suppose I like comedy because I find unrelieved drama unendurable. Take Kroetz's *Michi's Blood*, for example, which I think is a really good play. It was beautifully done by Peter Hinton here in Toronto, but when I saw it I knew I could never write a play like that about abortion. The issue is too painful and Kroetz's treatment of it leaves me with no sense of escape. With humour there is a sense that things could be different. For example, I think that the humour in *Smoke Damage*, a piece which many spectators told me was "very scary," is what made it possible for them to look at subjects like mass murder. When I've watched workshops or performances about rape and abuse that were presented with unrelenting seriousness, I've found it unbearable and I've shut off. I couldn't listen any more. It is part of my nature to want to give a little bit of relaxation, to entertain, and to make you laugh.

The whole business of the female clown is, of course, of political importance. The major teachers of clown don't use female clowns. There is no frame of reference. The funny woman is still not that socially acceptable or publicly acknowledged. When I am auditioning women, they constantly cry. I think it was Ann-Marie MacDonald who was told at the National Theatre School that she would never be a professional actress because she couldn't cry on demand. Society, patriarchal society, tends to associate women with suffering, with tears.

To be able to laugh — at yourself or in someone else's face, despite everything — is the ultimate empowerment, as the battered women who saw *Anna* proved to me. After all, the battered women we met were the survivors, the ones who finally made the choice to leave. And the fact that they were constantly approaching their hideous situation with a sense of humour, albeit a black sense of humour, was very impressive: a real testament to the human spirit.

RM: IN *ANNA* WHAT WE SEE, FINALLY, IS FEMALE RAGE DIRECTED OUTWARDS. THERE'S SOMETHING TERRIBLY GRATIFYING IN THAT. PEOPLE APPLAUDED SPONTANEOUSLY, WHICH IS UNDERSTANDABLE IN A DEPRESSING KIND OF WAY. IN A *TORONTO STAR* INTERVIEW IN JUNE OF 1984 YOU SAID THAT "THE WORK HAS NO FINAL MESSAGE" AND THAT IT DIDN'T PRESCRIBE VIOLENCE AS A SOLUTION FOR VIOLENCE. AT THE SAME TIME DON'T YOU THINK THE PLAY TREATS MARIANNE BACH-MEIER AS A CHAMPION OF WOMEN'S RIGHTS AND WOMEN'S HONOUR?

BR: What we tried to do was present a dialectical piece. We wanted to show the heroism of her act, it's impossible to avoid or ignore it, but we also wanted to show that Marianne was a real woman, a normal woman with dark sides to her. We were not saying, "Yes, you should shoot the guy who killed your daughter." In fact, the more we worked on the piece the more it became clear that Anna's tragedy started the moment she was born. In the play we mention that the murderer had claimed that the girl had said that her father had abused her. This information came from the trial records. When we first started on this project we thought, "Oh, that's too much. How dare he say that. This is just blaming the victim." The irony is that the longer we worked on it the more we found out about child abuse, and the more convinced we were that she had been abused by one of Marianne's boyfriends. In fact, a psychologist came up to us after the show and told us that it was quite possible that the child was behaving in what could be considered a sexually provocative manner because children who have been sexually abused do that. They will come and rub themselves up against you because that's how they have been taught. I remember going really weak upon hearing that and realizing that this child had already been burdened in this sexist society with being abused at the age of three or four or whenever it began.

It has always been important for me to initiate a discussion at the end of a work, to raise questions for debate rather than to give answers. That's why I said *Anna* has no final message. I personally hate being told what to do and what to think, and so in my own work, how can I presume? The only "answer" we could give in *Anna* is the answer "Get out" to the battered woman's question of what she should do. In their complicated situation that answer is the strongest positive choice. It's also important to me to show in my work that the world is a complicated place and not a place where there is only black or white. Perhaps this is what is most Canadian about my plays. The more that I travel between cultures, Germany, England, the Soviet Union, and the States, the more aware I become of the extreme polarization that exists in these places, the defaming or falsification of the other person's view or world. In Canada we have a sharp awareness that there's something in between. That might seem like a boring or bland middle-ground but it isn't necessarily. It's potentially a fertile ground where the black and white rub up against each other and discussion ensues.

RM: AT ONE POINT THE CHARACTER OF MARIANNE IN *ANNA* SAYS, "I'M GLAD HE'S DEAD BUT I WISH I HADN'T DONE IT." BOTH STATEMENTS, THEN, ARE PERFECTLY TRUE?

BR: Yes. I suppose the play could in some women effect a catharsis of their violent impulses. When we played it in prisons and in shelters, women especially responded to the scene where the wife is lifting the pan above the guy's head. They cheered and shouted, "Hit him!," "Shoot him!, "Kill him!" What was very curious was that a male reviewer from Carleton University wrote that we were espousing the total extermination of the male gender. It was so telling because we have seen so many films and plays where women are graphically tortured and killed and in *Anna* the most that's ever done is that someone points a finger and says, "Bang." It's only a finger. There is no blood, there are no screams and it is always a fantasy. Yet the fact of these fantasies was so shocking and powerful that a man felt personally attacked. Ironically, when we toured *Anna* in England men came to thank us for having created a play which didn't make them feel attacked on all fronts. It seems some English feminist writers are unrelenting. Take Sarah Daniel's *Masterpieces*, for example.

In any event when we created the work we weren't thinking about men. We were thinking about women under attack: what do we do when we are attacked, not why are men attacking us or what shall we do to men. It is a very woman-oriented work. I was really taken aback when male friends of mine said, "I feel guilty after the show." I'd just say, "If the shoe fits. . . ." I mean, that's their problem.

RM: I WAS VERY MOVED BY THE IMAGE WITH WHICH *ANNA* ENDS: THE POURING OF THE GLASS OF MILK. ONE OF THE ACTRESSES IN THE 1985 SUMMER EDITION OF THE *CANADIAN THEATRE REVIEW* DESCRIBES IT AS AN IMAGE OF ABSENCE WHICH, OF COURSE, IT IS, SINCE NO CHILD COMES RUNNING TO DRINK THE MILK. DO YOU RECALL HOW THAT IMAGE CAME TO BE?

BR: I certainly do. I also recall that people responded to that image in amazingly different ways. Some spectators described it as an image of tears, others experienced it as a scream, and one woman said to me, "You know what was great? When at the end you opened the fridge and there was blood pouring down." People projected their own fears and concerns onto the image.

I know that when I started working on the play I had a picture in my mind of a woman carrying cookies and milk for her child. I never considered it as an ending, just a jumping-off point. In fact, we tried a number of different endings, terrible ones, like turning to the audience and screaming. Then, out of the blue, during an improvisation of mine, the image simply arose out of my unconscious. It came from deep within me and it was immediately recognized by most of the company as the right image.

Another image in *Anna* which elicited a diversity of response was that of the nails, which came out of an improvisation in which I had to tell Marianne's story in three minutes, using any one prop in the room. There happened to be some nails in the corner of the room and for a reason I can't explain I began to lay them out in a circle as I recited salient facts regarding Marianne Bachmeier's life. It was a case of the prop inspiring the action which became a universal action. People said, "It's like nails in the coffin" or "It's the nails in the cross." One woman said, "It's a metal object, a hard object that penetrates." Someone else remarked, "You pull the nails out of the house and it falls down." For me it meant defining the subject or marking out the territory.

The very funny and erotic bread image in *Lolita* also evolved in a curious way. It was inspired first by a picture in Marcia Resnick's *Re-Visions*, a book of photographs of female adolescents dedicated to Nabokov's Humbert who, in our opinion, rationalized his sexual attraction to young girls by calling them teases. The picture was of a girl crushing a loaf of white bread between her thighs with a caption reading something like, "She learned the facts of life from a friend during a trip to a bread factory." The choreographer, Louise Garfield, asked Maureen White to do a movement study with the bread and without her pants, and she did, bless her. The movement study was very abstract, though, so we decided we would not use it. We also didn't like the nudity. Yet, the picture stayed with me and when we were trying to resolve a different section of the work, I took the bread and said, "Look at this," and I began playing with it in a way that was inspired by watching Maureen. As I mentioned earlier, it was a most successful image.

RM: DO YOU HAVE ANY SPECIFIC ARTISTIC GOALS FOR YOURSELF?

BR: No. It's a matter of one project at a time and one project leading to the next. I don't have a five-year plan like some people I know. I think my ultimate goal, which has motivated all my work, is to see how art can change the world, in however limited a way.

RM: ARE YOU AMBITIOUS?

BR: I think I am very ambitious but I don't think I am a careerist. I don't know what kind of recognition I'll ever achieve and I don't actively pursue fame. I think the present is a time for re-evaluation, of deciding what it is that I really want to go for. For years I've wanted to make films even though the problem with film for me is that you don't have the direct dialogue with the audience that you do in theatre. I have to find out if I really do want to write for film, I suppose.

RM: WHAT IS YOUR GREATEST STRENGTH AS A WRITER?

BR: I think that I am good at originating a concept and at finding a different theatrical language for each play. I am original. My work is definitely my work. I'm not covering other people's ground.

4. Playwright Sally Clark

Michael Cooper

Sally Clark was born in Vancouver in 1953 and has lived in Toronto since 1973. She has been Playwright in Residence at Buddies in Bad Times Theatre, Theatre Passe Muraille, the Shaw Festival and Nightwood Theatre. *Moo* was nominated for the Dora Mavor Moore Award for Outstanding New Play in 1989, and won a Chalmers Award in the same year.

I suppose, these days, it's all in one's credibility. If you are short, you have less credibility than a tall person. If you are a woman, you have less credibility than a man. If you are short, a woman and wearing a straitjacket — well, forget it, you have no credibility at all.

Moo in *Moo*

Produced and published plays:

Lost Souls and Missing Persons. Toronto: Playwrights Canada (copy-script), 1984.

Moo. Toronto: Playwrights Canada, 1989.

Produced plays:

Ten ways to abuse an old woman. Premiere at Vancouver Fringe Festival, 1988.

Jehanne of the Witches. Premiere at Tarragon Theatre, 1989.

The Trial of Judith K. Premiere at Canadian Stage Company, 1989. Originally commissioned, conceived and produced as *Trial* with Tamahnous Theatre, Vancouver, 1985.

Sally Clark Interview
by Judith Rudakoff

JR: IS WRITING FOR RADIO VERY DIFFERENT FROM WRITING FOR STAGE?

SC: Yes. I much prefer writing for theatre because I desperately need to communicate with people, to know that my work is being "received." One of the reasons I stopped painting was that painting didn't give me that chance to communicate. I would have an art show and people would look at my paintings, but that was never enough. I wanted people to *do something*, to applaud. . . . It was never a satisfying experience. It's the same with radio. I enjoy the radio play-writing, but it's like sending material out into a void. Unless you're sitting in the room with a person who's listening to the radio play, there's no feeling of connection or communication.

JR: DO YOU FIND AUDIENCES DIFFERENT COAST TO COAST? FOR EXAMPLE, *MOO* HAS HAD PRODUCTIONS IN VICTORIA, CALGARY AND TORONTO.

SC From a playwright's point of view, audiences are all the same. If they love the play, they're a wonderful, intelligent group of people. If they hate it, then they're a bunch of dull-witted deadbeats.

JR: OVER THE PAST FEW SEASONS YOU'VE HAD PRODUCTIONS AT FACTORY, THEATRE PASSE MURAILLE, TARRAGON AND CANADIAN STAGE (FREE THEATRE DOWNSTAIRS): ALL OF THE THEATRES ASSOCIATED WITH THE FIRST SURGE OF CANADIAN PLAY-WRITING IN THE ALTERNATIVE THEATRE BABY BOOM OF THE EARLY SEVENTIES. HOW DOES IT FEEL TO BE PRODUCED AT *ALL* OF THEM?

SC: I'm quite happy! I think it's a positive situation for theatre when companies don't ally themselves with a fixed "stable" of writers. For a period, in the eighties, you got the feeling, that the theatres were divided into very separate camps. And that an association with one of those theatres meant that you wrote in a particular style.

JR: THE WALLS SEEM TO BE TUMBLING DOWN. IS THERE ALSO A CLOSER CAMARADERIE AMONG CANADIAN PLAYWRIGHTS THESE DAYS?

SC: Yes, I feel that way. I was in Banff in the spring of 1988 and again in 1989 and I met a lot of writers there that normally I couldn't have gotten to know very well that quickly. Two weeks of

Banff is a far better way to learn about people than six years of bumping into them at theatre openings in Toronto. That intense period of daily contact helps a lot in terms of breaking down barriers. I came to realize that communication is possible even if we're all writing in totally different styles, about totally different issues, saying totally different things.

Now that might have something to do with Banff. . . . It really is different from most places. The Indians have always said that Banff is the spiritual centre of North America. You're isolated there, in the mountains. The air is clearer. You have nothing to think about except the play you're working on. Daily responsibilities vanish: they even provide your meals.

And when you relax and get into the work, the sense of competition seems ridiculous. Where you're from stops being an issue. What you thought was important back home just diminishes.

And it's not just the place. John Murrell finds the time to speak individually to each person about his or her play. He seems to be able to enter into the work wholeheartedly. That's something that I find difficult to do with other people's plays. But John can move from play to play and have a very intense involvement with each piece. Maybe it's through John that the atmosphere of trust and generosity at Banff survives.

JR: ARE THERE OTHER PEOPLE WHO HAVE HELPED YOU?

SC: Lots. Clarke Rogers, Jackie Maxwell and Robert Rooney have all spent hours and hours talking me through my various drafts to help me work out what's missing. I owe an enormous amount to Clarke, because if it hadn't been for him, I wouldn't have become a playwright.

My first play, *Lost Souls and Missing Persons*, has thirty scenes and twenty-two characters. When I first submitted it to theatres for their consideration, their response was, "You're crazy. Nobody's going to produce it in a million years. . . ."

And it looked like they were right. And then Clarke said that he was interested. We met to discuss the play and, well, with Clarke it was like a mini course in play-writing! He wanted more dramatic conflict, more action. It was a case of first-play problems: you know, pages and pages of people chatting and nothing actually *happening*!

JR: ALL YOUR WORK HAS A QUALITY THAT I COULDN'T DESCRIBE UNTIL I REALIZED THAT YOU WERE A PAINTER. MANY PEOPLE WRITE EPISODICALLY OR IN SEGMENTS, BUT YOUR PLAYS ARE LIKE MANY RELATED PAINTINGS COME TO LIFE. THE AUDIENCE ENTERS INTO THE FRAME OF THE PICTURES AND SOMETIMES THE FRAME IS AJAR, AT AN ANGLE. . . . SOMETHING IS ASKEW IN THE WORLD OF THE PICTURES THAT MAKES IT ALL THE MORE INTERESTING. IS THIS A CONSCIOUS STYLISTIC CHOICE?

SC: Well, I always go for contrasts. I like to put light with dark. For example, in *Moo*, I wanted to contrast Young Moo with Old Moo, what happens to people when they're young and what happens to them when they're old. And the difference in their reactions. Or a how a love affairs can change: the initial phases are filled with freshness and then later it gains weight or becomes twisted. That's what Act Two of *Moo* is all about, how the changes alter love.

There's even contrast in the way I portray obsession in *Moo*. There are always two sides to every story, even when you hear of, for example, a man like Harry being mean to the woman involved, treating her badly. Many men may perceive Moo as a victim, a poor woman who wasted her life. But what I was trying to write was the story of a woman who drove the man to do these things to her. She possessed a strength that scared Harry and caused him to commit these acts against her. It's just one of those twisted relationships where he knows that no matter what he does to her, she can take it. It's the outside world who keep trying to make her out to be a victim. And her family too. They're the ones who finally browbeat her into succumbing to their will, and they drive her to see herself as a victim. The minute she decides that, it's game over for her.

When I painted I used to go out with a man who hated plays. I would drag him to the theatre anyway and he'd tell me again and again that his idea of theatre was Elizabethan: that people in the audience should eat popcorn and throw it at the stage. He claimed that theatre had died because there was just nothing *happening* on stage to keep it alive. Theatre, he thought, was just four people in a room shouting at each other. In a way, I agreed with him: I also thought that not enough action was taking place on stage.

Take William Inge's *Picnic*, for example. The whole first act is spent talking about the picnic and the whole second act is spent discussing what happened after the picnic. But you never get to see the actual *picnic*! I wanted to put the crises, the action back on stage.

JR: ARE THERE ANY PLAYWRIGHTS WHO HAVE INFLUENCED YOU?

SC: I used to love Bernard Shaw when I was sixteen. Now, I don't think I like him any more.

JR: WHAT MADE YOU OUTGROW SHAW?

SC: His people just talk, talk, talk. And then another character will enter and say, "Stop talking. You're talking too much. Let *me* talk."

I used to hate Chekhov, but now I adore him.

JR: WHAT DO YOU ADORE ABOUT HIM?

SC: I love the fact that he portrays life, but he's careful to include that wonderful element of chaos. People shoot each other, and yet in the next scene you see them with a band-aide over their head wound. In a tragedy, you would have someone shot and that would be the end of it. Chekhov always has them staggering back on stage.

JR: THERE'S WHAT CRITICS KEEP CALLING YOUR "BLACK WIT AND MORDANT HUMOUR"! DO YOU THINK YOU'RE WRITING COMEDY OR TRAGEDY?

SC: I think I'm writing tragedies. But I think they're funny, too.

When I first wrote *Moo*, I didn't think it was funny. I had very serious intentions. There were gag lines, but when I wrote them, I took them seriously too. If I write anything, I have to believe it, be totally serious about the issues and the events. If I try, consciously, to be funny, it falls flat.

But, you know, I don't think I really do take life all that seriously, which is probably why I like to set up the problem of writing a tragedy and then constantly undermine the tragic elements.

JR: AND UNDERMINING THE CLASSIC POSE OF THE VICTIM. MOO AND HANNAH IN *LOST SOULS AND MISSING PERSONS* AND JEHANNE IN *JEHANNE OF THE WITCHES* ALL SHOULD BE PERCEIVED AS VICTIMS, YET THEY ARE STRONG AND, THOUGH THEY ALL DIE, VICTORIOUS OVER THOSE PERSECUTING OR HARASSING THEM.

SC: I sort of wanted Jehanne to survive. Clarke had posed that as a challenge to me. He wanted me to write a play about a strong woman because he perceived Hannah and Moo as weak! I disagree with him about them.

JR: IT'S THEIR STRENGTH THAT TERRIFIES THE MEN AND ATTRACTS THEM AT THE SAME TIME.

SC: Yes. I think he wanted me to write a play about a woman who wasn't victimized. So I picked Joan of Arc. The Big Martyr! But in one sense, I really believe that Jehanne isn't the victim, certainly not in my play: the victim is Gilles de Rais and the play is his version of the events. It's as if he's desperately trying to re-write her history.

JR: AND YOU LIKE TO SHOW THE DISTURBING SIDE OF THE KNOWN STORY TOO.

SC: That's the nature of drama. Showing a situation and then asking, "Well, what if this awful thing happened?" *Status quo* being disrupted.

JR: DO PEOPLE EXPECT THAT TO BE YOUR PENCHANT? YOUR ROLE?

SC: People used to think I should be a kindergarten teacher or something like that. I guess because I look quite calm.

JR: ARE THEY EXPECTING SOMEONE IN A LONG BLACK CLOAK CLUTCHING A DAGGER?

SC: After they've read my work? I don't know. People are sometimes offended or shocked by what I've written. That doesn't motivate me: I don't write to shock or to offend. But the writer in me doesn't really care what people think.

One of my favourite writers, Jean Dutourd, talks about writing as going down into the ocean and digging up either treasures or rubber boots: you don't ever know what you're going to find. And while you're down there, the world doesn't matter. You really don't care what people think of you and you're not trying to please any one. You're writing because you're investigating.

JR: YOU STARTED AS A PAINTER. WHY DO YOU WRITE?

SC: I get a thrill out of it. When I painted, I never got the same thrill. I could be calm and distant as a painter.

I never really thought of myself as a writer for years. I wrote at university, when I was doing a degree in art, and people said they liked the plays. And then, when I was having a difficult time getting a gallery to exhibit my paintings, I kept telling myself that if I could find a good story to tell, then I would write a play. So when I did find the story, I wrote the play.

I was never able to paint from my imagination. I had to work from "life." That's a severe limitation for a painter. In my paintings, I always tried to tell a story.

I also write to solve mysteries. Good stories have a mystery at their root. When I start a play, all I know is that there's something about it that needs to be solved. Often I don't know what that is.

Lost Souls and Missing Persons was based on the death of someone I knew. She lived one sort of life and then, one day, just died. Out of the blue. Much of that play came out of me trying to put the pieces together, to complete the puzzle.

A lot of my plays present that sort of mystery. Like in *Jehanne of the Witches*, Joan of Arc becomes the best friend of Gilles de Rais who is Bluebeard and is later accused of murdering a great number of young boys. I had to figure out the connection.

JR: DO YOU FEEL A GREAT SENSE OF SATISFACTION AND A CHALLENGE MET WHEN YOU SOLVE THE MYSTERY?

SC: I never really feel like I've solved it. If I'm lucky, I'll have isolated the elements of the mystery. It's sort of touch and go. All the way through the writing process I'm never quite sure if it's going to work out. I'll just know instinctively that there's a sense that one particular element has to be put up against this other element. I won't know what's going to happen when I do that, though.

I have an idea, usually, of what the ending is going to be, but I won't ever know how they all get there.

JR: HOW MUCH INPUT DOES THE DIRECTOR HAVE? WHAT ROLE DOES SHE OR HE TAKE ON?

SC: Director/dramaturges are very helpful. Particularly in clarifying problems in a play. I usually do a first draft on my own. After that, I'm desperate to talk to someone about it.

Most of the best work I do with a director is one on one. I prefer to spend time talking to one person about a script. That way I understand what their point of view is, where they're coming from. Then I can decide what advice to take and what to reject.

Workshops help in that they let me hear what works and what doesn't. For the most part, actors have been really helpful to me.

JR: YOU'VE HAD WORKSHOPS IN SEVERAL THEATRES. DO YOU PREFER STAGED WORKSHOPS WITH AUDIENCE OR CLOSED READINGS?

SC: Both are useful. The only criticism I have is that you never like to think you're being auditioned to be produced by a company.

It was in the first Factory Theatre workshop of *Moo* five years ago that we discovered that it was a comedy! I thought it was a riot: I felt vindicated. I was hoping it would be funny in places, but the actors had all been quite serious about it. You could see the surprise on the actors' faces when the audiences burst out laughing.

After I wrote my first play, my friend Camille Mitchell held an informal dinner party *cum* play-reading. She was an actress at the Shaw Festival at the time, so she asked her actor friends to come and read my play. That helped me a great deal. I heard people reading and got a good idea of what worked and what didn't: of what to do next.

JR: IT'S VERY DIFFERENT TO HEAR ACTORS READ THE WORDS THAN IT IS TO HEAR THEM IN YOUR HEAD, ISN'T IT?

SC: Yes. Mrs. Cape in *Lost Souls and Missing Persons* is a good example. I'd imagined her to be this Gorgon figure. Then I heard Pat Hamilton read her in a workshop at Banff years ago, and she sounded so sweet. It made the role much more frightening. She was so "nice" outwardly, and Pat made her seem to be trying to do her best.

JR: LET'S TALK ABOUT THE CAPE FAMILY. THEY ARE DANGEROUS BECAUSE THEY SEEM HARMLESSLY ANNOYING.

SC: It's almost a question of charity and where that leads. You try to help people like the Capes, but if you don't really like them then you're not helping them.

Years ago I got into a situation where I tried to help someone I didn't like. It's fascinating how the tables got turned. I started out thinking I was doing a good thing and then began to think, "Well, I'm not happy. Maybe I'm being a horrible person. I'm making fun of them through my charity."

What interested me in the relationship between the Capes and Lyle is that he got sucked into their world and then got blamed for being better than them. He got blamed for being who he was. Once again, it's a case of being victimized by victims.

JR: DO YOU THINK THAT TRULY HONEST PEOPLE HAVE A CHANCE OF SURVIVING IN A WORLD THAT'S BUILT ON CONVENTIONAL MORALITY?

SC: There's an upper/middle class politeness that I like playing with in my plays. The types who adhere to that politeness are absolutely no match for people who actually *want* something. In *Lost Souls and Missing Persons*, Lyle is one of those polite people and he's no match for the bulldozers like Mrs. Cape.

I always find it funny to watch polite people trying to ignore the fact that they're being bulldozed. They usually try to clamber out of the situation. Politely.

In *Jehanne of the Witches*, Joan is a holy fool. In fact, so is Nesbitt in *Lost Souls and Missing Persons*. They're honest and that alone protects them. Hannah is also protected, but only when she's Zombie, when she's honest. No evil happens to her until she comes to consciousness. The gods look after people who can't look after themselves. . . .

JR: HANNAH IS PROTECTED UNTIL SHE PUTS HER CIVILIZED FACE BACK ON.

SC: She starts to put it back on. She begins to feel ashamed at what she's done. She's affected by the moral world when she realizes, "Oh my God, I've been with this stranger. Who is he? I don't know." The irony is that she's quite protected when she's in the situation she identifies as danger, but the minute she leaves, she's no longer protected. And then she suffers the fate she probably would have suffered in the first place.

JR: SO THE AMORAL PEOPLE WHO MAKE THEIR OWN RULES ARE SAFE AS LONG AS THEY FOLLOW THEIR INSTINCTS. THE MOMENT THEY START TO PLAY THE GAME BY OTHER PEOPLE'S RULES, THEY BECOME SUSCEPTIBLE TO DANGER.

SC: Yes. It's a "loss of innocence." That's the moment that fascinates me, that loss of innocence.

Joan loses her innocence. It's one thing to have power, but it's another thing to pursue it. And Joan goes from having power to wanting power to keeping power to maintaining power. That's ultimately her downfall: that she can't be a man or a young boy all her life, which is really what she wants. Or at least she's persuaded by Gilles de Rais that that's what she wants. . . . I don't know that Joan actually would have wanted power to that degree, but he infected her with the desire.

JR: SO HANNAH'S POWER COMES FROM INNOCENCE. WHERE IS MOO IN TERMS OF POWER?

SC: I guess I was on the same wave length when I wrote those two plays. Both Hannah and Moo are wanderers. Hannah makes an interior journey backwards. She's re-examining her life, so while she's Zombie she's going back in time. Moo's journey is physical, exterior travel. She's tracking down the object of her desire. Hannah's tracking down the reason for her attraction to the object of her desire. She's trying to find the root of it.

Moo does what you do if you're involved in a love relationship that should be right, but for some reason isn't. Moo is an examination of how much you can apply yourself to make it right. Moo's answer is to apply all her will and determination and make this man love her. And, in fact, he does love her, but because she's so wilful about it, he's all the more determined not to love her. I'm really fascinated by the plain old-fashioned battle of the sexes.

JR: HOW DO MEN REACT TO *MOO*?

SC: Some men have told me that they think of Moo as a victim. They see the play as a sad story about a sad woman. None of the women I talked to think that at all. They think it's really funny. They're primarily interested in the sisters and Moo's relationships to them. They perceive Harry as a secondary character, not a vital element to the play. Women will say, "Well, it's about the family, the son. Oh yes, and then there's that guy. . . ." Men, on the other hand, think of the Moo-Harry relationship as the absolute pivotal point of the play.

JR: CLARKE ROGERS IS DIRECTING *JEHANNE OF THE WITCHES* AT TARRAGON IN THE 1989-90 SEASON. WHAT'S IT GOING TO BE LIKE TO HAVE A MALE DIRECTOR ON A PLAY ABOUT JOAN?

SC: In a weird way, Clarke suggested the idea for the play in the first place. He didn't just say, "Do a play about Joan of Arc," but he did say, "I want a play about female power and witchcraft." I took him to mean *wicca*, the ancient religion, more than contemporary witchcraft. These days there's a whole resurgence of interest in the Goddess, and because I didn't know anything about any of it, I started to do a lot of general reading.

The play itself came about in a strange way. When I responded to Clarke by saying I wanted to write about Joan of Arc as a witch, he looked at me as if to say *"What* are you on about?!" And a year earlier, I'd thought about writing a play about Bluebeard. Not Gilles de Rais, but the fairy tale Bluebeard who murdered his wives.

Now, in these Goddess books that I was reading, you're told to ask for what you want, and you will get it. So I asked for an idea for this play. I'd been reading for about six months and I just didn't know what to do. I got stacks of books from the library about different types of strong women, like pioneers, for example.

Then I went to an occult book store to pick up a book, and the man running the store looked at me and said, "Bluebeard was Joan of Arc's best friend." Just out of the blue, he said that! And I gave a start, and he said, "They were best friends, and if you want to go after an interesting relationship, then that's the one to go after."

Then he showed me a copy of Margaret Mitchell's *God of the Witches.* Mitchell is an anthropologist and her theory is that both Gilles de Rais and Joan were witches.

Both of them were burned at the stake. Gilles de Rais saved Joan's life twice before. He could have saved her that third time too, but he didn't. According to the witch cult, she was the Divine Sacrifice. Later in his life, Gilles became obsessed with Joan. He wrote a mystery play about her which became the first non-secular play written and produced in Europe. He revolutionized theatre! He actually rented the entire town of Orleans for six months, hired 550 actors and invited people from all over Europe to attend. He paid for all of this with his own money, and spent his entire fortune on the production.

Mitchell also believed that Gilles de Rais was innocent of the murders of all of those young boys. He even hired one of them to play Joan in his play. When the play was produced, the Church became angry and accused him of witchcraft. He was burned at the stake nine years after Joan's death.

Gilles' theatricality was incredible. First he denied his "guilt" when accused of witchcraft and murder, then he did a sudden turnabout confession. His confession was so moving that the parents of the dead children began to weep and forgive him. They then formed a procession and accompanied him to the stake. The stake became a shrine where, once a year, mothers would beat their children. It was also a shrine for expectant mothers to pray for milk. The shrine was operational up to the time of the French Revolution.

For me, the challenge was figuring out how to put the two people and their stories together. What was going on? How did this situation come about: Joan became a sacrifice to male-dom and Bluebeard ended up being a sacrifice to female-dom.

So walking into that book store got me right into the heart of that play!

Clarke helped me develop the play for about a year. I have a tendency to get stuck in history, immersed in detail. He always brought me back to the through-line. He really helped me through this play.

And what developed is clearly as much Gilles' story as it is Jehanne's.

JR: THEY'RE INTERTWINED. BOTH HAVE BEEN SACRIFICED.

SC: Yes. I think Gilles is innocent, except in the play, I've made that ambiguous. It's more interesting theatrically if he's guilty.

JR: HOW DO YOU INTERPRET JOAN'S THREE VOICES?

SC: After all the reading I did, I see them in the same light as me asking for a topic and having the man in the book store give me one. Mitchell explains the voices as real people who were spies helping Joan gain power in court. I find that explanation banal and not nearly as interesting as her actually hearing voices. I want the mystery of voices in my play.

It is fascinating to think that some people hear voices that tell them to commit murder while others hear voices that tell them to go out and save France!

JR: WELL, WE'VE HEARD OF THE MUSES FOR THOUSANDS OF YEARS. . . . WHAT ELSE ARE YOU WORKING ON NOW?

SC: I'm working on a play that will play with visual imagery in a theatre context. It's also about loss of innocence and where image and reality overlap.

I suppose it's similar in a way to what concerned me in *Jehanne of the Witches*. That's how I write, I guess. I tend to get onto a certain issue or idea and have to keep writing until I've solved it.

JR: THERE'S A BARRIER BETWEEN REALITY AND ANOTHER UN-CONSCIOUS LEVEL. WHICH LEVEL IS IN CONTROL CONCERNS US, DOESN'T IT?

SC: Yes. That's certainly what *Jehanne of the Witches* is about. There's Jehanne and there's the young boy, François, who plays her in Gilles' play. One is beloved and one can't be reached. I've always like that idea of the wrong person being in the right body.

JR: WHAT HAPPENS WHEN IT'S THE RIGHT PERSON IN THE WRONG BODY?

SC: Maybe that'll be my next play!

JR: DO YOU THINK OF COMBINING YOUR PAINTING AND YOUR PLAY-WRITING?

SC: Actually, I'm trying to do that in my current play, *Life without Instruction.* It's about a seventeenth-century Italian woman artist named Artemesia Gentileschi.

Her father was a painter and had apprenticed her. Her paintings are very strong: similar to those of Caravaggio. She was schooled in his style, in fact. I'm using the paintings as subplots to reflect her life.

She did one, for example, of Susannah and the Elders (the Bible story), and I'm sure that the girl in the painting is her. She usually painted herself. In it, her father and a male friend of his are leaning over her in a really sinister way. She painted this before her father's friend raped her. There is a conspiracy between her father and his friend that she somehow knew about before it happened.

JR: *THE TRIAL OF JUDITH K.* IS A FEMINIST ADAPTATION OF KAFKA'S NOVEL, *THE TRIAL.* HOW DOES THE ADAPTATION DIFFER FROM ORIGINAL WRITING?

SC: In an adaptation, you have to combine your sensibility with the original author's. It's very hard to tread the fine line between respecting the original author's intentions and being totally swamped by them. My play, *Trial* (that I wrote as a commission for Tamahnous Theatre in Vancouver), was an adaptation. It was their idea to have Judith K. as the protagonist instead of Joseph K.

In terms of structure, I think it was too similar to the novel for it to work well as a stage play. Robert Rooney was interested in producing it at Toronto Workshop Productions, but he felt it needed work. We worked very hard on it together at Banff, and my new draft, *The Trial of Judith K.*, is now quite different from the novel. I would now call the play "loosely based" on Kafka's novel, rather than an adaptation.

JR: KAFKA'S WRITING HAS ALWAYS SEEMED TO ME TO BE THE MALE, DARK SIDE OF LEWIS CARROLL'S *ALICE THROUGH THE LOOKING GLASS* OR *ALICE IN WONDERLAND.*

SC: Yes. And that was what was wrong with my first adaptation! Judith K. falls down the hole (the arrest), and one weird, unrelated event after another happens to her. Kafka's *The Trial* isn't tragedy; it's like suspended animation or a waiting room. Granted, a lot of twentieth century theatre focuses on the theme of the Waiting Room, but that's not the sort of play I wanted to write.

At one point, I tried to inject the Medea story into the play. Don't ask me why. It seemed like a good idea at the time. Well, it didn't work.

Adaptations are usually from novels, and the structure of novels is like a veneer. Events and conflicts don't repeat. In adapting you have to re-make the piece so people can reappear.

I love the mystery of the story. I always like to leave people up in the air for the first fifteen minutes of the play, not letting them know what's going on. And I enjoy scaring people. A lot of time that suspense comes about from putting what seem to be unrelated elements together and then slowly threading them.

JR: DO YOU CONSIDER YOURSELF A VANCOUVER PLAYWRIGHT, A TORONTO PLAYWRIGHT OR A CANADIAN PLAYWRIGHT?

SC: I've lived in Toronto since I was twenty. I grew up in Vancouver. I suppose that in a way I'm like David French, who is living in Toronto, writing about a place that he left when he was six years old. Whatever I write about and my sensibilities are Vancouver-based: you can never escape your background and it forms the root of what you're writing.

So I guess I'd have to say all of the above.

5. Playwright Judith Thompson

Michael Cooper

Born in Montreal in 1954, Judith Thompson graduated from Queen's University in 1976 and National Theatre School (Acting Programme) in 1979. Her first play, *The Crackwalker*, premiered in 1980 at Theatre Passe Muraille. Her second, *White Biting Dog*, won the Governor General's Award for Drama in 1984. Her third full-length play, *I Am Yours (1987)* won the Chalmers Award. Playwright-in-residence at Tarragon Theatre, Judith has also written for radio, television and film. *The Other Side of the Dark* won the 1989 Governor General's Award.

Did you ever start thinkin somethin, and it's like ugly . . . ? And ya can't beat it out of your head? I wouldn't be scared of it if it was sitting in front of me, I'd beat it to shit — nothin wouldn't stop me — but I can't beat it cause it's in my head fuck.

Alan in *The Crackwalker*

I — didn't mean that I mean — jeesh what's wrong with me I mean — I want to know what it is you have when you walk into a room you — make me feel as though I'm flying in my sleep, you know? Do you — know what that is? Maybe. . . .

Pony in *White Biting Dog*

Produced and published plays:

White Biting Dog. Toronto: Playwrights Canada, 1985.

The Other Side of the Dark. Toronto: Coach House Press, 1989. Includes *The Crackwalker*, *I Am Yours*, *Pink*, and *Tornado*. *The Crackwalker* was originally published by Playwrights Canada (Toronto, 1981).

Judith Thompson Interview
by Judith Rudakoff

JR: IS WRITING PLAYS A COMPULSION? A BATTLE? A JOY?

JT: The initial impulse is a joy.

JR: WHAT ABOUT THE REST OF THE PROCESS — IS IT A BUSINESS OR A VOCATION?

JT: Theatre is a vocation. If it was a business, I'd be the stupidest business-person in the world! It's just not lucrative. I suppose it might be if I'd write the kind of hit play that would be produced in all the huge regional theatres, the ones with thousands of seats. It's not that I don't think I could write that type of play: I just haven't. I have to be honest and follow through with my instincts when I'm writing and that's not the direction my instincts are taking me right now.

When I write, I'm like the Eskimo with a sculpture: chiselling away until I come to the jewel, the shape. It's hard, hard work and it's only in the refinement that I find the nuggets.

It's not like it was before I had children. Now, I have four hours a day where I go to the office that Tarragon has given me, and I write. And it becomes like automatic writing. Stuff just comes out! Some of it is garbage and through my learned knowledge of structure I do something with it.

JR: WHEN WE SAT ON A PANEL TOGETHER AT THE GOETHE INSTITUTE/TORONTO FREE THEATRE GERMAN THEATRE SYMPOSIUM IN 1987, SOMEONE ASKED YOU THE USUAL QUESTION, "WHY DO YOU WRITE" AND YOUR ANSWER AFFECTED ME GREATLY. YOU SAID, "IT'S NOT A QUESTION OF WANTING TO OR NEEDING TO WRITE: IT JUST POURS OUT LIKE BLOOD."

JT: Yes, it does. But it pours out *when I sit down to work*. In the past five years especially, since I've had children, the writing has had to become a job. It's how I make a living.

JR: DID YOU CHOOSE THEATRE, OR DID THEATRE PICK YOU? COULD YOUR FIELD HAVE JUST AS EASILY BEEN SHORT-STORY WRITING OR POETRY?

JT: The theatrical medium is where I'm happiest. It's what I breathe, what I know. I've been involved in theatre since I was very young. My mother was involved in theatre and I was in a play for her when I was eleven. For me, it was like being apprenticed to a trade.

I'm doing a lot of film-writing now, but that's a separate medium. Film-writing is like having a second trade. I'm just learning about it, and that's taking a lot of time.

Writing for live theatre is what I have an instinct for. You know you're good at something when your unconscious knowledge of it is far beyond your conscious knowledge of it. It's when I surprise myself that the piece works!

JR: WHAT'S THE DIFFERENCE FOR YOU BETWEEN WRITING FOR FILM AND WRITING FOR THEATRE?

JT: The main difference is that in film I think with my eyes and dialogue is disposable. Dialogue is the essence of theatre.

JR: URJO KAREDA ONCE SAID THAT ONE OF THE MOST EXTRAORDINARY ELEMENTS OF YOUR WORK IS YOUR ABILITY TO GIVE AUDIENCE MEMBERS A MOMENT DURING EACH PERFORMANCE WHEN, INDIVIDUALLY, THEY WILL SAY TO THEMSELVES: "HOW DID SHE KNOW THAT SECRET ABOUT ME?" IT'S UNCANNY HOW YOU CAN REACH INTO OTHER PEOPLE'S UNCONSCIOUS, HOW YOU CAN GET IN PAST THE CIVILIZED MASK.

JT: I do believe in a collective unconscious. I believe that we can all relate to everything. Somewhere. Somehow.

And then there's truth. The concept of truth is not limited to our society. The dream exists in other societies.

JR: CIVILIZATION IMPOSES OUTSIDE BARRIERS ON PEOPLE, SO THAT THERE'S A CERTAIN PERSON THAT WE SHOW TO THE WORLD. YOUR PLAYS EXPLORE PEOPLE TRYING TO FIND WHAT'S ON THE INSIDE AND ACCESS IT, DISCOVERING THAT THAT INSIDE IS A DIFFICULT PLACE TO GET TO. YOUR CHARACTERS SEEM TO WANT TO RIP OPEN THEIR CHESTS AND LET IT ALL COME OUT: SOMETIMES THEY CAN'T AND SOMETIMES THEY CAN.

JT: There's a difficult line between civilized and uncivilized in society. We have to keep the uncivilized part of ourselves under wraps: Plato was right. The old id, as Freud knew, has to be kept buried very deep. In murderers, the id is screaming.

When I write, my own conscious is very close to the surface. I look at it a lot and I spend a lot of the process getting to know myself, like psychoanalysts who learn their trade through being psychoanalysed themselves.

I was so far away from myself when I began in theatre that I don't think a word that came out of my mouth was true. Not a gesture. I do agree with Plato about keeping elements buried, but it's very important for us to keep in touch with what's going on inside. Once you're in your late twenties and thirties if you don't do serious work on who you are, if you don't acknowledge and meet fatality, then there is such damage that can be done. You have to really work. You have to think and work on yourself.

This begins to sound like I'm some kind of evangelist and I'm not. I'm more like an *idiot savante* at the first stage of the writing. I just try to get inside the characters and they become amalgamations of my relatives, my friends, my acquaintances. One person will say to me, "Dammit, I've always wanted to be the centre," and these bells go off and it becomes the central speech of the play — I sort of just *take* it.

I take things that I've seen. Things from when I was little. I'm like a magpie: I throw it all into the soup!

And then the play starts to develop its own structures and themes and *it* says, "No. I don't want this part. It may be a brilliant little metaphor, but throw it out! It's no good!" And I have to pick out all those things that don't belong. And often, I end up taking out all the things with which I began the play.

But what's left after that stage is what's grown up underneath it. Like when you put a band-aid on and suddenly the skin is grown over, the scab falls off and there it is: there's the play. Because, you see, all my first ideas, the ones I discard, were false — imposed — just me being clever.

The creation happens itself. I am somehow fortuitously plugged in. It all comes through the typewriter! It's such hard, hard work after the first couple of drafts, you know. With the first few drafts, everything does flow out, but then it's a case of refinement, refinement and refinement, sometimes for years.

There are times when I think that the reason I am successful is that I work really, really hard at it.

But I turn a lot of people off with my plays.

JR: THERE ARE A LOT OF PEOPLE OUT THERE WHO FEEL SOME-THING PENETRATING THEIR CIVILIZED SHIELD, AND THEY'RE NOT READY TO BE PROBED, THE SKIN HAS GROWN TOO THICK. THOSE ARE THE ONES, IT SEEMS TO ME, AT THAT MOMENT WHEN YOUR WORK TOUCHES IN, THAT TAKE OFF; THEY'RE THE ONES WHO WALK OUT.

JT: They claim to have been bored. Or that they don't know people who talk like my characters. And I have to respect them. Maybe for them it is boring. Maybe they don't like the plays. It would be arrogant of me to say that it was them and not me. . . .

Let's go back to my shocking people — I am always very, very shocked when people are shocked. The last thing I ever want to do is offend. I go out of my way to please little old ladies. I would never offend them. I'm not the kind of person who would say, "Well, to hell with you if you can't take a joke." I'm really conservative that way. I like to please. I'm careful of people's feelings. And yet, every time I write an adult play, it seems to become offensive to many people. . . .

I have these great aunts and I've spent hours and hours in their apartments looking at old books. And I have a great sense of family. So it's so horrible for me when I see these poor little old ladies — and I don't mean to be condescending to them — getting upset and walking out. I feel terrible. Because I guess I'm very naive when I write. It just doesn't occur to me that these characters would offend anybody because they're people and I care about them. And you just don't care about people because they're nice or they're pretty. . . .

I would like to reach more people with my plays if I could, but what do I do? Do I compromise, or is there another way? *The Wizard of Oz* reaches more people and it penetrates into the collective unconscious and our need for home: maybe I'll write a *Wizard of Oz*! Actually, I have been thinking that maybe I'll write a children's play because that way I wouldn't feel the instinct to be offensive. I have children and I know what they can tolerate and cope with.

JR: ARE PEOPLE SURPRISED WHEN THEY SEE YOU FOR THE FIRST TIME?

JT: It's funny. I'll be at weddings or functions and the person sitting next to me will think I must be racy or radical and talk to me in a vulgar way because of my plays. I just turn away, disgusted. I'm really very conservative in many ways. My characters say these things — I don't. I don't use that language. Unless I'm forced to. And then I'll qualify it.

A lot of people expect green hair.

JR: HOW DO YOU DEAL WITH THESE TYPES OF REACTIONS?

JT: Maybe I try to counteract it by dressing particularly conservatively. Sometimes I really admire those people with the green hair and I wish that I could make a piece of art out of myself, but then I realize that I just don't want to intimidate people, to draw attention to myself. Because if I did that, then they wouldn't talk to me. I like people to be open with me. I think that there are times when I unconsciously play low-status so that people will be comfortable with me. . . .

I do these things because I want to know about people. It took me years to learn to *listen*, rather than just wait till the other person finished talking. And I realized that there was a whole world of people out there saying things that I wanted to know. Now I listen and find out so much.

I have a real allegiance to the truth. About people. Some people say, "Well, diarrhoea is a fact of life, but we don't show that on stage. . . ." That's the old argument: psychological truths are different. Physical truths are one thing, we understand and see them; we do not know about psychological truths. We hide them.

JR: IN TERMS OF THE WRITING PROCESS, YOU ALSO LISTEN TO YOUR CHARACTERS, DON'T YOU?

JT: I have a really low threshold of boredom. So I act out parts and then I know when sections are too long. I cut, cut, cut.

It's really the only way for me, the acting out. And still, I forget and I don't do it and then I make the same mistakes in everything I write, every time. I have to go the long way around every time.

For instance, in *I Am Yours* there was a male character I was having trouble with and I thought, "Well, why not inhabit him for a while?" and then I realized, suddenly, how everything should be. Just by feeling like that character, by being him in that situation: that's how I knew exactly how it should be.

JR: CAN YOU GIVE ME AN EXAMPLE OF WHEN YOU DIDN'T IN-HABIT THE CHARACTER, ACT HIM OUT, AND WHERE THAT LED YOU?

JT: Cape Race in *White Biting Dog*. I don't think I fully in-habited him. I think he was half there. Or maybe he was there as a person but not . . . there's a real difference between character and characterization.

Character is what you do, your actions. It's truly who you are, especially in times of crisis. It's the choices that you make. Characterization is the person you present to the world.

With Cape, I just didn't get it. I didn't "go the distance."

You know, I suppose there's definitely an element of me in my characters. I don't know if that's just the part of me that taps into the collective unconscious, or if that's what makes me me.

It doesn't have to be true. Take Dee in *I Am Yours*, for example. I even heard people in the audience saying, "I understand she wrote this when she was pregnant and she was feeling very ambiva-lent. . . ." Never. Not for a moment.

On the other hand, Dee is not a complete character. I've got to go back. She's complete as a character *inside*, but not outside. I need something to help people in, to make her more appealing.

JR: WHEN PEOPLE TALK ABOUT YOUR WORK, THEY OFTEN TRY TO REASON IT OUT, TO EXPLAIN IT. DOES THAT ANNOY YOU?

JT: I love every take, every interpretation.

JR: EVEN THE ACADEMICS WHO SUGGEST THAT THE WHITE DOG IS OBVIOUSLY GOD SPELLED BACKWARDS . . . ?

JT: I think it's wonderful. There have been academics who have written papers that have revealed things to me. I don't pretend to be the author in the sense of the Knowing Creator. Often academics will find wonderful parallels and they'll say, "The street sign was 'Redwing' and the colour of the sky was red" when I chose the name because I just liked the sound of "redwing." Or because I saw a street sign that day when I was walking home from the grocery shop that said "Redwing.". . .

JR: ARE THERE OTHER WAYS IN WHICH YOU WORK THAT ARE IMPORTANT TO YOU?

JT: Unconsciously, there is some kind of structural working out that I'm not totally aware of. But it's there. I'm tremendously lucky that "it," that the images just happen for me. Sometimes when it doesn't work (for example, there'll be a song or something that doesn't fit), I'll consciously stop and say, "Well, there should be something in it about chickens." Or whatever.

There are times when I set out to write and I think, "Oh, sisters are interesting," and I'll write a monologue about pennies, and then one day I'll just sit down and write a plot outline, it'll just come. And I try not to think about it when I go home, because it's just too disturbing, and I close everything up and go home and fix dinner!

For me, the best things happen when I think. I get the chisel out and say, "Okay, crack the brain open." And I think, "Well, of course, *this* has to be *here.*"

As playwrights, we do all this for years and years and years and then people see it in two hours and they don't get one hundredth of what's in there. That's one reason I do appreciate those academics: because at least they take the time to see the layers and layers that would really take ten or fifteen viewings to penetrate. One might ask, is it worth it to write something so dense because, after all, people are only likely to see it once, and plays are difficult to read?

It is. Because that way it penetrates in a subliminal way. People will live with those images for a long time.

JR: DO YOU EVER HAVE THE URGE TO GO BACK AFTER A FIRST PRODUCTION AND REWRITE FOR THE SECOND PRODUCTION?

JT: If *White Biting Dog* was ever done again I'd do a lot of rewrites and I'd do a lot of cutting. We staged a scene for the 1987 Toronto Arts Awards with Shirley Douglas and Stephen Ouimette as Lomia and Pascal, a break-up scene. And it was then that I realized that I had just overwritten it. The writing was too self-consciously lyrical. I was intoxicated with lyricism. The play doesn't need all those strong images piled one on top of the other. That's what I'm learning from the cinema. Less *is* more.

The poor audience: people who are trapped in the theatre and they have to listen to some writer who is just showing off, flexing her muscles. . . .

JR: DO YOU THINK THAT PLAYWRIGHTS SHOULD EVER DIRECT THEIR OWN WORK?

JT: Writers should be able to direct their own works. They know the theatre. Essentially, I've directed all of mine. And I'm not a great director. I understand my plays, though. I understand them well and I'm pretty good with physicality, but I do stupid, terrible things with blocking. For instance, in NYC I had all three monologues at the same spot, till at the end the Artistic Director came by and said, "Judith, say, how about if we move them a-round?"

I understand everything about my plays. And I love it when someone has a better idea than I do. I love someone to come in and see things in a directorial way and turn it upside down, do wonderful things . . . it just hasn't happened yet.

It's not that the people who direct my plays haven't been good — because they have; it's just that perhaps their own visions were overwhelmed by mine. Because they had respect for my vision, they didn't allow their own to emerge.

Steven Bush did a wonderful production of *I Am Yours* in Ottawa in 1988. It was more visceral than Derek Goldby's premi-ere production at the Tarragon. Derek's production was problematic because it was really a co-direction with me. There were brilliant performances in it, but at the same time the actors felt stifled by us in a way.

There used to be a lot of new plays where the playwrights really didn't know what they were doing: they didn't know the theatrical medium, and they needed the actors desperately, to show them what the play was. I need the actor to play the piece, and to play it brilliantly, and to inhabit the work like Yehudi Menuhin inhabits a Bach piece. Menuhin is no less an artist because he doesn't write the notes.

I can't seem to convince actors that I have tremendous respect for their art, but that I don't need them to tell me who the charac-ter is. I know and I'm telling them. They can't say to me, "But this guy smokes." He does not smoke. I'm telling them. He comes from my unconscious and it would be sort of like them telling me that my mother wears wigs. She does not. I know. I feel like telling them, "You write your own play."

I do need them to bring their heart, their emotion, their ex-perience and to play it. There's a million things for them to find and play within the borders of their art.

Now the second, third, fourth productions: they do what they like. But in the premiere production I think there must be a mandate to present the writer's play.

JR: DO YOUR CHARACTERS BELIEVE IN ANYONE? LET'S TAKE SANDY IN *THE CRACKWALKER* AS AN EXAMPLE.

JT: Sandy believes that there's a right way to be and she's extremely Calvinist. She believes that the salt and pepper should be kept up in the second cupboard. She believes that when you butter toast, you butter to the edges. She believes that you have a cup of tea at ten o'clock. You don't wear mismatching socks, you wear matching gloves, you have your buttons done up, you have your clothes cleaned, you have your supper at five.

In other words, the quotidian is what saves her from the abyss.

She believes that if you buy everything you're taught and you live the way you are taught to live, you will be saved from the monster that's hovering around the periphery of civilization.

She's awfully surprised that she's not safe and her husband leaves. She keeps trying to observe these little laws and here are the monsters, yawning, right in her living room.

That scene where she's in bed with Theresa staying over and she goes out on the balcony and screams and screams and then comes back in and says, "It was nothing." Well, that's because it *can't* be anything. There are no monsters. I think maybe that's why we teach children about monsters: so that when they're eight we can turn around and tell them, "There are no monsters." And it's not till they're twenty-five that they realize, "Yes . . . there are. . . ."

I am still really truly surprised when I find out that policemen are sometimes corrupt. Because I believed what I was told about them. Like Sandy. She really believed all those things and she's very kind. She accepts Theresa for what she is. She says, "No, you're not retarded, you're just a little slow." And once you describe someone, they're okay. Sandy's a big pigeon-holer. "She's a little slow, but she's got a warm heart." Then that's all right.

So she believes in civilization, that it can be maintained. If you learn how to make a new drink then that's an achievement — and it is. And it's something she's done. She believes that you can put on eyeliner a different way and it can change your life.

JR: HOW WOULD YOU DEFINE "THE ABYSS"?

JT: The abyss is death. It's what you don't know. It can be terrible conflict at, for example, work. I live such a smooth life: I've made sure of that. You see an abyss when you're falling, in that dream where you're falling and falling and there's no bottom.

JR: EMILY DICKINSON'S CONCEPT OF THE ABYSS WAS DEATH, AND FOR YEARS SHE'D GO VISIT DYING PEOPLE. SHE WANTED TO SEE WHAT HAPPENED AFTER THEY WENT OVER THE EDGE, INTO DEATH.

JT: Everybody reads her poems at funerals. That wonderful poem about the "leagues out to sea, sweet intoxication." I want her poems to be read to me when I die: they're such a comfort. But do you think they're real? Do you think she ever found comfort watching all those people die?

JR: NO. I DON'T THINK SHE DID. THAT WAS THE PROBLEM. WHAT SHE DID DISCOVER WAS A NEW DEFINITION OF GOD: A NON-CHRISTIAN VIEW OF GOD AS THE "COLUMNAR SELF" SPIRALLING EVER INWARD TO A POINT AT THE CENTRE OF THE SELF.

JT: God is a newborn baby. Truly. You can really see God in a newborn baby. And it stays with them for a long time.

God is in every person — that's really hard to remember sometimes.

I do believe that God is in every one of my characters showing me herself. At little moments.

That's as scary as it is beautiful.

God is the innocence of a newborn baby; when people show that part of themselves, that eternal flame that's guarded; when they show that that's a moment of pure beauty, when they let you see it. Some people's flame seems to have gone right out. . . .

Spontaneity — that's what we look for on stage. Bring on a dog or a baby and everyone's blown away. The search for that spontaneity is religious.

JR: DO YOU CONSIDER YOURSELF OR YOUR CHARACTERS OPTIMISTIC ?

JT: I think I'm very optimistic, yes. I think I'm not cynical or pessimistic at all — I should be more cynical than I am. Pony, in *White Biting Dog*, believes in the good in everybody. She's not stupid. Obviously, though, you become more cynical as you become more experienced.

JR: OR AS YOU ENTER MORE INTO THE REAL WORLD. DO YOU FIND THAT THE CHARACTERS WHO ARE MORE ROOTED IN REALITY DEPEND MORE ON REALITY AND ARE LESS OPTIMISTIC?

JT: If you have the good fortune to come from a good and loving home, you're encouraged and loved and get a lot of attention. Then you go into the world and people are nasty. I think that there is a sadistic impulse in everybody and that's where torture begins.

JR: CAN YOU GIVE ME AN EXAMPLE FROM THE PLAYS?

JT: Alan, in *The Crackwalker*, is tortured by his own mind, his own fears, the cauliflower. He's tortured by his lack of self esteem because he can never quite match up. He'll be feeling really good, and then somebody will be haughty to him because his coat has a stain on it. People won't treat him as an equal, can't get it through their heads that the person lying in the gutter is no different than they are at all. They are actually fooled by the hype that there is such a thing as "better."

JR: PEOPLE OFTEN TALK ABOUT YOUR CHARACTERS IN TERMS OF THEIR SOCIAL GROUP. . . .

JT: My characters just don't have a particular social group.

JR: LET'S PHRASE THAT DIFFERENTLY: DO YOU THINK THAT YOUR CHARACTERS CAN ESCAPE THEIR UPBRINGING?

JT: My characters can't escape the effects of environment, because they'll always, always be with you. But just because your parents didn't read doesn't mean that you can't. Although you might be less likely to want to.

JR: AT THE END OF *THE CRACKWALKER*, DO YOU THINK THAT SANDY AND JOE ARE GOING TO CHANGE THEIR LIVES? WILL CALGARY MAKE A DIFFERENCE?

JT: No, Calgary to Joe and Sandy is like Moscow — pie in the sky. Joe will repeat his mistakes. It's very hard to change.

JR: OBVIOUSLY YOUR UPBRINGING HAS HAD SOMETHING TO DO WITH WHO YOU ARE AND WHAT COMES OUT IN YOUR WRITING. HOW DO YOU THINK LIVING IN TORONTO FOR A GOOD NUMBER OF YEARS AND HAVING CHILDREN WILL AFFECT THE WRITING YET TO COME?

JT: Having children had a huge effect on my writing. I have become more in touch with myself and with wonder. It's just helped me. I've always been kind of a child myself so maybe having children has made me into more of an adult.

It's also helped me in the sense that with children around you, you can't be solipsistic.

JR: DO YOU TAKE YOUR CHILDREN TO SEE THEATRE?

JT: I do take my children to theatre. And when I was a child I always went.

JR: IF YOU COULD BRING A NEW AUDIENCE INTO THE THEATRE, WHO WOULD YOU WANT TO ENTICE? WHAT WOULD YOU OFFER THEM?

JT: I want the people who go to hockey games at Maple Leaf Gardens to go to plays. I don't blame them for not going, it's generally very disappointing. To me, in any event. But we're all striving to make it better. We are all willing to admit that there are many disappointments, *but* there is this, somewhere in there, this golden egg, this moment we're all striving for, this moment of pure experience. What I call Truth. And when it *is* there. . . .

I'm having an ongoing argument with a Marxist friend. Marxists all are very snide if you say you think there is such a thing as Truth. They don't believe that there's any such thing as a moment, say, in theatre or in any art that transcends time, culture, generation, place. They think it's all contextual. They believe that we are moved because we are taught to believe that, for example, mothers should love their babies. They think that everything is placed and understood within an historical context. They don't believe anyone can be free of that.

Now, if that's true then I might as well throw all my stuff in the garbage and go home.

And I just find it enraging. How could it be true? Where does that leave the Grimms' fairy tales? My daughter is moved by them. They're timeless. And that sense of timelessness, that truth: that's what we're all striving for.

I keep telling my Marxist friends that context does help to bring the audience into the moment; it does help to lead them there. If you recognize yourself, then you're more likely to identify a little bit. Some people say, "Oh, Judith, your dialogue is so great." Well, dialogue is nothing, it's just an ear, it's just dressing to help people into the moment.

Actors always say, "Oh, I like your words." Well, it's the third, fourth, fifth thing down the line for me if we're talking about what makes a play work. Its those moments, those timeless moments that make the difference — the dreaded word: Truth.

When there is Truth in a play, when one of those moments happens, in any play, no matter how messy its structure is, or how flawed its thinking is, then I'll praise it to the sky.

JR: IS THERE AN ARTIST, EITHER OF OUR TIME OR NOT, WHO WRITES WITH THIS TRUTH? WHO HAS THESE MOMENTS?

JT: Howard Brenton. Lawrence Jeffery. Sally Clark. Joan MacLeod. Colleen Murphy.

I was, of course, also influenced by Tennessee Williams, Edward Albee, Mickey Mouse, My Favourite Martian, Mr. Ed, the Talking Horse — it's true! Really. Because we grew up watching them everyday on television. Ours was a typical late-fifties, early sixties household, so I can't deny it: I must have been heavily influenced by all that pap. Not that Mickey Mouse is pap!

Mickey Mouse: why do we, as children, respond to that little mouse! Truth, again.

And there's also great Truth in the Grimms' fairy tales. They influenced me greatly. Anyone who looks closely at my work can see that. But again, we're talking about tapping into a collective unconscious. They do, and I hope when my plays are working they do the same kind of thing. I think the Grimms' fairy tales gave me the courage. I didn't use to think you needed courage! People used to say, "Oh Judith, you're so brave," and I'd think, "Brave, you don't have to be brave to have a character killing a baby on stage. That's just what the character does. That's what happened." And the Grimms' fairy tales are *worse* than anything I write! Far worse.

JR: WHAT'S YOUR FAVOURITE FAIRY TALE?

JT: I don't know which my favourite is. They're all the same tale, in a way. There are actually about three tales.

And the major recurring character in most of them is the Bad Mother, the Wicked Stepmother. I think it must be little girls' Electra conflict coming out: Freud was right.

I am a devoted Freudian in some ways. I've read all his work. I went through all of it in about a year and a half and audited a course on him when I was on a Canada Council B-Grant. He does have that fairy-tale desire to make everything fit into his scheme. It doesn't.

On the other hand, in fairy tales you also have the Blue Fairy and the Fairy Godmother, because the kids, the daughters, of course, *do* love their mothers and need them.

Did these authors know this? I doubt it. In fact, I never understand what *I* write a lot of the time. I'm just amazed at it myself.

JR: HAVE YOU NOTICED THAT IN YOUR PLAYS, MOST OF THE TIME, IF YOU HAVE A MOTHER, THEN YOU GIVE HER A SON?

JT: I guess I do have mothers and sons in my plays. I wonder why I do that. . . .

JR: WELL, LET'S TAKE ONE OF THE LESS OBVIOUS MOTHER-SON RELATIONSHIPS: THERESA AND HER SON IN *THE CRACKWALKER*.

JT: When I was working as an Adult Protective Service Worker, I met a couple who had had a son and the father had killed him.

That was the kernel of that story, of those characters.

You know, maybe I would have done better to make Cape a woman. . . .

Of course, the obvious answer as to why I write about mothers and sons is that I was brought up a Catholic and there's one big mother-son relationship!

I had been thinking, before writing *White Biting Dog*, about manipulative people, sociopathic people and why they are the way they are. I know a few and by coincidence they all happen to be male. Men have a different sense of what power is than women do.

I looked at a religious card the other day and it said, "He has risen" and I thought — can you imagine growing up with, "She has risen"? Can you imagine the difference that would have made to who you are? She has risen.

JR: OFTEN YOUR CHARACTERS SEEK SHELTER OR DRAW STRENGTH FROM THE WOMEN IN YOUR PLAYS, EVEN IF *THEIR* SITUATIONS ARE LITTLE BETTER.

JT: Yes, people do come to the women for strength. To the mother in them. Yes, you're right, Sandy acts that way too. Sandy fixes everything. Theresa fixes Alan. Pony, Lomia do. Not in *I Am Yours*, though. In that play Mac was the only fixer.

It startles me when my plays come out because I never think they are a map of my unconscious. I really do believe that they are a map of the collective unconscious.

JR: DO YOU WORK WITH THE DESIGNERS OF YOUR PRODUCTIONS? DO YOU SEE A PLAY IN THE SAME WAY THAT YOU HEAR IT?

JT: I feel sorry for whoever designs my plays: they're so filled with voices in the dark. Not so much any more. And I do have some, a handful, of strong visual images for each play.

In *I Am Yours*, all the designers could really do is make an acting machine, so that with all the short scenes it wouldn't be clunky. Jim Plaxton did a nice job. Cathy Norman did a lovely job in Ottawa and actually made the environment quite pretty. There was less distance for them to travel. Fatter and wider. Beautiful. It really worked.

I tend to say things to designers like, "I see it sparkling." You know, luralex sets!

I'm really developing that visual side of myself because I'm working more in films. I'm thinking visually and it's going to help my next play.

JR: THERE HAVE BEEN SOME STRONG VISUAL IMAGES IN PREVIOUS PRODUCTIONS, FOR EXAMPLE THE BIG DRAINPIPE CENTRE STAGE IN THE PREMIERE PRODUCTION OF *THE CRACKWALKER* AT TORONTO WORKSHOP PRODUCTIONS.

JT: The big drainpipe in *The Crackwalker*. I don't know if I'd like that again. I loved it then. In a way I don't like it because I hate the notion that *The Crackwalker* is about the underbelly of society. They're not that horrible. They're not that different from anybody. It's infuriating.

Well, they're not the wealthy, privileged class — that's true. But how is Sandy different from most of the women in the audience? A little less education maybe. . . .

And all of us have a little of Theresa in us: the innocent, the child who wants to be protected and have no responsibility.

And Joe. It doesn't matter what class the man is from. There are a lot of Joes everywhere. And Joe is not stupid. None of them are. Even Alan isn't stupid, just emotionally troubled. In fact, he's probably the brightest. But that's how people make themselves comfortable, by saying, "Oh that play is not about me, it's about the underbelly."

The underbelly to me would be like, I don't know, the mob, drugs. Underbelly in the sense that it goes on all around us and we don't know.

JR: ARE YOU PROTECTIVE OR SELFISH OF ANY ASPECT OF THE WORK? EITHER IN THE PROCESS OR THE DEVELOPING OF CHARACTERS OR DURING THE REHEARSAL PERIOD?

JT: Well, I cut a lot on my own. I love to take the red pencil and cut. But in the rehearsals for *I Am Yours*, Derek Goldby cottoned on to me early on and told the actors, "Don't ever ask Judith to cut a line or she'll never cut that one."

Actors get quite angry sometimes when I cut, they think I'm cutting *them* out. I'm not. I'm just cutting the play. But if anybody tries to make me cut a line I never will. It's stupid and childish and I can't help it.

I'm very protective of Truth. There's that word again. And when I know that a character wouldn't do or say something or has to say something, then wild horsemen couldn't make me change it. I just won't. That's the only thing I'm strong about. I'm a wimp in every other way. But when it comes to the work and what's right or wrong, nothing can persuade me. Because I know it in my bones.

JR: WHAT'S THE STRANGEST PRODUCTION OF ONE OF YOUR PLAYS THAT YOU'VE EITHER SEEN OR HEARD ABOUT?

JT: It was strange to hear the Chicago production of *The Crackwalker* in thick Chicago accents, because I thought of it as so southern Ontario. But of course that doesn't matter. It was strange to me that there was a production of it translated into Hebrew in Tel Aviv. Talk about no context. That's one for our side. Here are people living in a war-torn country. What are they going to care about these characters on welfare in a peaceful country getting enough to eat and not dying, not getting shot? So what's the problem? What's to worry about? That's what I would have thought would be the reaction. But they related to it tremendously.

JR: DO YOU CONSIDER YOURSELF EITHER A CANADIAN PLAYWRIGHT OR A FEMINIST WRITER? IS THERE A DIFFERENCE IN PERSPECTIVE THAT COMES WITH EITHER OF THOSE TITLES?

JT: Well, according to the Marxists, there must be! I suppose it depends on how different you think essence of male is from essence of female.

In terms of male or female perspective, I suppose that a lot of people might say that my writing is very male. It's full of rage and a lot of women have had that stamped out of them. I think that's why there are fewer women writers. And I notice that when we audition actors, many women have trouble with real, pure rage. It's seen as masculine territory. Or maybe it is masculine and I'm just butch! Rage isn't nice. It's one of the seven deadly sins. I don't get angry much, really. I'm not an angry person, but I could get angry. But there's a lot of that kind of feeling in my plays and I think that's why they're so offensive to so many people. I'm glad I started out so excessive because by my late middle age I'll just be "kind of strong," whereas other people who started out subtle just go to mush. Real Pablum.

JR: HAS IT BEEN HARDER FOR YOU TO GET PRODUCED IN CANADA BECAUSE YOU ARE A WOMAN WRITER?

JT: It's probably been easier for me being a woman playwright because many theatres like to say they're producing women's plays. What's tough for me is the rehearsal period. I've been referred to as a ball-breaker and there have been rumours that directors hated me. Well, I just speak my mind, the Truth. If I was a guy, I'd just be a man saying his piece.

I don't consciously address feminist issues. Ever. But I might say to myself, "When I was growing up, I liked men who guided me, who took the wheel." My girl friends and I would talk and say that we couldn't stand it when a male said, "May I kiss you?" How wimpy and awful. And this was terrible. Where did this come from? And because it was true of me I would think it was true of a lot of women.

And then I want to know why. So I create a character who goes to the extreme of masochism. And I'm certain that a lot of feminists would take issue with that and say that you are not to portray a masochistic female, because that's perpetuating a notion that's incorrect. To that I would say, no, it's examining an issue that's *true*, and until you examine what *is*, what exists, you can't do anything about it. Until you open up the wound and find that bullet and say, "Yup, the bullet is there," you can't get it out. If you pretend the bullet isn't there, it's going to stay there and it's going to erode the whole body, the whole system.

You've just got to tell the truth and leave it at that. The horrible Truth.

Luckily, I'm not apolitical, but I try not to concern myself too much with politics. I mean, I vote NDP but I can't be political because it would ruin the work. To be political is to bend the Truth. I can be a recorder of the Truth.

JR: CAN YOU DEFINE "GRACE" AS OPPOSED TO "TRUTH"?

JT: Truth is simply what *is*. It happens to you through not doing anything. For example, you feel hatred although you've been pretending to feel love. Or you feel the impulse to do something. That's Truth.

Grace is something you achieve. Through work. And Grace is something you have to work and work at. It happens through penitence, through sight. Through seeing who you are and changing things. You achieve it through humility.

JR: YOU'VE CALLED *WHITE BITING DOG* A PLAY ABOUT GRACE. CAN YOU BE MORE SPECIFIC ABOUT THAT?

JT: Pony achieves Grace because she understands when she falls in "love" that something has possessed her, taken her over, and that that something can wipe out all her moral character.

In other words, she knows that for this love, if he asked her, to kill someone, or never to see her family again, she would comply. Because she was possessed by this infatuation, this love, she decided that it wasn't worth the anguish and that she would have to kill herself in order to conquer this possession. If you have a child murderer, the only decent thing he can do is kill himself. Obviously, he's possessed. I don't know how many people walk around with this urge and don't do anything about it. Maybe many, maybe none. Radical evil, once it enters you, seems to be stronger than most human beings.

Anyhow, Pony had the strength to conquer that radical evil. Now I'm certainly not advocating suicide. This is all in the abstract, a metaphor. But I am talking about killing the radical evil, conquering it at extreme risk to yourself. That's why I had to have it as a suicide in the play. But there's a side to people and to my character that would rather be all alone than be with a person who would cause you to do harm to others. Working through that can bring you to Grace. It's that difficult.

The old man in *White Biting Dog* also achieves Grace, also at the expense of his own happiness. Lomia and Cape, on the other hand, are amoral human beings who didn't even take the first step. You have to work and work and pray.

And that's what I was talking about at the beginning of this interview. You can't just get up out of bed, go to work, come home. As a writer, this is what I'm always thinking about: how we really have to do this work on ourselves. And that's why I think theatre can be very important. It's urgent that people see good theatre with those moments I call Truth. It will help them do the type of thinking I'm talking about. It will prevent those black holes of people who are fifty-five and walking around and not a word they say is sincere and you can't believe it. They don't listen. They have no Truth. Or Grace.

6. Playwright Joanna McClelland Glass

Born in 1936 in Saskatoon, Ms. Glass has recently returned to Canada after thirty years in the United States, where she raised three children and established her career as a novelist, playwright and screenplay writer. In 1986-87 she received a Rockefeller Grant and was playwright-in-residence at the Yale Repertory Theatre. Ms. Glass now lives in Toronto.

The women cry, but the land just goes on, year after year. Nothin' but death's gonna drive me off this land.

Walter in *Artichoke*

People tell me . . . used to tell me . . . that you were a pretty girl. I look at you, and try to see it. You know what I see? Me. The results of my brutality. You're like a little sapling, forced to grow sideways, around an impediment.

Cam in *Play Memory*

Produced and published plays:

Canadian Gothic and *American Modern*. New York: Dramatists Play Service, 1977.

Artichoke. New York: Dramatists Play Service, 1979.

To Grandmother's House We Go. New York: Samuel French, 1980.

Play Memory. In *Plays by Women*. Edited by Diane Bessai and Don Kerr. Edmonton: NeWest Press, 1987.

Produced plays:

Santacqua. Premiered in New York City at the Herbert Berghof School in 1969. Produced by the Herbert Berghof Playwrights Foundation.

Yesteryear. Premiered in 1989 at the Canadian Stage Company, Toronto.

Joanna McClelland Glass Interview

by Rita Much

RM: MANY OF YOUR PLAYS, *PLAY MEMORY*, *CANADIAN GOTHIC*, *ARTICHOKE*, AND THE NEW ONE, *YESTERYEAR*, ARE SET ON THE PRAIRIES WHERE YOU WERE BORN AND RAISED. WOULD YOU DESCRIBE YOUR-SELF AS A REGIONAL WRITER?

JG: That's hard for me to answer. I've spent the last thirty years entirely in the United States, whereas, as we speak, I've been back in Canada only one year. Certainly the "prairie" plays are regional, but the remaining work doesn't fit into the Canadian context.

RM: WHEN ONE READS YOUR PLAYS, ONE GETS REALLY STRONG IMPRESSIONS OF THE LAND AND THE WORK THAT IS REQUIRED, JUST FOR THE PURPOSE OF SURVIVAL, ON A DAY TO DAY BASIS. DO YOU CARRY PART OF THE PRAIRIES WITH YOU WHEREVER YOU GO? IS THE PRAIRIE LANDSCAPE, EMOTIONAL AND GEOGRAPHICAL, ENGRAINED ON YOUR PSYCHE?

JG: Very much so. The interesting thing is that for some years when I was starting out in the States, I was simply labelled a Cana-dian playwright. That was a very mixed blessing. In fact, it was a bit of a drag. I was lucky enough to get an agent, Lucy Kroll, right after I'd written *Artichoke*. She has been my agent all these years and has become a kind of surrogate Mum to me. She had an awful time. People would basically open a manuscript, see Saskatchewan and close it. That's probably another whole subject, the American attitude to what goes on up here. And in fact, it's probably pushing it to even call it an attitude, because it's mostly just ignorance.

To answer the question of regionalism, I never really thought of myself so much as a Canadian as I did a Saskatonian. I grew up in that city, that city was all I ever knew, and I left at eighteen. I had worked for one year as a writer in radio in Saskatoon, and then I went to Calgary, primarily to work with a very well-known woman of the theatre in the west, Betty Mitchell. I got myself into a couple of her plays and in one of them, *Anne of the Thousand Days*, I got the lead. Out of that at a Dominion Drama Festival, I was given a scholarship which I took to the Pasadena Playhouse. That was in fact a great mistake because the Playhouse was running on its last legs, and I stayed there only a year. Then I moved to New York, got married in 1960 and had three kids. After the kids were born I began writing. So I've missed nationalism, I suppose I could say.

RM: WHEN ONE READS WALTER'S TRIBUTE TO THE LAND IN *ARTICHOKE* IN WHICH HE TALKS ABOUT WHAT THE LAND MEANS TO HIM AND HIS RELUCTANCE TO LEAVE THE FARM, ONE GETS A VERY STRONG IMPRESSION OF YOUR LOVE FOR THAT PART OF CANADA, THAT PARTICULAR AREA OF THE COUNTRY.

JG: Yes. Some of it is love, some of it is just, I think, the magnet of one's formative years. I think that's an indelible time, and I think that's the reservoir that nearly everyone goes back to in writing. A great deal of what's in *Artichoke* comes out of the fact that my mother's brother owned a large farm on the prairie, a very primitive place, and all through my childhood I was taken there every summer. And so I culled from that a great deal of the *Artichoke* experience.

RM: CAN YOU TALK A LITTLE MORE ABOUT YOUR CHILDHOOD? WERE THERE ANY OTHER WRITERS IN THE FAMILY?

JG: None.

RM: WERE YOU TAKEN TO THE THEATRE?

JG: No. I never quite know how to answer the question of influences. I suppose there are two major influences — Lucy Maud Montgomery and my parents, whom I write about in *Play Memory*.

My mother was illiterate. She could not read or write. She had this unbelievable routine worked out, a kind of actor's exercise in how to look as if you know what you are doing whenever she was confronted with a menu in a café or a hymn book in church. She had been taken out of school in the second grade to raise eight younger kids, and she was an extremely sensitive woman who cried on hearing the radio news about people starving in Africa or wherever. Offsetting that illiteracy was this rather incredible father. He wasn't a well-read man, but he had grown up in an Irish-Scots family. They came to Canada about five generations ago and from them came a love of language, a remarkable gift of the gab, which comes out in the character of Cam in *Play Memory*. It was particularly Canadian, that a man like this who was basically a travelling salesman, in charge of some other guys, read poetry and knew quite a bit of Shakespeare. My Dad had been to the theatre a few times in his youth in Nova Scotia but I don't think he ever went after he moved to the prairies in 1911. Basically, I grew up listening to the stories he brought home from his travels. These men drove over a hundred miles every day. They stopped at all the little prairie towns and they would pick up bits and pieces of funny things and sad things, and we would get it all on the weekend. I'm drawing on that in my new play, *Yesteryear*.

As for Lucy Maud Montgomery, I was introduced to the entire *Anne* series in the fifth grade by a teacher called Miss Wilson. It was not until that point that it ever occurred to me that I could go to the library and get books. It's very hard to describe to you what kind of a revelation that was, but it was an enormous revelation, and of course I adored the *Anne* stories. They opened a door for me. I realized that there were people who spent their time doing this, filling these pages. And then I lost that idea for many, many years. I didn't actually begin to write until after my first child was born, other than the writing I did for radio and television in Canada. That was called "continuity writing," advertising, for used-car commercials and dry cleaning.

Another important teacher was a Mr. Mayer, who taught me in grades ten and eleven. He was extremely passionate about literature. This is specifically Canadian, too, because the literature was Shakespeare, Shelley, Byron, Keats. In the States, for example, my American ex-husband, who got a Ph.D. (in physics), had gone to a technical college in New York where their English lessons consisted of bits and pieces out of the *Reader's Digest*. I remember how amazed he was that I had not been to college yet knew Shelley's "Ode to the West Wind." As a matter of fact I used my Canadian education to handle suddenly being dropped into Yale society where most of the women were girls from Smith or Radcliffe who were either going with Yalies or marrying them. Quoting "Ode to a Nightingale" on occasion gave me some sort of standing in the community.

So I think that there were no really predictable influences, like a lot of books in the house. Probably the major reason I became a writer was the problem with my father, the alcoholism and this dreadful business of household things being taken away — what I would now call a divestiture of family that we went through. We weren't aware we were going through it. We thought it was just a bad patch. But it went on for a long time and what happened is that I withdrew very much into myself, into my room, and into my imagination. I think I decided very early on that the real world is pretty untenable and whatever I created for myself would be better.

RM: AS A RESULT OF LIVING IN THE STATES FOR SO MANY YEARS, SOME OF YOUR PLAYS ARE SET THERE. *AMERICAN MODERN* IS SET IN MANHATTAN AND *TO GRANDMOTHER'S HOUSE WE GO* IN CONNECTICUT. DID YOU FIND IT DIFFICULT TO WRITE IN AND ABOUT A FOREIGN CULTURE? WAS THIS SOMETHING THAT YOU HAD TO WORK AT VERY HARD?

JG: Not really, but it all evolved over a period of time. The first plays, *Canadian Gothic* and *American Modern*, were done at the Manhattan Theatre Club in the fall of 1972, quite successfully, and then again in the spring of '73. *Canadian Gothic* was my first attempt at going back to my roots. It seems to get produced somewhere every ten minutes because it needs only three chairs and four actors. *American Modern* is not all that frequently done. Together they illustrate, probably better than anything else, what I was going through at that time. I was very comfortable with the Canadian turf that I was writing about and I was also exploring the American. So *Canadian Gothic* is a very traditional, very accessible piece of writing, and *American Modern* isn't. In *American Modern* I was deliberately trying to be inaccessible, and to be problematical. I was also trying to delve into the whole business of psychiatry as well as the energy, the freedom, the lack of inhibition of Americans. In these two plays I was juxtaposing cultures.

RM: DID YOU FIND THAT THE DISTANCE FROM THE PRAIRIES HELPED YOU TO WRITE ABOUT THEM BETTER?

JG: Oh, I think that there isn't any question. I think that if I had never left Saskatoon I would never have written a word. When you have hindsight it not only illuminates things, it expands them. My exposure to Canadian theatre in the year since I moved back from the States has led me to conclude that more of this expansion is needed, that much Canadian play-writing is too introspective. There's too much navel-gazing and the canvas still isn't quite big enough. On the other hand, because of this marvellous Canada Council subsidy, it is a great joy to be able to see things that don't work. The whole problem with play-writing is that you spend a very long period all by yourself in a room somewhere. It's much like being a composer who sits for months and then hasn't any idea of what the sound is going to be. He doesn't know the instruments, or the quality of the instruments, that will be used. The whole business of collaboration in the theatre is a very dicey one. You basically hand a script over and a number of other personalities come in and have a tremendous impact on what you have written. So unless you can get things that don't work put on you can't truly learn your craft. You can't learn it in your room. And I don't know how much you can learn from readings. Very little, I think, because readings are nearly always inaccurately cast. More often than not it's a matter of a group of actors in your living room. And then you go away and mull it over and make cuts and rewrite according to what you heard. The fact that in Toronto so much gets on that is flawed, but worthwhile, is good. You know that another two or three plays down the line the playwright is really going to hammer something home that will be well crafted and focused.

Naturally, there is a negative side to subsidy. One hears a great deal about the incestuousness of the people who run the Council, give the money, etc. I get the sense that theatre here is even more of a closed shop than it is in the States.

RM: WHY DO YOU THINK THAT IS?

JG: There would seem to be two reasons. First, most of the funds that enable the work are controlled by a small group of people who reside primarily in the East. Secondly, the shop seems much more "closed" because the shop is much smaller. The English-speaking "centres" seem to be in Toronto and Vancouver. The pool that professional theatrical people can dip into is limited and the network that serves that pool is tighter. In the States there's a group called LORT, the League of Regional Theatres. These are non-commercial, non-profit theatres. After *Artichoke* was done at the Long Wharf Theatre, the manuscript was sent to approximately eighty LORT theatres, and was eventually produced in about fifty of them. Obviously what I'm talking about here is what's always talked about: numbers. Canadian population versus American population. Or, in a nutshell, the extent and scope of one's opportunities.

If I may digress for a moment, I'd like to make an observation. There is a structural organization in LORT theatres that I think doesn't occur in Canada. All of these theatres have both a business manager and an artistic director and they have equal power and input in the running of the theatre. They are really a team. The business manager doesn't just look for subscribers and count the box office. He is not a separate, fiscal entity. He is in no way subordinate. He helps choose the season, he has a say in casting, sets, costumes, he oversees the public relations and advertising, sometimes right down to guiding the design of the posters for the plays, he oversees the running of the physical plant. The artistic director is then freed of all the minutiae. I bring this up because what I am seeing, as I enter the Toronto theatre environment, is artistic directors who are quite overwhelmed with minutiae. There is no way that one person can function well in both spheres.

RM: LET'S DISCUSS THE SUBJECT OF YOUR BACKGROUND A LITTLE MORE. HOW EXTENSIVE IS YOUR ACTING EXPERIENCE?

JG: I did some acting in Saskatoon early on, starting out with pantomimes and things like that. After two years with Miss Mitchell and a year at the Pasadena Playhouse I was put into something called the Warner Brothers grooming program. I was out at Warner's nearly every day and I got, in a very short time, at the age of twenty, a bellyful of what Hollywood meant. I realised in that year that it wasn't going to be my cup of tea because I couldn't take the rejection. I had altogether too much pride. I was really insulted at the treatment of actors in film, especially pretty young women. It was quite devastating to me because I thought I knew a little bit about the theatre and I felt that I was disciplined. I felt that it was hard work and that it was an art, not an industry. Then almost overnight I was turned into a starlet at Warner Brothers. There was a

TV program in the States at that time called *Wide, Wide World*. The star of the program, a man called Dave Garroway, came out to Hollywood and selected twelve starlets that were going to "make it." And I was one of those chosen. I was quite thrilled because there were thousands of pretty young girls but at the same time I remember, very clearly, going on camera and feeling that I just had to get out of it. I felt diminished by it.

RM: DID YOU TEAR UP THE CONTRACT?

JG: No, I didn't have a contract. It was just a grooming school where we were given long speeches from old film scripts, and a director to work with. The prize at the end was supposed to be a film test. I worked for about two months on the Donna Reed scene in *From Here to Eternity*. Donna Reed plays a prostitute from Oregon and she has a big scene with Montgomery Clift where she talks about why she became a prostitute and her terrible childhood in Oregon. I remember working on that day after day, thinking that it seemed completely removed from anything to do with the theatre — and, to use that lofty word again, art. It struck me that I had better leave.

Then when my husband was at Yale I acted in a few amateur productions written by a man who became a very close friend, Austin Pendleton.

RM: DO YOU THINK THAT YOUR ACTING EXPERIENCE IN ANY WAY INFLUENCED YOUR WRITING?

JG: Only in a reverse kind of way, in that I was a very inhibited actress. I carried with me a certain repression that I thought of at the time as being particularly Canadian. My name was McClelland, and I had grown up in a social order where it was important to have a name like that rather than, say, a Ukrainian or Polish name. Very much of my growing up was all about how you behaved in public and about good manners and civility. In fact, about all the things that Americans consider rather dismissable Canadian things. I'm still very torn about all that. Part of me cherishes my heritage and part of me wishes that Canadians would take the tethers off and let go — dare a bit more. To answer your question, I learned quickly in my writing to try all sorts of things, to be adventuresome. For example, I would give all the gents very bad language, arguing internally that it was the gents saying it, not me. I really let loose in a way I never would have been able to as an actress.

RM: WOULD YOU LIKE TO ACT AGAIN?

JG: Never. I haven't thought about it since my first child was born.

RM: YOUR PLAY-WRITING DEBUT OCCURRED IN 1969 WITH *SAN-*

TACQUA, WHICH WAS PERFORMED IN GREENWICH VILLAGE. HOW DID IT COME TO BE WRITTEN?

JG: When my husband was a graduate student at Yale I worked as a secretary at a big factory in New Haven called the Winchester Western Arms and Ammunition Company. When I first walked into that plant I still had very Canadian eyes or, I should say, very Saskatonian eyes. I thought, "Isn't this peculiar. All these people are Jewish." And of course they weren't, they were Italian, some of them second or third generation, some of them first. In the most menial positions in the factory were blacks. Suddenly I was dropped into a whole new social situation, unlike anything I had ever experienced before. I knew nothing about blacks or Italians and there was an enormous discrepancy between my working life and my social life, which was Yale and its world of enormous privilege.

So *Santacqua* tackled a big Italian family, the patriarch of which was head of the union at a big factory. I sent it to Austin Pendleton. Austin had left Yale for New York at that time. He'd gone in as a green kid and Jerome Robbins cast him immediately in Arthur Kopit's play, *Oh Dad, Poor Dad, Mama's Hung You in the Closet and I'm Feeling So Sad*. He was studying acting at the Herbert Berghof School with the illustrious Mrs. Berghof, Uta Hagen. He decided that he wanted to direct *Santacqua*, and he did. That was my first production, at the Berghof School, in a hundred-seat house.

It was a three-act play and the first two acts were pretty good. The third was dreadful. I didn't know how to tie it all together. I was ignorant of the specific constrictions of the theatre — having only dialogue to tell the story, having only a minute and a half a page, having endless financial restrictions in costumes and sets. But this revelation was as important as the previously mentioned one of discovering the libraries. *I had an audience.* And they listened attentively and cared about my characters for two acts. And then, in the third, I disappointed them. And boy, did they let me know. I lost them. It was visible in that they withdrew their attention and tuned out. It was audible in their coughing and squirming. As they say, "If it ain't on the page, you can't put in on the stage." The playwright's curse is that you never really *know* if you've got it on the page until you get it on its legs in front of an audience.

RM: AS A FEMALE PLAYWRIGHT DID YOU HAVE A DIFFICULT TIME GETTING YOUR FIRST PLAYS STAGED? *SANTACQUA* SEEMED TO HAVE BEEN QUITE EFFORTLESS.

JG: That was very much because of my friendship with Austin.

RM: DID YOUR DOMESTIC LIFE OR FAMILY RESPONSIBILITIES IMPINGE ON YOUR WRITING IN A SIGNIFICANT WAY?

JG: I had my first child in 1963 and almost immediately became pregnant with twins, so I lost about five years there. I had three in diapers. My ex-husband, Alex Glass, had just gotten out of graduate school so we hadn't any money. I didn't have any help. I didn't even have a diaper service and there were no Pampers. There were about seventy diapers to wash a day. I felt an incredible exhaustion that went on for years. At that time we were living in Washington, D.C. during the L.B.J. years and Mrs. Johnson was out planting tulips and daffodils and beautifying America. I have no memory of any of that. Alex would come home and say, "Oh, it's just so great. I drove by the Jefferson Memorial and the cherry blossoms were out." I never got out of the house. Consequently, the writing that I was doing was very sporadic, without focus. In desperation, after getting all these kids to bed at night, I wanted to do something that was mine, that was just mine. I would try it for an hour or two and I would be aghast the following morning. I would think, "Oh, my God, this is terrible." It wasn't until the twins got into kindergarten that I took myself by the collar and said, "You're going to do this." I didn't really think of myself as a writer at that point. But there I was with my three hours to myself, so I started arranging my whole life around the three hours. And of course it stretched to about five hours when everybody got into school. So for a dozen years it was a matter of getting to the desk at eight in the morning when everybody left and leaving it about two o'clock when everybody came home, and then doing everything else: all the chauffeuring, the laundry, the groceries, the housekeeping, the whole thing. Then, after my divorce in 1976, I had the job of breadwinning, too.

RM: DID YOU FEEL SCHIZOPHRENIC IN ANY WAY?

JG: Quite totally, quite totally. I don't think my two lives as wife/mother and writer ever merged. Perhaps schizophrenic isn't accurate, though. It was more healing than that. It was more a salvation than a dilemma.

RM: BOTH NATALIE IN *CANADIAN GOTHIC* AND HARRIET IN *TO GRANDMOTHER'S HOUSE WE GO* ARE ASPIRING ARTISTS WHO HAVE TO FIGHT REALLY HARD FOR THEIR TIME TO PAINT. NATALIE, IN THE AFTERNOONS, WOULD GO OUT TO PAINT THE BRIDGE NO MATTER WHAT THE WEATHER WAS LIKE. DID YOU EVER FEEL THAT YOU HAD TO DEFEND THIS NEED OF YOURS TO WRITE?

JG: Yes, on two accounts, domestically and professionally. I didn't have an office, I wrote at home. When a woman works at home her work is often not taken seriously. You have to let your friends know that you are "off limits" for certain hours of the day. But you're there when the plumber comes, and the woman canvassing for the Lung Society, and the census taker, etc., etc. And the children intrude constantly, even when at school. I recall making trips to the school with forgotten lunch boxes, soccer gear, cheer-leading outfits. I'd say, "If your mother was in an office, you wouldn't make these calls." But they called, and I was at home, and I delivered. And frequently other women didn't understand. Certain friends looking for volunteers for school and civic committees felt free to call and make requests simply because I was at home. I'm afraid, when I said I was trying to write, they thought me a bit uppity. And after awhile you are, in fact, uppity. You're repeatedly sending out the message: Do Not Trespass.

Secondly, I had to defend not just the time to write, but the subject matter. My problem was that I wrote about the Canadian prairie from places like Detroit and Berkeley and finally, Guildford, Connecticut, where I lived for twelve years. I had to, along with my agent, convince people that there was universality in the writing, that there was worth in it regardless of its geography. Canadian play-wrights, you see, writing in a Canadian context, are basically preach-ing to the converted. Mine was a different, and to some degree tougher, battle. I was the missionary taking the word to the heathen.

RM: ARE MORE FEMALE ARTISTIC DIRECTORS NEEDED AT THE HELM OF THEATRES IN NORTH AMERICA? IS IT YOUR EXPERIENCE THAT IN GENERAL MALE ARTISTIC DIRECTORS RESIST PLAYS BY OR ABOUT WOMEN?

JG: That has not been my own experience. I think that the greatest lack in the theatre is people who are able to understand the process of the theatre. Most directors want a script delivered, ready. They give lip service to the development or process. But, you know, it's a hell of a pain in the ass, the whole business of creating a play. And it's especially difficult for actors in a virgin production because you're giving them dialogue and you're taking it away and you're trying to collaborate and you're not at all sure of what you're doing. In fact, altogether too much stuff gets into rehearsal prematurely, and it's too late for major rewrites. It's just altogether too late.

RM: DO WE NEED MORE DRAMATURGES?

JG: Personally, I haven't had the best experiences with them. Having never written a play themselves, having never gone through the panic of walking in on the first day of rehearsal and seeing that the posters have already been made, and the cast names are up, when the play is nowhere near ready, they can't be of great help. Actually, the best experiences that I've had as far as process goes have been with women who give you time with a kind of grace and a kind of élan that helps you go very rationally through a script and analyze what each character wants. I have had good experiences in going to either academic women or women working in the theatre, nearly always in some capacity other than directors (though they want to *be* directors), and getting help. You know, it isn't even help so much as a fresh eye and objectivity because of the loneliness of the writer. Because in the long weeks and months spent in isolation, you simply lose track of what the original intention was. It's very hard to find a male director who has the same degree of patience, who is as nurturing. I'm perhaps speaking very much from an American point of view here, but the directors who get work get quite a bit of work, so they basically fly from regional theatre to regional theatre. They are rarely prepared. They very rarely have done their homework. They weren't available when the embryo needed attention.

RM: IS IT EASIER FOR WOMAN PLAYWRIGHTS TO GET THEIR PLAYS STAGED NOW THAN IN 1969 WHEN YOU FIRST STARTED WRITING?

JG: I don't know. I can't honestly say that I have suffered any more than my male counterparts in getting my work put on. Of course, I've had great luck. After *Santacqua*, I sent *Canadian Gothic* and *American Modern* to my friend Austin. He took them to Lynne Meadow, who was just starting the Manhattan Theatre Club. While we were doing *Canadian Gothic* and *American Modern*, Austin ran into an old actress-friend, Maria Tucci, and invited her to see the show. She brought her husband, who is Robert Gottlieb, at that time the Vice-President and Chief Editor at Knopf. Two days later Gottlieb called my agent to ask if I had ever tried writing a novel. Lucy Kroll apparently replied, "She's getting very tired of toting Canadian things around, and being dismissed. She has talked of trying to do a novel that is half and half, that's about an American family that summers in the Canadian Rockies." He said, "Let's bring her into New York," and suddenly I had a foot in the door at Knopf. I had a contract for my novel, *Reflections on a Mountain Summer*. When I retrace all these steps myself, I can never find anything distinctly female or male, you see, in these things that have occurred. Of course, I haven't written anything that would be considered a flaming feminist agitprop piece.

I think it is very, very hard for anyone to "make it" or work in any of the arts. Theatre is a three-thousand-year-old form that is competing with half-hour sitcoms for the public's attention. You are asking some segment of the populace to wash their hair, and shave their legs, and get a baby-sitter and pay twenty to fifty bucks to go out and see this thing, this very special thing. Theatre has become somewhat anachronistic and elitist and therefore difficult to work in.

RM: DO YOU REGARD YOURSELF AS A FEMINIST PLAYWRIGHT?

JG: No, I don't.

RM: WHAT DOES THE TERM MEAN TO YOU?

JG: Unfortunately, it has a tinge of something abrasive about it. I feel that my life in a way is simply a testament to survival, the survival of a father and the survival of a husband.

RM: TWO MEN.

JG: Two gents, as it turns out, yes. But I think that life is just very difficult for most people. I suppose that one of my biggest gripes with women's liberation is that finally, when all is said and done, our only alternative, if we follow our biological imperative and we have children, is to hire another woman, generally poorer and darker-skinned, to do what we should have done in the first place. Of course, tomes have been written about the ensuing guilt. It seems to me that the buck stops at biology.

RM: DO YOU THINK THAT WOMEN WRITE DIFFERENTLY FROM MEN BECAUSE WE LIVE IN A MALE-DOMINATED SOCIETY, OR DO YOU THINK THAT IT'S MORE OFTEN THE CASE THAT WOMEN TEND TO CHOOSE DIFFERENT SUBJECT MATTER? MEN WILL WRITE ABOUT POLITICS, AND WARS AND SO ON, AND WOMEN ABOUT THE FAMILY.

JG: We can only function out of our own frame of reference and our frame of reference, for most of us, is pretty narrow. Men don't experience motherhood, labour, this innate nurturing, nesting thing that we have, so they can't understand, never mind write about, the daily battleground women get tested on. Nor do they value it. But I'm a great believer in the magic of the imagination and I think that the best writers have the kind of androgynous centre that sees it all and understands it all.

RM: YOU HAVE WRITTEN TWO NOVELS — *WOMAN WANTED* AND *REFLECTIONS ON A MOUNTAIN SUMMER* — AND YOU HAVE WRITTEN FOR RADIO, FILM AND THE STAGE. WHICH IS THE MOST DIFFICULT FORM?

JG: Oh, I think there isn't any question that the theatre is the hardest. I might think differently if I wrote poetry. I guess there isn't anything that has to be more precise than a poem. Film, on the other hand, gives you tremendous freedom. You have this marvellous ability to go to three cities in one page or have three meals in one page. You have this wonderful flexibility that you can't possibly have in theatre. The novel is also a freeing experience and I know a lot of people believe that it is only in fiction that one can really address large themes and dig into topics and analyze and search for truth. I don't have a strong opinion on that, because a novel just seems to me to be this wonderful taking off of the tethers. You've got five or six or seven-hundred pages, if you can fill them, if you can sustain it. I had a very interesting experience when *Woman Wanted* was bought by big-time American producers before it was even finished. The producers, Zanuck and Brown, have made some very good films: *Butch Cassidy and the Sundance Kid*, and *The Sting*. But where they really made their money was on the *Jaws* films. I had a very uncomfortable meeting where Zanuck was clearly the Hollywood contingent and Brown very much the New York literary contingent. I had to present an oral thesis to let them know how I was going to finish this novel. I told them, because I'm very bad at "pitching," in Hollywood terms, that there were three possibilities for the ending. And of course Dick Zanuck didn't much care for that at all. They don't like possibilities. They want it nailed down right there and delivered in 120 pages. And movie budgets are intimidating. In Hollywood, the bottom line is seventy-five thousand dollars a page. And they want about a hundred and twenty pages for a screenplay, so you've got nine million before you hire any stars. Those are just daily operating costs. Now, it's quite alarming to sit down to a blank piece of paper with that figure in mind.

RM: DO YOU HAVE PLANS TO WORK IN FILM AGAIN?

JG: I'm about to start another screenplay as soon as *Yesteryear* opens. An independent New York producer, Charles Evans Productions, the people who made *Tootsie*, sent me a book about a love story set in the late sixties, between two American kids. The reason I am very interested in the story is that the boy is a draft resister who comes to Toronto. I don't think anyone has addressed the issue of the numbers of kids who came up to Canada. Like the character, I'm looking at Canada and what it means to be a Canadian pretty much with American eyes. I think the boy's observations could be quite illuminating.

The problem, from a dramatic point of view, is that the love story takes place primarily in letters that are written between Connecticut and Toronto — Ward's Island, actually, which is where the boy moves. It's also challenging because the sixties were the years when I was so overwhelmed with babies, so there is a great deal of research I have to do on the Vietnam War. To look at the question of the kids who said no, who felt that moral imperative at the time, intrigues me.

RM: WHICH IS THE MOST ENJOYABLE FORM TO WORK IN?

JG: I think the most enjoyable is writing for film. But I have to qualify that, too, because there simply isn't any experience anywhere in writing akin to live theatre. No two performances are ever precisely the same. Actors forget lines, lights explode, sets fall down. If a film is made of your screenplay — and only three out of every thousand that are written get made — you don't have the same control as you do when a play is produced. No dialogue can be changed without your approval. You have to be in on casting sessions. You have all kinds of say. The business of taking the money and running in Hollywood is kind of true in that God knows what they are going to do with your screenplay. If they have got a Meryl Streep in there at six million dollars a picture and there are lines she wants to rewrite, she will rewrite them.

RM: I WANT TO ASK YOU A VERY DIFFICULT QUESTION. WHAT INSPIRES YOU TO WRITE A PLAY? DO YOU START WITH A PICTURE IN YOUR MIND'S EYE, OR IS IT A PHRASE, AN EXPRESSION, OR A MEMORY?

JG: It's different on every project.

RM: HOW LONG WILL IT SIT BEFORE YOU ACTUALLY PUT PEN TO PAPER? WHAT'S THE PROCESS OF WRITING A PLAY LIKE FOR YOU?

JG: That is so hard to answer. I remember washing dishes some years ago when the first line of *Reflections on a Mountain Summer* came to me: "Somewhere in the Canadian Rockies there is a summer resort called Buena Vista." Now, I had worked as a waitress at Waterton Lakes when I was fifteen, sixteen, and seventeen. So we were talking almost twenty years after that time when this line came into my mind. I simply sat down with that line and began writing, though I really didn't know where it was going. After about three or four lines, I decided the entire book should come out of a sixty-five-year-old man.

RM: *PLAY MEMORY* IS HEAVILY AUTOBIOGRAPHICAL. WAS IT A VERY PAINFUL PLAY TO WRITE?

JG: Yes, it was. And it still is painful to see it, though I had a wonderful experience this summer concerning the play. I came across an article in the *Globe and Mail* about an amateur group in B.C. called the Powerhouse Theatre, mounting a production of *Play Memory*. They played for two weeks in Vernon and then went to Salmon Arm where they won "Best Play" and several other prizes, which then qualified them to go to Victoria, where they won "Best Play," which then qualified them to go to Halifax. I went to Halifax to see them and they were quite marvellous, especially the Cam. I think there were fourteen plays being done in seven days and, once again, they won. Now they are going to Monaco in the summer of 1989 to represent Canada in an International Drama Festival.

It's wonderful for me to be representing Canada in an international competition, but it is also highly ironic. Here I must address the knotty problem of my citizenship. When I got married dual citizenship was not available. I was marrying an American and I thought, of course, that I would be married forever. My ex-husband had strong political convictions which I eventually absorbed, and I wanted to vote. So, three years after I married I took American citizenship. The Playwrights Union of Canada has twice invited me to join, and twice withdrawn the invitation when I told them my citizenship. I recently went down to the Canadian Stage Company to sign the contract for the commissioned play, *Yesteryear*. It was full of clauses that said, "This is in accordance with the rules and regulations of the Playwrights Union of Canada." We had to strike all that out because I can't be a member. Now, in the U.S., if you bring in a play from Sri Lanka and have it produced off-Broadway, you're invited to join the Dramatists' Guild. They want your participation in theatre-at-large and, obviously, they welcome your dues.

Equally jarring was being in the running for the Governor General's Award for *Play Memory* which Malcolm Black directed here at Theatre Plus. It was wonderful for me that the play had come home, that it was on its own turf. The whole business of the Ukrainian bootlegger in the Broadway production was never entirely understood because that was synonymous with prohibition in the States. It's such a very Canadian play to me. Anyway, I heard through the grapevine that all the votes were in for *Play Memory*. Then three days before they were going to announce the winner someone on the selection committee called me up to ask what my citizenship was. When I replied that it was American there was this little beat of time and then she said, "I'm afraid you are disqualified." I was numb all weekend.

It's so very strange in that I strove so hard for so long to get my prairie plays produced in the States and then I get up here and there seems to be resistance. In a *Saturday Night* magazine article the American critic Clive Barnes described me as having "the spirit of the prairie" in my writing. I thought, "Oh God, Canadians reading this will say, 'Oh well, that's an American saying that, so it doesn't have much credence.'"

So here I am, back in Canada, applying for Landed Immigrant status in order to live here. Getting chest X-rays and police checks and having to present lists of assets, etc., all the while with my Saskatchewan birth certificate in hand. All the while watching Third-World refugees come in by the thousands. It's a conundrum to me, personally, that I'm back but I feel quite peripheral. I'm really rather stretched right now, figuring out where I belong.

RM: IT'S A QUESTION YOU SHOULD BE ASKED IN A YEAR OR TWO WHEN YOU ARE MORE SETTLED INTO THE CANADIAN THEATRE COMMUNITY.

YOU BROUGHT UP THE SUBJECT OF CRITICS. DO YOU READ REVIEWS?

JG: Yes, I do. I don't really understand people who say that they don't. Actors, yes, because it can be totally debilitating if you have to go on the night after three or four guys have demolished you or the play. So I do read them, especially in the States where the critics are so important because the safety net of subscription audiences doesn't exist in the commercial theatre. The critics there can make or break you overnight.

RM: HOW MUCH DO THE REVIEWS OF THE LAST PLAY INFLUENCE THE NEXT?

JG: After bad reviews, it's very hard to go to the machine and face the blank paper. It takes tremendous stamina and ego, I guess, to believe that you are going to keep on doing this thing. I've got a bit of mileage on me now, and if you have gone through enough of this you realize that it's all so fickle, as one very pivotal experience taught me.

Before opening on Broadway, Hal Prince's production of *Play Memory* played for a month in Princeton. The *New York Times* sent a critic to write an "out-of-town review." Well, it was a review that you would die for. It was money in the bank. It compared me to Tennessee Williams, which is very funny, I think. It raved about the play, about Hal's direction of it, about the cast — everything. Immediately, the five-hundred thousand dollars needed to move it into New York fell into place on the strength of that review. But then Frank Rich, who is the kingpin at the *New York Times*, disliked the play. Clive Barnes at the *Post* adored the play. If we had gotten the Barnes review in the *New York Times* we would have run for months. If we'd gotten the *New York Times* review from Princeton out of Frank Rich, we would have run forever, but none of it happened. So it all seems terribly ephemeral after a while. Certainly, the good reviews are much easier to live with than the bad ones, but after a while it's just a matter of discipline. I think you have to write everyday; you can't wait for inspiration or a pat on the back or you are not a professional writer. It just isn't going to happen. You carve out four or five hours and you write. You may throw it away for three days in a row, but it'll clue you into something, give you some direction. I think writer's block is simply fear.

RM: MOST REVIEWS ARE STILL WRITTEN BY MEN. DO YOU FEEL THE NEED FOR MORE FEMALE CRITICS?

JG: Yes, I do. I don't know how you solve that. The problem is that female critics can actually be more resistant to women writers than male reviewers. No major New York or London newspaper has a female critic, but I have felt a certain double standard going on with female critics on smaller papers in smaller cities. Perhaps there's an analogy in the experience I had in an integrated neighbourhood during the five years I lived in Detroit. Lower-class blacks, after an arduous struggle to get out of the ghetto, somehow managed the down payment on a house in our well-integrated middle-class neighbourhood. They had arrived, they thought, and so did we, the whites. But we were naive. Their new enemy was their middle-class black neighbour. The middle-class black went on the defensive and there was a great deal of criticism and disparagement of the new people. It was as if the middle-class black neighbour was saying, "*Now* you have to prove yourself. *Now* you'd better bloody well measure up because if you don't, you'll embarrass us. If you falter, we will be ashamed."

Some women critics have followed a similar pattern of behaviour. It's not that when we get there we want to step on those we have left behind, but I think there is a certain element of not wanting to be reminded. There probably is something really unconscionable here that has to do with the things we had to do in order to get where we are. Some kinds of selling out. Some kinds of ass-kissing. Some kinds of apple polishing that we can't think about because it's too painful.

To me there is frequently in female criticism a spite, a mean streak. I suppose we simply need more time. The pendulum has to swing further and we have to become more comfortable with ourselves. I think it's a matter of waking up in the morning with some sense of "all-rightedness," of going out in the world with some assurance that one is going to be accepted. Only out of that can you have freedom to have largesse of spirit. And, if I may be so bold and really stretch this metaphor, I think Canadians as a whole still need to achieve that kind of assurance. To accept and have confidence in what they are. To stop grinding axes and having chips on the shoulder. To stop seeing the southern giant as "the white overlord." I may still be naive, but I think "all-rightedness" and largesse will only come when this happens.

RM: IN *PLAY MEMORY* YOU SEEM TO BE TAKING ON PATRIARCHAL SOCIETY, ARGUING THAT POWER AND MONEY, WHICH ARE IN MANY WAYS ITS HIGHEST VALUES, ALSO CONTAIN THE SEEDS OF ITS DESTRUCTION. WHEN CAM LOSES HIS JOB, THE MAIN SOURCE OF HIS IDENTITY AND THE THING THAT MOST GRATIFIES HIS EGO, HE GIVES UP. IT'S THE WOMEN WHO SURVIVE.

JG: Yes. One sees it so clearly at any Christmas party of executives. It all falls in line according to rank, according to salary. And women don't experience that because we've got this very fundamental biology. How much we earn is not our reality. Home is our reality. We have got to wipe the bums and get the food on the table and be sure the fridge is stocked.

We are rooted in a way men aren't, but unfortunately our care-taking is taken for granted. For example, we were living in Berkeley when *Artichoke* was done at Long Wharf in New Haven and my mother-in-law came to pitch in with the kids while I went off for a month to New Haven. It was my first time out in the big time, Colleen Dewhurst was in the cast, and I was both nervous and guilty about my family. I vividly remember going home and opening the door in California to finding one of my twins looking up at me and saying, "There's no mayonnaise!" That was my greeting after a month away.

RM: WHAT VALUES DO THE DAUGHTER AND MOTHER IN *PLAY MEMORY* REPRESENT?

JG: Something very, very elemental that I associate with my mother and the prairies, something deeply rooted in the land. The odds against what one might call a civilized life on the prairies were enormous. That farm that I went to every summer had no plumbing or electricity. There was something called a dry well where everything that needed to be kept cold in the summer had to be taken. Provisions were lowered down on a rope, brought in before every meal and after every meal taken out. All the butter, milk, meat. All the water had to be hauled. Just washing dishes or doing the laundry was a very difficult task. So when my father became a chronic alcoholic, my mother didn't fall apart. She went to work in the kitchen of the Oliver Lodge, an old folks' home in Saskatoon.

It was my father who had the advantages and, I think, an enormous talent for what he did. For many years he had the respect of males in the community and the admiration of the women. But he had to have everything on his terms. There's a passage in the play where the mother wants to fight for the crumbs, and Cam says, "No." When he is axed from his job, he simply pulls down the blinds and closes the door. I suppose it's a death wish.

RM: IRONICALLY, CAM FEELS HUMILIATED ABOUT WHAT HIS WIFE AND DAUGHTER ARE GOING THROUGH IN ORDER TO FEED THEMSELVES AND KEEP THE HOME TOGETHER WHEN, IN FACT, THERE IS TREMENDOUS DIGNITY IN WHAT THEY ARE DOING, IN SPITE OF THE FISH SMELL THAT SO BOTHERS JEAN. WHEN YOU WATCH THE SPECTACLE OF A TWELVE-YEAR-OLD GIRL TAKING ON ADULT RESPONSIBILITIES, ALL YOU CAN FEEL IS ADMIRATION AND RESPECT FOR HER.

JG: Yes, but Cam's philosophy, encapsulated in his remark that even pigs respond to the dawn, is also deserving of admiration. I am really impaled on those two points of view. One wants so much to aspire and to be like Cam, but this elemental thing, the getting up in the morning and doing battle, which I associate with women, keeps intruding. In my life I have had a huge portion of the getting up and doing battle. But, luckily, through some freakishness of fate, I've become a writer and that gives me the embodiment, I think, of the things that Cam wanted in life: the pursuit of something a little higher than the three squares a day and the nine to five.

RM: AT THE END OF *PLAY MEMORY* JEAN MANAGES TO TRANSCEND THE SUFFERING CAUSED BY HER FATHER'S BETRAYAL OF HER TRUST. IS CAM IN ANY WAY A TRAGIC FIGURE BY THE END?

JG: He's a character that people really don't want to see on the stage. We all know that he exists in life, we've got him in our neighbourhood, but he's a very alienating character. He doesn't have a good message. He says, "My way, or no way."

His is a particularly male problem: as Cam says in the play, his name was on the door, he had an expense account and the company car. He had authority. All these plums were withdrawn and a vacuum remained, which is tragic.

All the expectations in the male world, sexually, professionally and financially are in the thirties, the forties, and then there is a dropping off. There is the down side. Women in their late forties have to cope with the problem of the empty nest, but for many the last third of life is a time of ultimate fruition. I look upon the next ten or fifteen years with great anticipation. Now, once a mother, always a mother. There are still the phone calls and the problems. So one is always involved, but now there is a certain detachment and a certain freedom. My first thought in the morning no longer is, "Is the dinner in the fridge? Is it in the freezer? Do I have to shop?"

Of courses, a great toll has been taken. There always is in a divorce, in the falling apart of ties that bind, and in the rather incredible attitude I had that I could support everybody as a writer. I've had to do quite a lot of grubbing about for money. I had a real crisis about five years ago when all of my children were in college — expensive American colleges. Out of the blue I was offered the position of head writer on a soap, starting at a salary of $350,000. All of my friends said I should do it for three years and then go back to the theatre, but the truth of the matter is that you have no credibility left afterwards. You can't go back and work for nothing at the Factory afterwards. The temptation was great but, finally, I told myself, "You got a Guggenheim Fellowship for your work last year. You mustn't sell yourself out for this huge bundle of money."

RM: IN ALL YOUR PLAYS YOU SEEM TO PULL THE RUG OUT FROM UNDER THE AUDIENCE'S FEET, TO UPSET THEIR EXPECTATIONS OF A STEREOTYPE PORTRAYAL OF WOMEN. IN *ARTICHOKE* MARGARET COMMITS ADULTERY INSTEAD OF SMILING AND PUTTING UP THE GOOD FRONT AS IS THE TRADITION OF WIVES WHOSE HUSBANDS HAVE BEEN UNFAITHFUL. PAT IN *AMERICAN MODERN* EXPERIENCES AN AL-

MOST EXISTENTIAL CRISIS DUE TO THE LACK OF FULFILMENT IN HER ROLE AS HOUSEWIFE, AND IN *TO GRANDMOTHER'S HOUSE WE GO* THE MOTHER REFUSES TO PLAY THE ROLE OF THE SELF-SACRIFICING MATRIARCH. AND, OF COURSE, IN YOUR NEW PLAY, *YESTERYEAR*, THE MADAM OF A BROTHEL TURNS OUT TO BE THE MOST INTELLIGENT AND THE MOST COMPASSIONATE PERSON IN THE PLAY. DO YOU CONSCIOUSLY SET OUT TO PORTRAY WOMEN IN A NONTRADITIONAL MANNER?

JG: No, I guess I just don't buy that traditional has to mean relegating females to kitchen sink dramas. Bernard Shaw's women, Oscar Wilde's, Shakespeare's, Chekhov's, James Joyce's Molly Bloom, these are strong, idiosyncratic women with sharp senses of humour. Yes, these are all male writers, but their women have enormous appeal to me. Again, it's a matter of mind-set and frame of reference but perhaps it's mostly selection. I knew women like that on the prairie. I also knew long-suffering drudges. For me there is little appeal, and even less drama, in the latter and I haven't selected to write about them.

RM: WHAT ABOUT THE SIGNIFICANCE OF THE TITLES *AMERICAN MODERN* AND *CANADIAN GOTHIC*? THE LIVES OF THE TWO CHARACTERS IN *CANADIAN GOTHIC* REALLY CONSTITUTE SOME KIND OF STOICAL ENDURANCE. THEY'RE GOING TO CARRY ON. THERE'S RESIGNATION MAYBE, THE FATHER WITH HIS BLINDNESS AND JEAN WITH HER LOT, BUT THERE'S NO DESPAIR AT ALL. WHAT SPECIFICALLY DID YOU WANT THE TITLES OF THESE PLAYS TO ENCAPSULATE?

JG: I think *Canadian Gothic* refers to the fact that Canada is a very new country. All of this verbiage that I'm using about "fundamental" and "elemental" seems to me to be not just a Saskatchewan thing but a very Canadian thing. The play is about what I think the prairie stands for and my mother as a pioneer on the prairie stood for. And my mother's mother, my maternal grandmother, who homesteaded and lived in a sod hut, and ate potato soup made from the skins of potatoes for a whole year. I'm very in touch with all of that. When my mother died at seventy-one, the little headline on the obituary said, "Pioneer Dies." That was a strange thing to receive in the States, because it spoke of the newness of Canada. Canadians seem closer to their origins.

The title *American Modern* refers to, in part, the inevitable softness that sets in when there's just too much. When the basic things — food, shelter and so on — haven't had to be worried about in a long time. I think that what the kids did, predominantly in the States in the sixties, the giving the finger to all of that, is a kind of luxury that you only have when the prior generations have gone through all the elemental stuff. Time after time throughout history there is decline and fall. The intention gets muddied. Traditions, tenets, commandments, if you will, get muddied. Things become diffuse. Man's innate greed and selfishness take over. We always seem to be in this box of a prison between the flesh and the spirit. Between good and evil. I think this is as old as Man, and I think that nothing new under the sun can be said about it. Sometimes God, or Fate, comes in with a plague or a war or some sort of disaster that clears it all out and you have to start all over again.

RM: IS BECKETT AN INFLUENCE ON YOUR WORK? IN *CANADIAN GOTHIC* THE THREE CHAIRS RECALL BECKETT'S URNS, AND IN *ARTICHOKE* LILY AGNES' HAT SEEMS REMINISCENT OF LUCKY'S HAT IN *WAITING FOR GODOT*.

JG: No, I think there's something very Beckett in my psychology, but I'm too "languagey" a person to compare to Beckett. Why write unless you heighten the language? Writers are wordsmiths, so I'm often impatient with Beckett's minimalism.

RM: MANY OF YOUR PLAYS DEAL WITH THE THEME OF LOST INNOCENCE. FOR EXAMPLE, IN *PLAY MEMORY* JEAN GROWS UP AT THE AGE OF TWELVE; IN *ARTICHOKE* GIBSON WANTS TO RECAPTURE HIS YOUTH ON THE FARM; AND IN *YESTERYEAR* DAVID AND MILLIE ARE IN A WAY RELIVING THEIR PAST ROMANCE.

JG: Yes, it is a recurring theme and an important one for me. I think it's a matter, finally, of our mortality, of not going gently into that good night. So much of our lives is gauged around the three score and ten, the finite. I have always been intrigued with the idea of how differently we would live if we knew that the lifespan was, let's say, a hundred and fifty years. Would we go to school at forty? How would we map it all out? So the recapturing, the going back to what once was, the wanting to recapture is due to the pressure of time. It's what goads us on.

RM: WHAT IS IMPORTANT IN YOUR WORK NOW THAT WASN'T WHEN YOU STARTED TO WRITE?

JG: I think I want to write a feminine piece now. I would like to write a play with four women: a mother-in-law, some semblance of me, the mother of the character based on me, and a daughter in her twenties. It's hard to say much more because the piece is in an initial stage now. It's a very uncommercial work and it's a very languagey work. By languagey I mean that there's a static element to it that doesn't make it particularly dramatic. In this play I want to examine a whole bunch of issues that I have already examined, because they are of endless interest to me, from the points of view of these four ladies who are gathered together because the husband of the character based on me has died.

RM: WILL IT BE A COMEDY?

JG: Oh, no. But there will be comedy in it because I feel very strongly that theatre has to entertain. When one writes a novel one knows that if they hit a boring patch they are going to the john or they'll get a beer or make a phone call, and come back and perhaps just skim over a few pages. But in theatre one has a captive audience — the immediacy of the theatre has to be always entertaining.

RM: ARE THERE SPECIFIC PLAYWRIGHTS WHOSE WORK YOU ADMIRE?

JG: I adore Chekhov. There are probably more contemporary film-makers that turn me on than playwrights. Fellini in *8½* has his finger so squarely on the button that it's almost Shakespearean to me. I think we've gotten so narrow — David Mamet and his sordid little men, for example. It just irritates me.

RM: DO YOU HAVE ANY ADVICE FOR WOMEN CONSIDERING A CAREER AS A PLAYWRIGHT?

JG: To persist. To write every day. And to expose yourself to as much as possible. Hemingway said something like, "Know as much as you can about everything." I would give that advice especially to women. You have to keep your interior vulnerable, because your *feelings*, finally, are what you're trying to get on paper. But you must, at the same time, develop a tough hide against the nay-sayers. We have always to remember that thirty publishers, count 'em, thirty, turned down James Joyce's *Dubliners*.

So above all, persist.

7. Playwright Ann-Marie MacDonald

Nick Seiflow

Born in West Germany in 1958, Ms. MacDonald graduated from the National Theatre School in Montreal in 1980. In 1986 she appeared in the internationally acclaimed film *I've Heard the Mermaids Singing*, and in 1988 she received the Chalmers Award for Outstanding Canadian Play for *GOOD NIGHT DESDEMONA (Good Morning Juliet)*. Ms. MacDonald currently resides in Toronto.

The best of friends and foes exist within:
Where archetypal shadows come to light,
and doff their monster masks when we say "boo!"
Where mingling and unmingling opposites
performs a wondrous feat of alchemy,
and spins grey matter into precious gold.

Chorus in *GOOD NIGHT DESDEMONA (Good Morning Juliet)*

Produced and published plays:

This is for you, Anna (contributor). In *Canadian Theatre Review*, 43 (Summer 1985).

Smoke Damage (contributor). Toronto: Playwrights Canada, 1985.

Clue in the Fast Lane. Toronto: Playwrights Canada, 1986.

GOOD NIGHT DESDEMONA (Good Morning Juliet). Toronto: Coach House Press, 1990.

Ann-Marie MacDonald Interview

by Rita Much

RM: CAN YOU TALK A LITTLE ABOUT YOUR BACKGROUND, YOUR FAMILY AND UPBRINGING?

AM: I was born in West Germany in 1958 at a Royal Canadian Air Force base. Because of my father's profession, we moved around most of my childhood. My parents are from Cape Breton Island, which is a kind of spiritual home for me. Haunting my imagination was this mythic place called Cape Breton which we would visit every now and then, and mythic relatives who were all larger than life because I didn't grow up seeing them very much. They were my own personal Pantheon. I endowed the place and people with an aura of magic, of mystery, and even now I still feel a longing to return. I would love to have a place there; the landscape really feels like home.

My parents also idealized Cape Breton, the home they had left behind for what were bloody good reasons. Mainly it was too small, too lacking in opportunity and too full of their relatives — all things they later romanticized from a safe distance. I don't think they would have ever chosen to go back there. They loved to miss it too much. As a result, I had early training in the life of the imagination. Curiously, I've lately been getting cast as a Cape Bretoner. I did a feature set in Cape Breton called "Island Love Song" for CBC, and now I'm doing "Where the Spirit Lives," which is a CBC independent co-production in which I play a teacher from Cape Breton. Ironically, no one knew anything about my Cape Breton roots when the part came up. It's funny how these things happen.

I went to high school in Ottawa, spent one year at Carleton University, and then attended the National Theatre School for three years. When I graduated in 1980 I came to Toronto to begin my acting career.

I have a theatrical family in the sense that they are pretty dynamic or expressive people, but not in the sense that anyone is in the theatre. I'm happy to say that they are very supportive of my career.

RM: WHAT WERE THE HIGHLIGHTS OF YOUR THREE YEARS AT THE NATIONAL THEATRE SCHOOL?

AM: Attending the NTS was like taking awful medicine that does you good. It was exactly what I needed to do, but thank God it's

behind me. My training there gave me a firm foundation for my acting
career. I had some wonderful teachers, Pierre Lefève, for example,
made some wonderful friends and basically grew up. It was my coming of age. The highlights were character mask work with Lefève,
Ionesco with Derek Goldby, and creating and performing original text
with Michael Mawson. Now, of course, my approach to work has
changed both as a result of my own politics — feminist — and as a
result of the creative autonomy that I've developed over the years. For
example, when I was a young actor at NTS, I figured that the ability
to cry on cue or to come across as a genuine hysteric was some sort
of touchstone of authenticity. That's an indication of the kinds of roles
women are so often faced with: emotional barometers and the representatives of vulnerability and instability in general.

RM: HOW DID YOUR TRAINING AS AN ACTOR AND YOUR ACTING
CAREER PREPARE YOU FOR WRITING PLAYS?

AM: Well, acting and writing were always dual passions for me
ever since I was a little girl. I never really thought of them as separate
until I reached the age where you are supposed to think of specializ-
ing. I opted for acting because I wanted to launch myself like a rocket
on the theatre scene and the acting life and community, it seemed to
me, had the energy that was required. Writing is solitary. So much of
the motivation must come from within. When I arrived at the NTS I
felt like I was jumping into my theatrical career feet first, that I was
committing myself to a life from which there was no turning back.
Those years of training also healed me. I needed to focus my energies,
and putting acting front and centre helped me do that. I don't think I
would have started writing for theatre a moment sooner, because I
think my career as an actor has been the most natural thing in the
world for me. It had to happen first.

The transition from acting to writing was organic, smooth. My first
effort was the Nancy Drew serial, *Clue in the Fast Lane*, on which I
collaborated with Beverley Cooper. We worked under pressure-cooker
conditions, writing a piece one day, producing it and performing in it
six days later. We did everything and we did it impossibly quickly. It
was a hell of a time. I suppose I do a lot of things in that crash kind
of way. I'm determined that the play I'm working on now isn't going
to be hurried.

RM: IS THIS THE WORK YOU ARE WRITING WHILE PLAYWRIGHT-IN-
RESIDENCE AT THE CANADIAN STAGE COMPANY IN TORONTO?

AM: Yes. It's called *The Arab's Mouth*, which is a title that
dropped into my head from the ozone. Months later, when researching
the origin of numbers, I discovered what "the Arab's mouth" actually
is. In ancient Arabic numeration, the symbol for wholeness is a

mouth, drawn as two concentric circles. This fit in thematically in a way that's somewhat uncanny; the piece is about discovering truth through integration, rather than through separation. It's set in 1899 and it's about a family with some terrible secrets. Each character knows part of the truth but none of them knows the whole truth until the end, and they are all obsessed with protecting each other from what they think is the truth. Typical family behaviour, really. It's set in Scotland. The central female character is named Pearl MacIsaac. She's a well-educated spinster of independent means and she's one of those people, more common in the last century, who can be taken seriously and who is good at a lot of things: a Renaissance woman. Pearl is an amateur scientist. She is capable of coming to the same conclusions by examining a fossil as she can by staring at the heavens through a telescope. The central idea is that all knowledge is connected. I'm toying with the idea that her prime enthusiasm is mathematics because the essential irrationality of numbers really fascinates me. At certain points Pearl will accidentally, naively, refer to huge discoveries like quantum reality. I am reading a book by Stephen Hawking, the Cambridge astrophysicist, in which he says that the knowledge that the universe is expanding is knowledge that any scientist could have come to anywhere from the late eighteenth century on. They *didn't* come to it, because the implications of it were just too staggering. Our thought systems were way out, our world view wasn't such that we could contain it.

I'm still very vague about the work right now. I haven't written much. I'm buying books like crazy and getting very excited and making notes but I haven't really started. I've got the concept and I have ideas, some of which come to me out of the ozone, but it's up to me to do what I consider "breaking rocks." I've got the jewels, but I have no idea how they fit into the setting or framework of the play.

RM: IS PEARL A PART THAT YOU WOULD LIKE TO PLAY?

AM: Probably, but I doubt if I will. I think I'll want to see someone else play the role, for a couple of reasons: first of all, I can come to opening night with a flask of Scotch and pace at the back of the audience like a real tortured writer and make rude introverted noises whenever anybody doesn't understand my work; secondly, there's something quite thrilling about seeing a favourite actor breathe life into one's work. I learn a lot just by watching and listening.

RM: WHERE DO YOU GET YOUR DRAMATIC CONCEPTS FROM? DOES "THE OZONE" MEAN "OUT OF THE BLUE"?

AM: In a way the ideas come out of the blue and in a way they don't. In a way everything is culled from the unconscious. Suddenly, something flashes to the conscious mind and says, "Aha, I'm here!"

I'll hear a word or see a face that starts me off. It's almost embarrassing to admit but I tend to think of titles first. I don't think that some great spirit is writing through me and all I have to do is sit at my computer. *Au contraire*, it's really bloody hard. But I get a very strong sense of what the play's about, who it's about, and what the tone of it is. And ultimately I believe that the central images and ideas really are gifts from out of the blue. I just trust that some ideas are important. I go with them and find out later just what they mean. I choose a title, then discover why. I decide that a central character is an amateur scientist, then, through research, discover why the whole business of science is so important to me. I suddenly realize why I've been obsessed with dogs and the Jackal, Anubis, which in Egyptian mythology is a guide through the Underworld, which suggests transformation, which is a kind of alchemy, which is science, which brings me back to the meaning of the universe.

I also find out why I bought what I wore to the last Dora Mavor Moore Awards ceremony. Before I got my idea for *The Arab's Mouth* I bought an outfit with a jackal motif all over it! At the time I just thought it was neat and I felt good in it at the awards. Now I think, "How fitting. Every aspect of a gal's life, including her party dress, should add up." Only now do I see the patterns that were emerging and leading up to the idea for the play.

RM: DID YOU HAVE ANY FORMAL TRAINING AS A WRITER?

AM: No.

RM: ARE THERE SPECIFIC WRITERS OR PLAYWRIGHTS WHO HAVE INFLUENCED YOUR WORK?

AM: There are well-made plays and there are well-made educations and I don't have a well-made kind of education because I've never been the type of person who loves to read plays. I don't love to read plays. I like to watch them. Sometimes I love to watch them, but most of the time I find it's *work* to watch them. I don't get a generalized delight from the theatre. I get a very specific, occasional, thrill. In general, I'm probably pretty hard on it because to me it's the source. It's endless. It has infinite possibilities. I don't think I know nearly enough about theatre yet and I haven't seen nearly enough yet. I've been so busy concentrating on a number of projects, going very deep inside them, that I haven't had much time to surface and take in what other writers are doing. When I was at the NTS I probably saw two plays.

I suppose I am starting to surface a bit now because now that I have a body of work, both acting and writing, I can finally think, "Well, yeah, I guess I'm part of the community and I should see what I'm doing in relation to what other people are doing." For the first time I am voraciously curious about what everyone else in the world is up to. I want to see everything Pina Bausch and Robert Lepage do because, in contrast to what I do at my computer these days, their work is more movement and image weighted. The kind of theatre which can only be created "on one's feet" is as important to me as the work I do at home. As a performer-creator, this is the kind of work I want to continue to explore. *This is for you, Anna!* is like that. *Boom, Baby, Boom!* and *Serpent Kills* wove elements of dance-theatre into a narrative text in a very exciting way. DNA Theatre is doing that, too. Theatre Columbus is doing some of my favourite work around these days. They are developing shows via clown-based creation and performance styles while incorporating text that gets more ambitious and interesting all the time. Take *Paranoia* and *Doctor Dappertutto*, for example. I want to see every which way that opera can possibly be performed. I want to see dance. I want to see movies and theatre and dance and opera combined because that to me is tremendously exciting: visions of mutant, recombinant theatre.

As for favourite writers, I admire Judith Thompson, George F. Walker, Sally Clark, Howard Barker, Tennessee Williams, Anton Chekhov, some ridiculous Jacobeans, and Shakespeare, to name a few. But I rarely sit and read a play. These days I read science and history. I love nineteenth-century novels. Dickens was a brilliant dramatist. I'm glad I wasn't born a Brontë but I am eternally grateful that they lived and wrote. Findley, Atwood, and Davies are my favourite contemporary novelists.

RM: AFTER YOU GRADUATED FROM NTS YOU BECAME IMMERSED IN THE FEMINIST FRINGE THEATRE MOVEMENT IN TORONTO. CAN YOU DESCRIBE YOUR INVOLVEMENT IN THE NIGHTWOOD PRODUCTIONS OF *THIS IS FOR YOU, ANNA*?

AM: In the winter of 1983 I had just done a show called *Generals Die in Bed* at Theatre Passe Muraille, which began a long association with that theatre. That was a piece that had been collectively created but I came into it during the second production, so I didn't contribute very much to the script. However, it gave me an exciting taste of what collective creation was like. Banuta Rubess saw the show, which is how I met her. When she described her idea for *Anna* to me I said, "Wow, I'd love to do this!" At that point I knew that I was going to be committed to radical theatre and I had reached the end of whatever I had to learn from or contribute to mainstream theatre. I'd done *Dreaming and Duelling* by John Lazarus at the Young People's Theatre, which was directed by Christopher Newton, I had worked with Robin Phillips on *The Wars*, and I had made a commercial and a TV drama. I did one of everything that year and when that year was over I had a ton of money and no concept of how hard it would be to get that kind of loot again. I then went to Germany to stay with my sister and spent five weeks looking at castles, eating cream puffs and gratefully allowing my sister to look after me. I know now I was very depersonalized, numb, and depressed. I had had a "successful" first year and a half, and I felt lost. It was a big shock. I spent the rest of the summer at my parents' place and the rest of the year waitressing and reading and not liking anything. That was also my year of reading a lot of feminist literature. I realized that I couldn't put it off any longer. It was something I had to do and I knew it was going to change me, that there would be things that I wouldn't ever be able to do again. When I broke the "fast" I broke it at Passe Muraille with *Generals Die in Bed* and then I went right into *Anna*.

So *Anna* was my first truly collective experience as well as my first feminist theatre experience and for me it is a seminal work and a major turning point personally, artistically and politically. Meeting Maureen White, Banuta Rubess and Kim Renders changed my life. Creating a show and a style from the ground up, collectively to boot, is one of the hardest things in the world to do. You go on faith a lot of the time. We did a million improvs, endless research, many workshops to create *Anna*, for example. In the end we really could not say which idea belonged to whom because any idea had been explored and transformed by each of us until it belonged to all of us. And sometimes the most sublime ideas have their origin in a mundane accident; the "nail story" in *Anna* was born because in our rehearsal space there happened to be a pile of nails lying in the corner. If we had rented a swankier space perhaps the nail story would never have been.

RM: DO YOU HAVE A SENSE OF THE DIRECTION THE ALTERNATIVE THEATRE MOVEMENT IS GOING IN?

AM: I don't know anything about who is coming up, but I know that the trend in my own generation of fringe theatre artists is that we are all getting more differentiated, we are all getting more specific in what we do. Many of us are finding that we have one strength or two or three but we are no longer interested in working collectively all that much. There are however a lot of lessons learned from the collective process that we continue to apply. The lesson of dedication to a process is especially important to me because it's the cornerstone for creating my art. In fact, if I didn't have such a radical grounding in collective creation I wouldn't really stick to my artistic goals and have the personal ethics that I do have.

RM: DO YOU MIND BEING REFERRED TO AS A WOMAN PLAYWRIGHT?

AM: I don't care.

RM: DO YOU REGARD YOURSELF AS A FEMINIST PLAYWRIGHT? WHAT DOES THE TERM MEAN TO YOU?

AM: I'm a feminist through and through. I was born that way and then made it my business to understand it. It's a term too open to definition, really. There are all kinds of schools of feminist thought and obviously I'm going to be too feminist for some people and not nearly enough for others. For example, in a play like *GOOD NIGHT DESDEMONA (Good Morning Juliet)* there are a lot of sexist jokes which I find hilarious because of the context, but a purist might take offence. Yet the entire situation is a feminist situation. It's like the woman who's been done wrong and in the end she gets her own. What could be more feminist?

What being a feminist writer means to me is that there are certain bloody-well self-evident facts about women's place in the world and anyone who can read history with this in mind will figure out who is responsible for most crimes that have ever been committed on the face of the earth and that over fifty percent of the human race has been largely wasted or buried. There are a million other specific things which also make me a feminist. I'm a thinking, breathing individual, I am a political beast, I am a feminist creature. That goes without saying; it's woven through everything I do, though I don't write agitprop and I am not specifically issue-oriented at this point. In addition, being a feminist theatre artist doesn't mean I sacrifice aesthetics, as my participation in *Anna* and other shows demonstrates. I'm also a humorist and a humanist and I don't believe in cutting off anybody's anything.

RM: DO YOU THINK THAT ART CREATED BY MEN DIFFERS IN SOME WAYS FROM ART CREATED BY WOMEN, OR IS ART GENDERLESS?

AM: I do have a definite opinion on that. I think it's a mixed bag. For one thing, I think there are probably many more than two sexes, or that most people are more bisexual than they realize. Tanja Jacobs told me that when she was five years old and finally understood that there were only two sexes, she was horribly disappointed. I bet a lot of people have felt that. And when we discuss the issue of gender and art we must of course take into account that we live in a male-run society and that social conditioning is a contributing factor. You can definitely talk about general distinctions between a typically male aesthetic and a typically female one, but you might fail in a blindfold taste test.

What I personally don't like in a lot of writing by men is the undue solemnity, a kind of addiction to the dark, hopeless side of things — even an obsession with suffering and death. Stuff like that bores me because it strikes me as self-important and indulgent. Naturally, women also have their own brand of schlock which drives me bananas, too, and which I can be severely critical of, because as a woman I feel particularly mortified. I don't like generalized over-simplified solutions. I don't like gauzy feminism.

Also of concern to me is the obsession with perfection and symmetry which female writers have absorbed or inherited from male artists, mainly because men dominate the artistic scene. There's an irresistible male urge to make everything work, to make everything like clockwork and actually I am like that, too. If I am hard on that particularly male perspective it's because I've shared in it, internalized it. I'm addicted to perfection, too. Which leads me to wonder, "Is it really the exclusive preserve of the male?" I tend to project a lot, but then I was born with my gender in a knot.

Ultimately, although gender is important in art I don't think it is definitive. I think the only thing that is definitive is whether you want to get it across or not, "it" being the ideas in your heart and mind.

RM: YOU SAID THAT YOU ARE A HUMORIST AND NO ONE WOULD ARGUE THAT YOUR PLAYS AREN'T VERY FUNNY. WHY IS IT THAT SO MANY WOMAN PLAYWRIGHTS DO WRITE COMEDY?

AM: Well, comedy is a funny thing. I mean, it's the whole business of, "If I weren't laughing, I'd be killing myself." For me writing comedy is inevitable. Before I started writing and before I was really acting, I wanted to be a tragedian though I believed that comedy was the hardest thing in the world — it was what I most admired. Then I lost interest in tragedy, maybe because comedy seemed larger somehow. Comedy can contain tragedy but tragedy doesn't contain comedy. I am also obsessed with redemption and can't bear the spectacle of unremitting suffering. This is perfectly illustrated in *DESDEMONA* where Constance says something like, "I'm terrified of violence. I couldn't kill a fly. In fact, I tried to write a murder mystery but I couldn't manage to kill anyone off." I'm addicted to Perry Mason, he's the cornerstone of my personal trash, but I can't write that kind of stuff. The picture of the universe I am presenting in *The Arab's Mouth* is not an exclusively terrifying one. "Yes, there is a devil," I am saying, "but he is not necessarily what you think he is." The devil is that little place where the numbers don't add up one time out of ten. He's a trickster, a semi-divine, who can be your power or who can kill you, laughing all the while. In the Jungian sense it's a matter of incorporating the shadow to work for you rather than against you.

I think that women who write comedy are courting a lot of criticism like, "Who are you to be funny?" When you are growing up boys are the clowns and it's O.K. for a boy to get laughs but when a girl gets laughs it means that she's not attractive. She's weird. A guy can be everything and funny, too. Humour doesn't take away from his sexual attractiveness, but a girl is risking a lot. Comedy is a "bad girl" thing to do. Poking fun at institutions is iconoclastic and girls are not supposed to be rebels. When I write comedy I take an uncompromising view and try to weld as many people as I can into the experience. I figure it's open season on everyone and everything. I don't tear a strip off the unwitting audience, though. Like most women in comedy I am not that kind of comedian. I think that that kind of assaultiveness is peculiarly male territory. I take something people identify with or revere, like Shakespeare, and say, "Excuse me, while I turn this upside down." I would never lampoon something that I hated. It can only be something which fascinates me for some reason and if I'm fascinated by it then it means there is a deep attraction to it.

RM: HOW MUCH DO YOU THINK OF YOUR AUDIENCE WHEN YOU ARE WRITING A PLAY? DO YOU TRY TO ACCOMMODATE YOUR AUDIENCE?

AM: I write for myself and I write for my audience. I accommodate the audience to the degree that a dramatist must if he or she wants the play to be understood. This does not mean that I water anything down. I don't think all of the audience will "get it" all of the time, and I don't strive for that. I strive for clarity without gutting the piece, so that everyone has a chance at a satisfying experience. In *The Arab's Mouth* there are jokes and references for people who know more than average about science, and there are also jokes and references that are on a level with the old banana peel. What counts is that the unifying themes are very human, however bizarre, sublime, or ridiculous my means may be. If there is someone who is going to laugh only at banana peels, well, there will probably be one there because that makes me laugh, too. I have a very low corn threshold. I will laugh at just about everything if it's done well and well-timed and comes by surprise. In *DESDEMONA* I didn't worry about whether or not people would understand the whole business of tenure and fields of study. I figure they can ask questions or just enjoy the banana peels. As far as I'm concerned, my humour is not ghetto-ized and people who accuse me of that are probably ghetto-ized themselves. They are perfectly welcome to come out of their ghetto and have fun at my party. If they don't want to do that or it's not their cup of tea, that's fine. I don't write as a self-styled *enfant terrible* to alienate an audience. If I did I wouldn't be in theatre.

RM: I WANT TO ASK ABOUT THE PROCESS OF WRITING A PLAY. HOW MANY DRAFTS DO YOU GO THROUGH? HOW LONG DOES IT TAKE FROM START TO FINISH? DO YOU REWRITE DURING REHEARSALS?

AM: It took just over four months to write *DESDEMONA* from the time I sat down in my chair with my first reference book to the time of the first performance. That's quick. I did three drafts. They got the third draft the day of the first rehearsal and they had three weeks to rehearse it. It was a typical fringe process because of the tiny budget. Everyone decided they would just forge ahead and do the best with the script, which was over a hundred pages long. You can imagine how much I cut. I was there at rehearsals almost every day doing little re-writes if something didn't work. I didn't worry over them too much. If it didn't work for an actor I would simply change it. I thought, "I can be precious later. Right now it has to work." There were things that got changed in the first week of performance.

RM: YOU WERE OBVIOUSLY COLLABORATING CLOSELY WITH THE DIRECTOR, BANUTA RUBESS.

AM: Yeah, I have to have a very close relationship with the director, especially when the work is new. That is part of my credo, as well as working with actors I trust. If an actor says, "I'm sorry, I can't make this work," I might think to myself, "For Christ's sake, I could make it work." That's me at my worst. Normally, though, I agree. After all, in order for the play to be truly alive everyone has to feel good about it. I know the actors are on my side and it's imperative for me to have a strong rapport with them.

RM: DO YOU THINK YOU WILL EVER DIRECT?

AM: Right now I have two close friends, Banuta and Maureen White, whom I think very highly of as directors and as long as that creative rapport is there then I am very happy not to direct. I think that if I ever direct theatre it will be a matter of a necessary evil — because no one else sufficiently understands the play in question. In general, directing theatre doesn't appeal to me. Very recently I started to think I would like to direct a movie. I've actually had ideas of how I would do that but I've never had any ideas of how I would direct in theatre. I know how I *see* something when I write it but if I'm working with a director who has a strong visual sense I'm terribly excited that she can make the thing "look" better or talk better than I ever thought it could. In addition my directors are also my dramaturges, my editors, and that is very convenient. If I try something new in theatre I'd like it to be teaching textual analysis, editing, etc.

RM: YOU MENTIONED COLLABORATION WITH BEVERLEY COOPER

ON THE NANCY DREW PARODY. WHAT APPEAL DOES COLLABORATION
HAVE FOR YOU AND WILL YOU DO MORE OF IT?

AM: Not in theatre, though Bev and I are collaborating on a
screenplay and a series. I'm not interested in collaborating with
another playwright right now. I'm too excited about working on my
own. I am, however, currently collaborating with a composer-musician,
Nic Gotham, on a chamber opera called *The Nigredo Hotel.*

The idea of woman writers collaborating makes a lot of sense.
They don't have an old boys' network to rely on, so the gals have to
get together to do their own stuff. Women also don't have the luxury
of considering themselves heirs to the tortured-soul-artist mythology.
As Virginia Woolf put it, they need money and a room of their own.
In theatre, which is social, that translates into "money and a room and
a few friends." I've never felt as though I was less of an artist
because I was working collectively or collaboratively. *Au contraire*, I
was extremely proud of the fact that we were all risking these things
together. Nor do I think the final product is schizophrenic. For
example, *Clue in the Fast Lane* is just bigger than either Bev's brain
or mine — it's like the whole is greater than the sum of its parts. It is
one cohesive work, authorship is completely inextricable. There is only
one voice. I suppose Bev and I just work well together. We both have
strong egos and we fight for our ideas and we challenge each other
and disagree a thousand times, but I never feel that she ruins what
I've done. It isn't territorial. The bottom line for both of us about
something one objects to is, "If it's really going to upset you, we'll
keep it in." Ideas that are rejected simply find their way into another
piece. I don't think that anything is ever lost and I guess that is a
female thing, too, the whole process of recycling.

RM: YOU SAID THAT YOU WOULDN'T LIKE TO PLAY PEARL. WHAT
ROLES OR KINDS OF ROLES WOULD YOU LIKE TO PLAY?

AM: The only thing I'm really interested in doing in theatre is
something that involves more dance, like *Boom, Baby, Boom!* I'd like
to take non-traditional dance further in theatre. I'd also like to play
some version of Mephistopheles, as I am very drawn to comic,
demonic parts. Maybe I'll have to write that myself. I'm afraid I still
get cast as the "nice girl," which I find boring.

RM: ARE THERE ANY CLASSIC ROLES THAT YOU WOULD LIKE TO
PLAY ON THE STAGE OR IN FILM?

AM: I'm playing Ophelia in a film version of Stoppard's *Rosen-
crantz and Guildenstern Are Dead.* And every now and then someone
tells me I should play Hamlet. I haven't really thought about it but I
think it could probably be fun.

RM: OF COURSE THERE IS A LONG TRADITION OF WOMEN PLAY-
ING HAMLET ON THE STAGE.

AM: Yes. I'd love to play the great buffoons and tempters,
rather than the heroes and heroines. The part of Hamlet involves
both buffoon and tempter, which is why I am attracted. I don't know
if I want to ever play a great tragic role. I saw Glenda Jackson do
Phaedra and loved it. But tragedy on that operatic scale makes me
laugh and that's wrong. When Phaedra dies over the course of a
twenty-five minute speech I get so excited that she's going for it and
she's dying, but she doesn't die. She just keeps dying. So it's very
moving but it's also very funny.

RM: HAS YOUR SUCCESS IN FILM, PARTICULARLY *I'VE HEARD THE
MERMAIDS SINGING,* CHANGED YOUR ACTING CAREER DRAMATICALLY?

AM: This being Canada no one thing you do changes anything.
What it does change is some quite intangible thing called your profile, which may or may not mean anything. What it may mean is
that you go in for a drink somewhere and people ask you, "Weren't
you in such and such?" or the film acts as an ice-breaker in a meeting with the next director, but in Canada stepping stones are not
arranged in any kind of neat or causal fashion. I certainly had a
great time making the film and playing a type that is meant to be
both the silent spiritual presence and a discreet symbol of sexuality.
But I did find it extremely difficult to be that cool. I guess that's
why I prefer to play clowns.

RM: IN ADDITION TO WRITING FOR THEATRE YOU HAVE WRITTEN
FOR TV, AN EPISODE OF "STREET LEGAL," AND A PROPOSAL FOR A
SERIES, AND YOU HAVE WRITTEN FOR FILM, AN ADAPTATION OF *CLUE
IN THE FAST LANE.* WHICH IS THE BETTER FORUM FOR WOMAN WRI-
TERS AND WHICH DO YOU PREFER?

AM: They are all such different kettles of fish. My heart and
soul is in theatre. There's no question about that. Nothing compares,
I feel. Writers for TV seem to be just so much chopped liver in the
television machine and television is a very censorious medium. You
can't push an idea very far. As for film, you can put your heart and
soul into a screenplay but you might not recognize what comes out
at the end. There's too much money and too many people involved
and you lose control once you've done the actual writing. Theatre
gives the writer the most control. It honours the author, it's the
author's medium. It's also an artist's medium, because there's not a
hell of a lot of stuff between the artist and the performance. There's
not a lot of other technology, there's not a lot of money, there's not
a lot of other people getting in the way.

My heart and soul are in theatre also because I am an elemental
kind of person and the theatre is eternal. The audiences are small

compared to film, which isn't good in terms of getting one's message and ideas across and getting one's art across but I don't worry about that. If I ever win a Dora for writing I'd say in my acceptance speech, "My play would not make a good movie." There is this impression that theatre is somehow the poor cousin or the clever, endearing, bohemian sibling of film, when theatre is really the matrix. And I'm not looking for the illusion of reality. If I call for a fabulous effect, I want to see the strings. I want to see where the flash pot is. What I like about spectacle is that I know it's spectacle. I would love to write a play with seventeenth-century cloud machines. That's my idea of a great effect. I don't want anything seamless and I don't want anything fixed. I love the idea that theatre is never the same two nights running, that it has a million different incarnations.

RM: *CLUE IN THE FAST LANE* IS ABOUT TEENAGERS, THOUGH WRITTEN FOR ADULTS. MANY WOMAN PLAYWRIGHTS WRITE ABOUT YOUNG PEOPLE OR FOR YOUNG AUDIENCES. WHY DO YOU THINK THAT IS?

AM: I am fascinated by childhood and I have an idea for a film about a child. I think that because women raise our children they respect the wisdom of children, their freshness. Writing for young people or children is related to a comic sensibility as well. Who else is interested in children? Clowns and comedians. I like the whole idea of the world seen through the eyes of a naif. It never occurred to me until this moment but Constance Ledbelly in *DESDEMONA* is a naif and so is Pearl. I like anything that is not cynical. Cynics are ultimately lazy.

RM: YOU HAVE WORKED MAINLY WITH WOMEN IN THE THEATRE, BUT HAVE YOU EXPERIENCED A DIFFERENCE BETWEEN WORKING WITH WOMEN AND WORKING WITH MEN?

AM: When working with men in the theatre there is always a point at which I say, "Hey! I'm working with guys again." Working primarily with women has prepared me, I think, to work with men. It has helped me to become creative, confident and autonomous so that when I work with men I am not defending myself all the time or apologizing for my views or approach. Working in a feminist environment has made me a hell of a lot more gender-blind than I ever was before.

RM: YOU HAVEN'T EXPERIENCED MUCH DIFFICULTY IN GETTING YOUR WORK SHOWN. *DESDEMONA* WAS FIRST PRODUCED BY NIGHTWOOD AND NOW NIGHTWOOD IS PRODUCING A NATIONAL TOUR OF IT WHICH WILL END UP WITH A RUN AT THE CANADIAN STAGE COMPANY IN TORONTO IN THE FALL OF 1990. IN GENERAL, DO YOU THINK THAT WOMAN PLAYWRIGHTS MEET RESISTANCE?

AM: Oh, of course. Not much has changed in theatre in the 1980s. Part of my disillusionment in my early career had to do with the politics: the need to be ingratiating, the inability to speak the language of the people who run the major theatres, who are men, my failure to be the "right kind of girl," etc. etc. Since it's a boys' club, woman writers will always have a hard time until the *status quo* changes and that won't change overnight.

RM: HOW DO YOU RESPOND TO REVIEWS?

AM: Reviews are a sore point with me. Too many reviewers are men and too often they don't twig onto what the woman writers are doing — or saying. It seems to be almost a point of honour with some of the male critics in this town. I try, though, to let it all roll off me, the good, the bad, and the ugly.

Several reviews of *DESDEMONA* said it was "too long" (and I agree that it's a bit long, though I think that's a silly criticism of any play) and that it was "unfocussed." I seem to see these two criticisms of plays by women every time I read the bloody paper.

Male critics who liked *DESDEMONA* liked it for reasons different from the reasons I like it, and those who didn't like it missed the boat in terms of what the central issues were. They seemed to have come to the theatre prepared to see something they had decided on beforehand. I think the problem is that critics have a set of aesthetic criteria or touchstones, and woman playwrights, who are often challenging theatrical traditions, upset those criteria. For example, one man wrote that the play was a vague mishmash of Jungian something-or-other. Well, if you take the time to watch the play you'll realize that it's a Jungian fairy tale. The Shakespeare is the backdrop, the running joke, the means by which the piece is recognizable. It was the source. I was being mischievous by using Shakespeare as the source in the same way he used everyone else as a source. What the critic saw was this "new treatment" of Shakespeare. Few of the reviews acknowledged the resolution of the ending, how Constance incorporates the two lost aspects of herself and is made whole. Those that did "get it" were irritated by it because it wasn't Shakespearean enough. In 1989 critics come to the theatre prepared to see patriarchy challenged. "Fine," they say, "we can handle that. In fact, we are on your side." Then they say, "Well what is *this*? What are you saying? Isn't it a feminist play and if it's a feminist play shouldn't it be like *that*? And if it's a new treatment of Shakespeare, why are you going on about Jung?" So many people who didn't know anything about Shakespeare or Jung sat back and simply enjoyed themselves.

RM: HAVE JUNG'S IDEAS INFLUENCED YOU PERSONALLY AS WELL AS ARTISTICALLY?

AM: I've read a lot of Jung, who makes me uncomfortable when he strays into sexist territory, but he was on the right track. He just happened to be a man living and writing in a patriarchal society, whose values he had absorbed. I've also read many feminist Jungian texts and I suppose that in the sense of my interest in examining the psychic and physical relationship as well as that whole area of accidental discovery or synchronicity, I am a Jungian. Jung wrote a great deal about wholeness and that is what I want: physical, spiritual, creative "oneness."

RM: WITH NANCY DREW IN *CLUE IN THE FAST LANE* AND CONSTANCE LEDBELLY IN *DESDEMONA* YOU SEND UP THE WORN-OUT CLICHÉS ABOUT FEMININITY AND FEMALE SEXUALITY. IS PARODY ALMOST AN INEVITABLE PART OF THE PORTRAYAL OF WOMEN ON THE STAGE TODAY?

AM: It's like opening up a trunk that used to be full of instruments of torture and now everything has turned into toys. When you reclaim and transform ideas and methods that have been used against you as a woman, you become empowered. Subversion of this kind is healthy.

RM: IT'S A COMMON CRITICISM THAT FEMALE PLAYWRIGHTS DON'T CREATE CONVINCING MALE CHARACTERS.

AM: Well, *excusez moi*! Let's talk about some of the parts I've had to play. I feel like I've been crucified on the cross of the ingenue one too many times. Throughout theatre school I was forced to play a Chekhov character like a fucking gossamer thing, or a Shakespearean lady like a wimp. If you get a part with teeth in it it's usually negative: the character is a bitch or suicidal. I always heard that if a girl could cry she had to be a good actress. The guys never had to cry. They got a lot of words to say and a lot of fun things to do. They didn't have to be emotional to prove they were good actors.

Time will tell about the male characters in women's plays. Any slave class studied its masters a lot more closely than the masters ever studied the slaves. So women probably study men a lot harder than men ever analyze women. I tend to think that the portrayal of men by women is substantially truer to life than the opposite. Actually I'm fascinated by writing male characters. I have a male character who exists inside of me. I even know his name. I'll write something for him some day. Writing male characters is terrific. It's not a necessary evil or revenge.

RM: YOU MENTIONED *NIGREDO HOTEL*, THE CHAMBER OPERA YOU ARE WORKING ON WITH MUSICIAN NIC GOTHAM. CAN YOU DESCRIBE THE PIECE IN MORE DETAIL? WHAT DOES "NIGREDO" MEAN?

AM: It's an alchemical term for the part of the alchemical process in which matter is sealed up and cooked in its own juices. In Jungian terms it corresponds to the depression which can precede a breakdown and/or a breakthrough.

RM: WHAT ARE YOUR GOALS IN THEATRE?

AM: I have a huge amount of ambition. I want to write a lot of plays. I want to somehow make a major contribution to theatre, something that transcends gender, region, nationality. I hate the new misogynist art that has developed. Take the film *Blue Velvet*, for example. Take Cronenberg. Fine, great film-makers. Wonderful ideas. Good going, boys, but get your fucking metaphors off of my body! Find yourself a different vehicle. Fuck something else over. Don't tell me that it's not "really women." Well, it is because you're using my image. Get with it. I'm working on it. Where are you at? Why can't you work on it, too? I expect more of these people. I'm really sick of seeing the "in crowd" applauding this stuff. Don't they understand that the medium can't be divided from the message and that the metaphor is also the message? You can't divorce them. What I'm trying to achieve is unity. I look for the underlying weave or connection among disparate ideas and events. Perhaps there really is none. If there isn't, then I guess I'm trying to create it. Either way, that's what's ticking in my work these days.

8. Playwright Margaret Hollingsworth

Margaret Hollingsworth was born in Sheffield, England in 1939 and emigrated to Canada in 1968. Since then, her plays have been produced in Canada and England, and have also been seen on television, and been aired on radio, in Canada, England, West Germany, Australia and New Zealand.

If he were to come back tomorrow nothing would be changed. What happens outside does not affect me. Not accepting the darker side of man means not loving him enough.

Winnifred in *Poppycock*

Produced and published plays:

Mother Country. Toronto: Playwrights Canada, 1981.

Willful Acts. Toronto: Coach House Press, 1986. Includes *The Apple in the Eye, Diving, Ever Loving, Islands*, and *War Babies. Ever Loving* was also published in *The Penguin Book of Modern Canadian Drama*, ed. Richard Plant (Toronto: Penguin Books, 1984).

Published plays;

Alli Alli Oh. Toronto: Playwrights Canada (copyscript), 1979. Companion piece to *Islands.*

Operators/Bushed. Toronto: Playwrights Canada (copyscript), 1981.

Endangered Species. Toronto: Act One Press, 1988. Includes *The House that Jack Built, It's only hot for two months in Kapuskasing, Poppycock*, and *Prim and Duck, Mama and Frank.*

Margaret Hollingsworth Interview
by Judith Rudakoff

JR: WHAT DOES THE TERM *"CANADIAN* PLAYWRIGHT" SIGNIFY TO YOU?

MH: Straight off the top of my head, I think, "Ugh. Groan." Now that's partly because I hate classification and partly because we have so far to go. I prefer to think of myself and others simply as playwrights.

JR: DO YOU CONSIDER CANADA A SETTING, A FRAME OF REFERENCE OR A NEUTRAL PLACE FOR YOUR WORK?

MH: For me, it's certainly not neutral. It's my whole frame of reference. Canada is what I write about. Canada is where I come from; it's what feeds me.

JR: WHAT ABOUT THE OTHER COUNTRIES IN WHICH YOU'VE LIVED — ITALY, JAPAN, ENGLAND — DO YOU WRITE ABOUT THEM AS WELL?

MH: Yes. But very, very rarely. In my fiction I tend to write about other places as well as Canada, but my plays always, in some way, come out of Canada.

JR: WHY DO YOU THINK THAT IS?

MH: I find it easier to be autobiographical in fiction. In plays, I'm always trying to keep a distance, to be more objective. The characters in my plays often have very little to do with me. I wouldn't say that's true in my fiction.

JR: DO YOU THINK THE SPECIFICITY OF LOCALE IN THE PLAYS MAKES THEM MORE OR LESS PRODUCIBLE HERE AND ABROAD?

MH: In terms of Canadian productions, there's that horrible Canadian predicament that gets in the way: "It can't be interesting if it's about *us.*" Abroad, it's virtually hopeless to try to get a Canadian play produced. Try to read about Canada in any of the European newspapers. We don't exist.

When I lived in Italy, Canada was never even mentioned. In England, you still have to go to Canada House to find out what's happening here.

JR: THE EUROPEANS CONSIDER US A THIRD WORLD COUNTRY. ONLY NOT NEARLY AS EXOTIC OR INTERESTING. . . .

MH: They really do. They don't care about Canada. They don't consider us important.

One of the elements that I do find lacking (one that makes it so hard to write about this country) here in Canada is a cross-country sense of Canadian consciousness. For example, I wrote *It's only hot for two months in Kapuskasing* in British Columbia, and hardly anyone there knew where Kapuskasing was. Nobody I met knew what it was like to be in a small town in Northern Ontario. And not only did they not know: they didn't care! It becomes very hard when you're trying to write something about a country and the rest of the nation doesn't care.

JR: DO YOU FIND THAT AUDIENCES DIFFER DEPENDING ON THE COAST THAT YOU'RE ON?

MH: I can't say that I find a collective difference. I think it's a more individual difference. On the whole, audiences in Canada are responsive and non-judgemental.

JR: IN THE INTRODUCTION TO *ENDANGERED SPECIES*, YOU SAY THAT WOMEN ONLY HAVE A SMALL VOICE IN THE CANADIAN THEATRE. DO YOU THINK THAT'S LIKELY TO CHANGE? DO YOU THINK THERE'S A WAY FOR YOU TO CHANGE THE SITUATION?

MH: I see that situation changing somewhat in that a few theatres are producing more women's plays now. But the plays that are being produced still tend to be fairly conventional in style and content, they adhere more to what I would call the "male norm."

I just don't hear a lot of the female material getting through. What do I mean by "female" material? Well, it's stuff that you can find if you dig. I get it from female students. It's a different consciousness. It's not documentary material or one woman getting up and talking directly to an audience about her personal experiences in a one-woman show. I'm talking about plays that deal with women's experiences in an in-depth manner, written in a form that a woman will embrace.

No, I guess I don't see the male hierarchy in the artistic directorates of theatre in Canada changing. Even when the tendency is towards change, I think women become honed down very quickly to that male point of view. They have to if they're going to survive. I don't blame them for doing it; theatre is a male endeavour. It always has been throughout its history. And not just in Canada either — throughout the world. That's a dreadfully pessimistic answer, isn't it?

One of the ways in which we're trying to change the situation is through communication. For example, the recent conference of International Woman Playwrights which was held in Buffalo in the spring of 1989. It gave me a sense of incredible strength. Suddenly I realized that this problem is an international one. The support and energy from woman playwrights from all over the world, all in similar positions of frustration, made me feel, "Okay, now I can fight again, for a while."

And maybe, if we all work together, some things can change. That conference was an amazing experience: woman writers from China, from Africa, from Greece, all telling the same stories.

JR: WHEN YOU COME OUT OF AN EXHILARATING, SUPPORTIVE SITUATION LIKE THE CONFERENCE, AND YOU'RE FILLED WITH POSITIVE ENERGY AND HOPE, WHAT DO YOU DO NEXT?

MH: I came back to Canada, feeling revitalized and thinking about all the plays I was going to write and all the projects I was going to initiate. Basically, all I've done so far is help initiate the next conference, which will be here in Toronto.

I did also begin sending my plays around to theatres again (which I'd stopped doing), but not to any great effect. But that aside, I still, six months later, still feel strong.

JR: PART OF THE DIFFICULTY STEMS FROM THE DIFFERENCES BETWEEN MALE AND FEMALE NOTIONS OF POWER. THE FORMER IS ESSENTIALLY A POWER *OVER* AND THE LATTER AN EMPOWERMENT.

MH: I don't think one necessarily obviates the other. Power is power, after all. Male and female power can work really well together, and women can, I think, possess both types. I don't think many men have that female understanding of power, of sharing; not delegating — *sharing.*

JR: WOMEN TEND TO USE POWER DIFFERENTLY, USING IT AS A LEVER TO MAKE US ACT. ITS NOT USUALLY AN END UNTO ITSELF.

MH: You read *Poppycock,* which is basically about women and power. In that play I took it to the extreme to see the effect when creative women are linked with powerful men who subsume and subvert their power. It all disappears!

JR: IN *POPPYCOCK,* PICASSO SAYS THAT THERE ARE TWO TYPES OF WOMEN: "GODDESSES AND DOORMATS."

MH: He really is reported to have said that, you know.

JR: IS THERE A WAY AROUND THAT ATTITUDE?

MH: It requires so much work. I did a lot of research before I wrote *Poppycock.* For example, the way we use space. Compare the way in which women will sit and men will sprawl. See how often women smile compared to men. Look at their body positions when they are talking to men. Look around and see this in action, on subways, anywhere. How do you begin to alter that patterned behaviour?

When women do get hold of power in any major way it's not surprising that they sometimes take it to the extreme and become Maggie Thatchers.

JR: THEY'RE STILL OPERATING WITHIN A MALE-DETERMINED HIERARCHY.

MH: Realistically, they have to. It will certainly take a while before any change can be affected, but at least women are becoming more aware of this position. That's the first step.

JR: WHAT DO YOU THINK THE EFFECTS ARE OF BEING A MINORITY (PLAYWRIGHT WITHIN THE WRITING COMMUNITY) WITHIN A MINORITY (CANADIAN WITHIN A NORTH AMERICAN OR EUROPEAN TRADITION) WITHIN A MINORITY (WOMEN IN A MALE CULTURE)?

MH: It wipes you out, doesn't it? It's bizarre that anyone would want to work under those restrictions, really.

JR: WHY DO YOU DO IT?

MH: I don't any more. Not unless I get a commission.

JR: BUT YOU DO. YOU'VE JUST PUBLISHED A COLLECTION OF YOUR PLAYS IN AN ANTHOLOGY CALLED *ENDANGERED SPECIES*. AND I THINK IT'S OF PARAMOUNT IMPORTANCE THAT THE PLAYS YOU'VE CHOSEN TO INCLUDE HAVEN'T HAD PRODUCTIONS. THE VOLUME CERTAINLY STANDS AS A TESTAMENT TO THE IMPORTANCE OF THE PLAY SCRIPT AS TEXT AS WELL AS A RECORD OF A PERFORMANCE.

MH: That's right. I became so tired of having plays just lying around with nothing happening to them. It occurred to me a long time ago that I should publish them myself, but that takes a lot of money and energy.

As much as anything else, *Endangered Species* is a political statement from me. The more people I can get to with that statement, the better.

I didn't publish the volume with an eye to getting produced. I don't think getting published can affect that. Except perhaps in the universities or the schools. I can't think of a professional Canadian theatre that would produce those plays, frankly. But the book is out there and the work is going to live on as my statement, even when I'm not here.

JR: WERE THERE MANY DIFFICULTIES IN GETTING THE BOOK PUBLISHED?

MH: Only financial. And, of course, finding the time to edit it. The whole process was actually more fun than I imagined it would be. And I still get such a kick out of going to my Post Office Box every week to pick up orders. It keeps me going, knowing that I have a link out there, knowing that people are reading me and buying my plays. Otherwise, play-writing can be so isolating. And so debilitating.

I find sometimes that there are so many battles to fight and (particularly of late) I've just started retreating and thinking, "No. I have other things to do." If the theatre, to focus on one battle, is not available to me, then there are other ways for me to make a statement. Even though theatre is and always has been my preferred medium (I think it's the type of writing I do best), I can't go on bashing my head against a wall forever.

JR: ARE THERE ANY BRIGHT SPOTS?

MH: Academe. That's where the interested people are. That's where I get the most feedback, both from students and from the academics themselves.

I spoke to a class at the University of Toronto in January of 1989 for Professor Ann Saddlemyer's Woman Playwrights course, and I received letters afterwards from the students. One of them even followed up and came to my house to meet with me to discuss how she could try to find a way of producing my plays! She wanted to petition the theatres! What wonderful, positive energy.

JR: DO YOU THINK THAT THE NEXT WAVE IN CANADIAN THEATRE WILL COME FROM THE UNIVERSITIES?

MH: I don't know where else it's going to come from. As a country, we haven't nurtured our more mature playwrights, so they have, literally, fallen by the wayside. If you look at the names that were on playbills a decade ago, you'll find that about eighty per cent have disappeared. Only about three or four of our more senior playwrights have managed to survive after a decade. Where are the people like Lawrence Russell, Hrant Alianak, Beverley Simons, Michael Cook. . . . Will we re-discover them all when they're old men and women?

These playwrights were innovative and often outspoken. People who are writing now have to be *so* conservative, because that's what Canadian theatre demands of them.

You cannot have a theatre if you're ignoring the more mature writers. All the theatres seem to be looking for someone new whom they can sponsor and market and claim as their own discovery. In that way playwrights are locked into the theatre where they made their mark. It makes it hard for anyone who works outside Toronto to ever break into the Toronto scene. But playwriting is a long-term investment.

That dismissal of playwrights doesn't seem to happen so readily in other countries. It's a very Canadian phenomenon.

JR: DO YOU SEE IT AS BEING AN OFFSHOOT OF THE CURRENT LOVE AFFAIR WITH YOUTH?

MH: Partly. I do think that theatres are always looking to build up their own stable of young, new playwrights. "Stable" — what a horrible word. We're people, aren't we?

In a contemporary society where Promotion and Packaging are major elements of a successful career, what advantages can there be to being part of a minority? Any of the minorities you mentioned.

I can't think of any advantages.

JR: SO WHAT KEEPS YOU WRITING FOR THEATRE?

MH: I haven't had a new play produced since 1982. So why did I keep at it? I don't know.

The Green Line is probably the last uncommissioned play I'll write, and I'll have to publish it, as it may not be produced.

Two years ago I was very bitter about the situation here. I was upset and hurt. I'm not any more. I send the plays out, nobody ever responds and so what do you do? You can't let it get you down. I can comfort myself with the thought that at least they're not rejected.

The main thing is that I've always done what I know I have to do: write plays. Maybe I have to find another way of doing it, or another place to do it and if that does mean moving to England — well, I don't know what that means at the moment.

As long as I'm getting some reward somewhere (and I have arranged that for myself with film and other writing projects), I can keep going. My book of stories is being published in the fall of 1989 and I was nominated for an ACTRA Award this season. And I have two film scripts in pre-production. The theatre is just something I have to do, and so I do it. Fortunately, I've been commissioned to write a play for the Nanaimo Summer Festival for their 1990 season.

JR: WHAT KEEPS YOU BASED IN TORONTO?

MH: Nothing, really. Coming to Toronto from Vancouver is partly what put a hold on my career. I was doing fine in British Columbia, and still am. That's where my book is being published and that's where my stage plays still get performed and where my royalties come from for amateur productions.

For some reason, in Toronto virtually nothing has happened for me. I haven't had anything produced since I moved here except through Nightwood Theatre. So, nothing really keeps me here.

In fact, I've been back to British Columbia three times this year and I'm still, if you use classifications, a B.C. playwright.

JR: WOULD YOU CONSIDER MOVING BACK TO BRITISH CO-LUMBIA?

MH: I may. At the moment, being based in Toronto and going back there is working out. I think that if I really want to do theatre again in Canada, that's where I've got to go. But even in B.C., there isn't that much happening. There's so little government funding for the arts in that province.

JR: WHAT INTERESTED YOU IN THEATRE INITIALLY?

MH: I knew about theatre from an early age: I always had theatre around me. The only book we had in our house when I was growing up was *Hamlet*, and my father (who wanted to act professionally, and did perform occasionally) used to read it aloud all the time.

The first show I ever saw was when I was just a little kid. It was in the local church hall and I think it was an Agatha Christie mystery, or some such thing. I was entranced! I spent most of the play looking at the clock at the back of the hall, hoping it would stop so that the show could go on forever. I was hooked.

JR: WHAT WAS THE FIRST THING YOU EVER WROTE?

MH: I wrote novels from the age of five. I've still got the first one and it's only one line: "All the Jews were waiting for a Messiah." Jews spelled "joos" and Messiah spelled "mesir"!

I illustrated it, too, with a picture of my Sunday School teacher holding a cushion. And thus began a literary career!

I used to sit under our table (there was a long chenille table cloth over it!) and listen to the adults talking, and write my novels in chalk on the underside of the table.

And every year when it was my father's job to wallpaper the walls of a different room, my job was to strip the old paper off the wall, up to where I could reach. As my reward, I was allowed to write on the bare wall, so the walls of that house are covered with scribbling up to the height of a little girl. I still remember that pinkish plaster and I never see a pristine wall now without wanting to write on it!

JR: WHAT WAS THE FIRST PLAY YOU HAD PRODUCED?

MH: I won a national play competition in England and the piece received a production in the ruins of Coventry Cathedral. (Coventry was bombed during the war and the new cathedral was built next to the ruins of the old one.) I guess that was my first produced play. I was about eighteen at the time.

JR: HAS YOUR PLAY-WRITING CHANGED MUCH IN THE INTERIM?

MH: Actually, no. My style hasn't undergone any major changes: it was always heightened realism, perhaps more so in my earlier work. The language of my plays has always been condensed, poetic.

My second play, *The Tongue Is a Scorpion* (what a name!), was very condensed and stylized in the manner of the work in *Endangered Species*. It didn't quite have the underpinning of realism that those do.

Underneath it all, I'm probably a poet as much as a playwright. The problem is, I cannot write poetry to save my life! That's been my search, right from the beginning: to find a theatrical metaphor, a medium for a poetic drama that isn't self-conscious.

Because we have never had a strong theatrical tradition in Canada, poetic drama will always be deemed literary. So even though I'm writing earthy, gutsy material, it's relegated to that category.

I still maintain that audiences want to hear language and glory in it. But playwrights have to be cautious, because our theatre is cautious. One of the woman playwrights from China at the conference last spring said that there was no point at all in writing for the theatre unless one was controversial, or one's writing was controversial. I see little of that here.

JR: WHAT ABOUT THE ISSUE OF ISSUE-ORIENTED THEATRE BEING TARGETED AT SPECIFIC AUDIENCES. DO YOU FIND THAT LIMITING?

MH: It's a problem, isn't it? We're always in danger of ghetto-izing ourselves and just making women's theatre.

But, on the other hand, without theatres like Nightwood Theatre, we aren't going to get produced.

JR: DOES THAT SPILL OVER INTO THE PUBLISHING SITUATION?

MH: Well, the great thing about self-publishing is the control over the material. Nobody can breath over my shoulder and say, "That play doesn't belong in there."

JR: IS THEATRE WRITING THE SAME FOR YOU AS WRITING FOR FILM OR RADIO? ARE THE AUDIENCES THE SAME OR DIFFERENT?

MH: I don't think of the audience, really. That's too calculating. But the wonderful thing about live theatre is sitting in the audience and having them react to you, the playwright. Because that's what they're doing. Reacting to you. In film they wouldn't be reacting to *me*.

JR: AND RADIO?

MH: Radio is such an intimate medium. You're telling a story to one person. It's not an audience as such. It's much more like a written story. It's me and you. I can beckon to people, "Come closer and listen to this. . . ." Radio is wonderful because it's so abstract. It's like sending out smoke signals: they go out once (usually) and then that's it, they're gone. It's the most ephemeral of dramatic forms. And the most attractive in some ways. It's like sky-writing. I like it but I don't do it a lot. It doesn't pay much. (I have a very eighties way of looking at things at the moment.) And if I'm going to write things for practically nothing, then I might as well write for live theatre!

JR: TELL ME MORE ABOUT FILM-WRITING AS AN ALTERNATIVE TO THEATRE.

MH: It's very much like theatre in that you really write for the filing cabinet. The difference is that you get paid very well. I've been warned over and over that only one in ten commissioned film scripts gets produced.

There's probably less freedom. There are so many more people involved in the process, and you go into it with a different attitude. At least I do. I know it's not *my* piece and that it belongs to the producer. What I'm trying to accomplish is to understand what the producer wants the piece to say and then do that. It's just not the same as creating a totally original piece. Writers have no status in the film industry, and I've already learned that it's a really dirty business.

Once you've discovered what the producer wants, it's a lot like finding a pattern or a form, and organizing the ideas (visual ideas, mostly). Certainly to do that you need to be familiar with and understand dramatic form and character, narrative structure. But it is very different.

I particularly love the visual side of film-writing and the freedom it gives. I'm very happy doing the film-writing, but it is just a job.

JR: AS OPPOSED TO THEATRE WRITING?

MH: Theatre writing isn't just a job. I think it's a kind of obsession. A passion.

And the torment of the rehearsal period. Well, it's torment and exhilaration at the same time. You don't find that mixture anywhere else. And that combination is part of the reason why I do it.

JR: DO YOU SIT IN ON REHEARSALS?

MH: When I do (and I think I'm behaving myself . . .) and I just sit there, directors don't like it. They don't seem to like it when I speak either! The stumbling block may be that I present them with huge problems in my plays and they just don't want me to sit there watching them wrestle with those problems. Even when they solve them. Directors get self-conscious with me and find all sorts of reasons for getting rid of me!

They usually say it's because I'm difficult, but actually, I'm just fascinated by the process. When I sit there and watch, I'm not judging them. I must have a facial expression that makes people think I'm just a judgemental old witch.

During the rehearsal period, I enjoy watching those involved begin to uncover my mental process, how I wrote the play. They get quite excited, but they often don't know what to do with it when they've first found it. I should understand that no one likes to be watched when they're grappling with something and I should leave them to it: but I don't, because I'm so fascinated. It's like they're walking 'round and 'round in my head and I want to see how deep they can get, and if they can surprise me.

JR: AND YOU DO GIVE THEM CHALLENGES WITH YOUR PLAYS. THEY ALL HAVE SO MANY LAYERS.

MH: I like to have that sense of ambiguity. I work at knowing when to leave things hanging and I try not to always explain everything.

I think that *The House That Jack Built*, which was the last play I wrote in *Endangered Species*, is more straightforward. It's still got all those different layers to it, though.

JR: WITH WHAT DO YOU BEGIN? AN IDEA? A CHARACTER? AN ENDING?

MH: Never with an ending! I often start with an idea or a visual image. Right now, I've got this visual image of an orchestra sinking slowly under water. I don't know what I'll do with it; it could become anything.

For *The Apple in the Eye* I deliberately took a book of reproductions of famous works of art and randomly opened the book at five pictures. My goal was to write a play linking the five paintings. You would never know that I'd done that from the play if I hadn't told you, but you can actually find the pictures in the play. They're all either referred to or described.

Anything I write is patterned, underneath the surface, anyway. I find a link that isn't obvious between images or words or characters.

Sometimes, I'll take a word and then I'll spin from the word.

A lot of Canadian theatre is far more up-beat than I am: People want happy endings. They want *endings* above all else. They need things tied up and resolved. Now that's the buzz word these days: "resolution." Or "redemption."

I'm not particularly interested in either. Nor in being especially optimistic about something that *I'm not optimistic about*! And when people say, "I don't think anyone will want to go to the theatre to cry; they go there to be entertained," I say, "Well, too bad."

For me, the major function of theatre is to challenge and disturb. And it's great if we can entertain along the way.

I think that one is quite manacled when writing in this culture.

JR: WHEN YOU LEAVE THE ENDINGS AMBIGUOUS OR OPEN-ENDED, DO YOU MEAN TO IMPLY THAT THE CHARACTERS CAN ULTIMATELY CONTROL THEIR OWN DESTINIES, OR IS IT ALL MERELY FATE AT WORK?

MH: I should believe in Fate. That is, after all, what good old-fashioned dramatists believe in! That's what drama is all about: whether you act against Fate or not.

I guess I'd have to say that I don't believe in Fate.

JR: WHAT WOULD YOU SAY YOUR FEMALE CHARACTERS VALUE MOST?

MH: There's really nothing they share except a desire for a space of their own. Finding that space and putting their seal on it.

JR: A NICHE SOMEWHERE FOREIGN?

MH: All of them are trying to get away from something or someone, aren't they?

JR: THEY SEEM TO BE RUNNING TOWARDS OR AWAY FROM WHAT THEY HAVEN'T YET BEEN ABLE TO NAME.

MH: Ann Saddlemyer calls that place or thing "home."

JR: HOW DO YOU DEFINE "HOME"?

MH: Well, it certainly isn't simply "house"! It's a place you recognize and where you are recognized.

JR: AN ANCHOR?

MH: Maybe an emotional anchor, but "anchor" makes you feel weighed down and I don't think that is the sense of home that I mean.

Home is a place where you are not an immigrant. All of my woman characters are immigrants. But then I think that all women are pretty much immigrants in a male society.

The characters are all trying to suss out the rules of the male, foreign society and end up getting them wrong most of the time. For example, poor Prim in *Prim and Duck*: she wears a green fright wig and spends all her time trying to understand the rules, getting them wrong.

JR: DO ENVIRONMENT AND CIRCUMSTANCES SHAPE YOUR CHARACTERS OR DETERMINE THEIR ACTIONS?

MH: Yes. That's very important. Look at those three sisters in *Mother Country*. They're totally shaped by an environment they're not even physically in: England.

JR: YOU'VE LIVED IN ITALY, JAPAN, ENGLAND, CANADA. YOUR CHARACTERS ARE OFTEN TRANSPLANTED TO NEW HOME COUNTRIES. DO YOU THINK IT'S POSSIBLE TO LEAVE THE COLONIAL INFLUENCES BEHIND OR DO THEY JUST KEEP PILING UP, LAYER ON LAYER?

MH: Things become more or less important as time goes by, but I don't think you ever totally leave influences behind. They get buried, but you can always find them. Some circumstance crops up and "boom!," there it is: the past, even though you might not have thought about it for years. There it is. Clear as ever.

I find it interesting to see my past associations with Italian and Polish communities show up in my characters. In *Ever Loving*, for example. And *Operators*.

JR: WHAT ABOUT THE INFLUENCES OF FAMILY?

MH: I haven't really written about families very much. When I do, I've used them as allegory. Usually I write about people running *away* from the prison of family.

JR: LIKE ALLI, WHO ESCAPES HER TRADITIONAL FAMILY LIFE AND RUNS IMMEDIATELY INTO ANOTHER LESS CONVENTIONAL RELATIONSHIP?

MH: That second relationship isn't so much a family as a need for security, a need that most women feel.

JR: DO YOU BELIEVE IN THE POSSIBILITY OF NON-PARASITIC, SYMBIOTIC MALE-FEMALE RELATIONSHIPS?

MH: I think they're possible. At least I hope so! But whether or not they're possible for my characters, I'm not sure.

If those positive types of relationships were possible for my characters, then it wouldn't be drama for me. People ask me, "Why do you put your characters in such awful situations?" And I have to answer, "Because that's dramatic. It's not interesting if they're not involved in that type of situation."

JR: ARE THE WOMAN CHARACTERS VICTIMS?

MH: I don't like the word victim. I think that they are all trying to find their way out. And a lot of them do find a way out in eccentricity, or abstract flights of fancy that take them out of the real world. But I don't think that makes them victims. After all, they're active, they're in flight.

JR: YOU CREATE BOTH YOUR FEMALE CHARACTERS, INNER AND OUTER WORLDS, AND THE PLAYS PRESENT THE PERSPECTIVES OF LOOKING IN AND LOOKING OUT.

MH: Yes. Through all the layers. That's the other technique I work with in my plays: presenting the inner world. It's very difficult and I'm still finding different ways of doing it. It's technically challenging in production, too.

JR: I THOUGHT *WAR BABIES* TOOK THAT DEVICE A STEP FURTHER. WERE YOU HAPPY WITH THE WAY YOU DRAMATIZED INNER AND OUTER WORLDS THROUGH COLIN AND ESME 1 AND 2?

MH: I don't know. I think there are other ways of doing it. I don't really like dualities on stage: I mean I don't like two people representing one. There's got to be a way or a gimmick of dramatizing that split and getting right into the character and finding both parts.

It's funny that I do it more for the women than the men characters. But that's probably because I don't know what the male inner world is. I know what their outer world is and I can reflect that really well. But I'm just not sure what their inner world is. I'm not sure they care to know either. . . .

JR: SEARCHING FOR THE INNER WORLD IS REALLY A —

MH: — very female thing to do! It's a quest isn't it?

I don't know how many plays from a male perspective you can find that look inside. That inner world is an element that makes my plays very female and makes men afraid of them. No question about that!

I've actually had men say to me, "I don't like these inner voices. I don't think they work in the theatre." Well, I think they do work. Shakespeare uses them. He finds ways, for example in *Hamlet*, to look in.

JR: ONE OF THE WAYS YOU'VE EXPERIMENTED WITH DELVING INTO THE LAYERS OF THE CHARACTER'S PSYCHE IS THROUGH MASK AND CLOWN WORK. CAN YOU TALK A BIT ABOUT THAT?

MH: I think that mask and clown work has incredible potential to open up the various worlds of the characters. I've been disappointed because I think we didn't really know what we were working with in our rehearsals for *Poppycock*. We got scared and tried to handle the power of what we were seeing in rehearsal by using more conventional means, which, of course, you cannot do. You've got to give the work free rein and if it fails, it fails. You must realize that with mask work you are on the brink of discovery.

We were exploring areas in that rehearsal process that teetered on the brink of something very new and exciting. I kept getting this strange *frisson* that would go through me, telling me that this must have been what innovators like Peter Brook felt like.

But we simply weren't strong enough to carry through. We needed, as a group, to support each other more than we did. But there were deadlines to meet and a show to put on.

JR: WOULD YOU WORK THAT WAY AGAIN IF THE DEADLINES WERE REMOVED?

MH: What I would like to do is work that way again in rehearsal with somebody who was willing to go through it, not only in a visceral sense, but also intellectually. The process needs both and last time what was lacking was the analytical, intellectual approach. I supplied that to an extent, but I wasn't directing and I wasn't acting. So, once again, I was just sitting there, getting on everyone's nerves.

I did keep giving little bits of input, but that type of work needs somebody with a strong understanding of where it can potentially lead. The Theatre Resource Centre people, Richard Pochinko and Ian Wallace, were very instinctive in their uses of clown work. They didn't analyze; they didn't want to. It wasn't their thing.

But to take the work that step further, I think, requires vision *à la* Peter Brooke.

JR: IS THERE ONE EXERCISE OR A MOMENT THAT YOU EXPERIENCED IN THAT PROCESS THAT STANDS OUT?

MH: In the whole clowning process? Well, the clowning was really an interior journey for me. With clowning, you discover all sorts of things about yourself, and then you have to exteriorize them.   I discovered that one aspect of myself was the Mischief-Maker. And I think that character appears throughout my work. I'm an unbalancer, a rocker of boats. But in a nice way, I hope, not an evil way!

JR: THE MISCHIEF-MAKER SHOWS UP MANY PLACES AS THE TRICKSTER, THE FOOL. . . .

MH: Yes, the Wise Fool. That was a huge shock to me. I didn't know that that aspect was in me, yet through the clown work it showed up so clearly. So did an incredible childishness, which I suppress a lot of the time. It was wonderful to find that and inject it into the work.

But, again, you've got to have someone leading you who can interpret those discoveries or take them further. I'm not a good enough handler of people to do that myself: I'm a mixer; I'll mix people up or stir them up, but I'm not a leader in the way that's needed.

JR: THERE'S STILL A GREAT FEAR IN THE THEATRE OF RUINING INSTINCT BY FOLLOWING IT WITH INTELLECTUALIZING OR ANALYSIS.

MH: "Intellectualize" is a dirty word in Canada.

The best plays have to be both head and heart. You can't have one without the other. Most of the plays in Canada are heart with the odd head play. Very few are a combination.

JR: AND YOU'RE TRYING TO BLEND HEAD AND HEART IN YOUR WORK?

MH: I hope so. I do try and I'm learning. I think that the plays of mine that don't work are the plays that emphasize one or the other.

JR: DO YOU THINK THAT THERE'S A BIG DIFFERENCE BETWEEN WHO YOUR CHARACTERS ARE AND WHO THEY THINK THEY ARE?

MH: Of course. I don't think any of them really know who they are; it wouldn't make good drama.

JR: MANY TIMES THE PRIMARY CONFLICT IN YOUR PLAYS IS BETWEEN THE CHARACTER AND HERSELF.

MH: Right — in *Mother Country*, for example. I think mothers have that kind of internal conflict. I have very strong, rather evil mothers in my plays quite often, which is very unfeminist of me, isn't it?

JR: WHENEVER YOU INCLUDE PREGNANT CHARACTERS THEY'RE IMBUED WITH A SENSE OF THE MYTHIC. THEY SEEM LARGER THAN LIFE AND SEEM TO REPRESENT REGENERATION. ARE YOU CONSCIOUSLY CREATING EARTH MOTHERS?

MH: I prefer to avoid the word "myth": I'm not consciously doing anything. Much of Canadian Literary Criticism is a desperate search for the mythic. Come on out, wherever you are. . . .

The conflict (actually, I hate that term, "conflict." I won't use it. I prefer "the push-pull"), the push-pull, the liaison *is* between the character and herself. It's a push-pull between where she is and where she perceives herself to be. Again, that's part of the interior world.

JR: YOU CREATE A DETAILED MAP OF THAT INTERIOR WORLD, AND IT'S THAT MAP THAT FUELS THE PLAYS. IN THE SHORTER PIECES, THE MEN SEEM TO BE ADJUNCTS TO THAT WORLD: THEY'RE SHADOWY FIGURES OR DISEMBODIED VOICES, OR OFFSTAGE. . . .

MH: They're usually shouting directions to the women from offstage!

JR: YOU BUILD TWO DISTINCT WORLDS: MALE AND FEMALE. AND IT'S CERTAINLY THE FEMALE WORLD THAT IS THE MOST ENGAGING.

MH: The only exception to that, I would say, is in *Prim and Duck*. In that play the characters, male and female, are equal. But actually, that play is about ritual. I suppose that a lot of my plays are about ritual, about the unwritten rules that we all perceive. If we're socialized then we *must* know those rules. If we're not socialized (and many of my characters aren't) then we're always one step behind the rules, trying to find them. And that's what *Prim and Duck* is all about. Duck's the only one who can afford to be creative with the rules: he can make them up.

Frank knows exactly what the rules are. It's all very clear for him. Not so for poor old Prim. She just cannot get it right. Ever. She is always trying to learn what the man's rules are, but she doesn't even understand what happens when you take photographs. She worries about her insides getting photographed. And what if the photograph shows what she's just eaten? The terror, the absolute terror of being adrift in chaos is overwhelming.

And Mama can't get it right either, but she gets away with it simply because she's a mother. She's earned her status, and she lets them all know it. But in fact, she's as much at sea as the rest of them. She doesn't know whether the man in the shop likes her or doesn't like her, or what's going to happen, or why her daughter doesn't dress the way she must dress to play by the rules or why even when Prim tries the rules don't work for her. The two women, in different ways, are totally at sea.

JR: IT'S SAD, BUT I CAN'T HELP LAUGHING.

MH: Yes! It's supposed to be funny!

JR: THAT HUMOUR IS SO IMPORTANT TO THE PLAYS, AND YET OFTEN PEOPLE SEEM TO MISS IT.

MH: Oh God, yes. They don't have enough time to find it in rehearsal. In production they often miss it too. Those plays are so dense. There's only so much you can get to in our short rehearsal periods. All you can get is what the hell they're about. You don't get to try to put that burnish of humour on them. That would take another week. Often if you'll see the plays at the end of the run, you'll find the humour. For example, *War Babies* at Toronto Free Theatre changed tremendously during the run of the show. They finally got it right.

JR: THE SET WASN'T PARTICULARLY HELPFUL. IT WAS QUITE

OVERT IN ITS SYMBOLISM WITH THE STARK WHITE AND BLACK AND THE OBVIOUSLY BALANCED SEGMENTS.

MH: I think the play needs to be done on a bare stage, actually.

JR: WELL, IT TAKES PLACE IN THE RECESSES OF THE MIND. IT REALLY ONLY NEEDS SHADOW AND LIGHT.

MH: Hangings here and there and lights . . . a staircase. But nothing more. Constantly moving. Oh well, maybe next time.

JR: *WAR BABIES* HAS A REAL SENSE OF RENEWAL, OF FEMALE POWER IN A WAY THAT STRIKES A DEEP CHORD IN ME.

MH: Interesting. It was the women in the audience who got that feeling. So it's no good people saying to me that that distinction doesn't exist, that male and female reactions are all the same. It simply isn't true. A lot of the men in the audience were left quite cold by *War Babies.*

JR: IT ALL HAS TO DO WITH PLUGGING IN TO THE MATERIAL AND RELATIVELY LITTLE IDENTIFYING WITH LINEAR PLOT.

MH: Yes. I think that's what I'm trying to do when I'm writing. I try to appeal on a subliminal level so that people don't know what it is that's drawing them in or repelling them. Sometimes my plays get people really angry. And they don't know why. That's okay because it means that that play has worked. It has taken me a while to recognize that, but it's okay.

JR: IS THERE A PARTICULAR THEATRE SPACE THAT APPEALS TO YOU?

MH: To me, the space isn't important. I don't think there's any theatre space that doesn't work, frankly. Theatre will work anywhere if it's good. As long as you can see and hear the performers, there are no bad spaces.

I love theatres that are artificial. And theatres that have curtains that go up and down or that have a proscenium arch (preferably with a motto over the top that says something like *non nobis domine*). That's the sort of theatre I grew up with, like the Intimate Theatre in Palmer's Green in England. It was a repertory theatre and when I was growing up I used to go every two weeks when they changed the program. The curtain was so magical. I really do miss a curtain. That's so old fashioned, isn't it? Next I'll probably say that I miss three-acts . . . but I do! Or an organist. I miss anything that helps put you into that theatre mode. The kind of space I like least is the type that's designed to be everything. And as a result, it's nothing . . . .

Theatre is artificial. It's meant to be. It's magic. I don't want to think that I'm sitting in my living room. I'm not. And I'm not much interested in a bunch of actors performing a scene on the shop floor. Even in medieval times they had the sense to put the actors on carts.

JR: WHAT IS DANGER TO YOUR CHARACTERS?

MH: Encroaching emotionally is very dangerous to a great many of them. So is direction from the outside, particularly from men. In *War Babies* everything is dangerous. War is always dangerous and a lot of the plays are about war of one kind or another. Engagement of any sort is dangerous. It's easier for all of them to step back instead of engaging.

In *Operators*, the three women are dangerous to each other. The one with her six children and her happy life is very dangerous.

Knowing is dangerous. The exploding of mystery is one of the most dangerous things that can happen. Any myth, mystery or fantasy that we build up is meant both to disguise and shed light on reality. That's common to almost all of the plays.

Someone who deviates from the rules is terribly dangerous, like Jerri in *Operators*. She's really rocking their boat. And, of course, Christmas and Sarah are also in dangerous situations because they're breaking rules and making up new ones too. That's probably *the* most dangerous thing of all, breaking the rules. Not understanding them is dangerous. You've got to try to get ahead of the rules and understand.

JR: POOR PRIM NEVER WILL.

MH: No. Never.

JR: DO YOU THINK SHE'LL SURVIVE?

MH: No. I don't think so. Not a very hopeful character. Not a very hopeful play. I see *Prim and Duck* as a body containing worlds spinning within worlds spinning within worlds. Everything is finally in motion at the end. Some physicists have that theory, don't they? There's no order in the universe, only chaos, and to live in it, we must impose order. I think this is one of my favourite plays, which is why I keep coming back to it.

JR: AND *POPPYCOCK*?

MH: In *Poppycock*, what is dangerous is power. Absolute power. Those men. . . . The final thought of Dora Maar: "He [Picasso] put me in a Paris square and I'm now white from sparrows . . ." says it all: she is totally powerless. Men with that kind of all-encompassing power are incredibly dangerous. That power doesn't recognize love. All three of those women loved their men blindly.

JR: CAN MALE AND FEMALE CHARACTERS PERCEIVE AN EVENT IN THE SAME WAY?

MH: I suppose it's possible, but they don't in my plays. Do the two visions ever come together? No, I don't think so. I'm most interested in the differences. The battle zones. Drama is made for displaying that. We don't see enough of it dramatized from the female point of view.

JR: IS THERE A MAJOR DIFFERENCE IN MALE AND FEMALE POINTS OF VIEW?

MH: In *The Green Line* I've tried to crystallise the male-female points of view. The male thinks with his head: he's the benevolent one, the thinking man, the hero. The female character is almost like a mosquito. I hope that in the course of the play I turn the situation around and show the other sides of each of them. It's a power struggle between the male and the female set within a war zone. And it's a plea to break down the barriers, to try to understand them and then to break them — the green lines of demarcation. It's like the other plays I've written thematically, of course, but I've taken it a whole step further.

I've really talked about war in *The Green Line*, and what it is and how it's reflected in the relationships between the sexes. It's Old World and New World in conflict in that play too: another element that's in all my plays, but drawn into focus in this one. The woman represents the New World and the man represents the Old Ways of thinking.

In one of the first plays I wrote, *Bushed*, I wrote about men. The women have their place in that play; they're in a very female environment, a laundromat, and the men don't have their own place. The men dance around the outside of it and they're adrift. So that in a way set the tone for all of my men. It's there in *Mother Country*: the two men totally adrift in female worlds. They just don't know what to do.

In *War Babies*, Colin goes back to war because he doesn't know what else to do. Or how to fit into the female world. It's very threatening when the female world comes to confront him (with the pregnancy). Most of my men characters are in the same situation in the plays. Although this isn't entirely true in *The Green Line* where it's much more balanced and I'm calling out for a solution: Peace. Understanding.

JR: THERE'S A REAL SENSE OF THE GREEK PLAYS IN YOUR WORK.

MH: Yes. The inevitability, anyways. That brings us back to fate, doesn't it?

JR: AND THE GREEK CHORUS OF WOMEN IN *BUSHED!*

MH: I guess they are a sort of a chorus. Commenting on the men by their movement. In counterpoint.

JR: AND LET'S NOT FORGET "CASSANDRA," THE BABY BORN AT THE END OF *WAR BABIES.* . . .

MH: I couldn't resist. Now, in *The Green Line* the Greek influence is there in spades. I bring the gods on-stage.

JR: DO YOU THINK THE FUTURE HOLDS MORE PRODUCTIONS FOR YOU?

MH: Oh, theatre is always changing. These plays might get done. But I've stopped pushing. One of the reasons for that is that my plays cry out for good productions and very good actors. I could get them done by companies with no money and no time to rehearse and inexperienced actors . . . but there's really nothing to be gained by that.

The early plays, like *Bushed*, can survive that, but the later ones, like *War Babies*, couldn't.

JR: AND THE SPINNING. THERE IS A LARGE AMOUNT OF CIRCLE IMAGERY IN YOUR PLAYS.

MH: Yes. A lot of circling. That's supposed to be a women's thing, isn't it — this cyclical business. . . .

9. Playwright Mary Walsh

Steve Payne

Born in St. John's, Newfoundland in 1952, Mary Walsh has worked in live theatre, radio and television and is a founding member of the comic acting ensemble, CODCO. She has written, directed, produced and acted in such pieces as *Cod on a Stick*, *High Steel* (1985) and *Booze, Drugs and the Urge to Kill* (1988) and *Hockey Wives* (1988).

Danielle: *Brenda, there is an assortment of stains right down the front of your dress.*

Brenda: *Is there? Oh well, if I get lost in the woods I can always suck my dress.*

Hockey Wives

Mary Walsh Interview

by Judith Rudakoff

JR: DO YOU THINK YOU'RE OLDER AND WISER THESE DAYS, OR YOUNGER AND CRAZIER?

MW: I don't know. A little bit wiser maybe, but that could just be because I've hit that smug time when you're in your thirties.

You know, I always used to think that my life was "coming up," later on. And that theatre was just something I'd do until I got to my life. And then it struck me — *this is my life*. And then I realized that as writing *is* my life, I'd like to be able to manage it a little better!

I'd like to be more methodical and work at my writing every day. I will go through the most awful machinations to avoid writing: I will build tall buildings, scrub floors — all to avoid writing. I'd like to be able to sit down and work without having to have someone breathing over my shoulder, desperately waiting for the next page.

But then, on the other hand, I also think maybe if I achieved that state, the necessary edge might be gone. Because there is a process that goes on the whole time I'm putting off writing: the ideas are whirling around in my head. When I get to the typewriter, it all comes pouring out because of the "avoiding" time.

JR: SO IT ALL COOKS LIKE A STEW IN THE UNCONSCIOUS WHILE YOU'RE OFF BUILDING THE WORLD TRADE CENTRE.

MW: I always admire people like Anthony Burgess who can write a thousand words a day, three hundred and sixty-five days a year. Wow.

JR: IS THERE A GREAT DIFFERENCE BETWEEN WRITING SHORT PIECES AND FULL-LENGTH PLAYS?

MW: Oh boy . . . *yes*. But even in writing short pieces, I'll be the last one to get the work done.

JR: WHAT ARE YOUR WEAKEST AND STRONGEST SKILLS AS A PLAYWRIGHT?

MW: My greatest strength is dialogue and my greatest weakness is, I think, structure. The parts of *Hockey Wives* that I'm least happy with are the parts where I've imposed a structure on the material; I've forced it.

Maybe I should have let the material remain more unstructured, but *Hockey Wives* was one of the first full-length plays I'd written and experience is what brings the strength you need to say "No!" to other people involved. And there were a lot of people involved. . . .

JR: THERE CERTAINLY WERE: FROM THE INITIAL COLLECTIVE TO THE WORKSHOPS TO THE PRODUCTION.

MW: I started fresh, you know. The original playwright on the project had a very poetic voice, which we all know is different from my own! I'm much more prosaic. (The only poetic prose I've ever actually liked is Elizabeth Smart's work, *By Grand Central Station I Sat Down and Wept*.) So I began all over again.

At some point it's important to discover your own style. So next time maybe I'll be strong and say "NO!" when I have to. And maybe discover that I don't have a style, or that I'm wrong or that I'm no good at writing plays. But something. It's important to discover that "something" through making your own choices.

Sometimes, finding your *own* voice and style gets lost amidst the dramaturges and the directors and the actors and the workshops.

Our director at the CBC for our CODCO series has helped us a lot, in terms of editing the material and even as a dramaturge, so I'm not being arrogant to the point of suggesting that workshops are *never* useful. But I think that I was too new to the writing to take the best advantage of the workshop situation on *Hockey Wives*.

JR: I ALSO GOT THE IMPRESSION THAT IT MIGHT HAVE BEEN DIFFICULT FOR THE PEOPLE WHO HAD BEEN INVOLVED IN THE PIECE FROM THE BEGINNING AND HAD SEEN IT GO THROUGH SO MANY INCARNATIONS TO COME TO YET ANOTHER VERSION IN YET ANOTHER WORKSHOP.

MW: Yes. And of course, when you're doing something for the first time and you're in that situation, it's hard to demand respect, let alone feel comfortable.

JR: BUT SINCE YOU'D DONE SO MUCH WORK IN THE THEATRE BEFORE *HOCKEY WIVES*, IT'S SURPRISING TO ME THAT YOU'D FEEL INSECURE IN ANY WAY. WHY DID YOU DECIDE TO WORK ON *HOCKEY WIVES* IN THE FIRST PLACE?

MW: Because they asked me! You know how it is when you're a free lance in the theatre — though I think that now I'm beyond that stage — you accept *every* offer because you're worried that if you refuse you may never get another offer.

My whole life has been spent freelancing and you just get into a pattern: "Yes, I'll do that. Four things on Saturday. Yeah, I'll get those done."

So that was the initial reason for accepting the job. Then I met the women involved and I liked them all so much that I enjoyed the work in spite of myself.

JR: AND NOW YOU'RE THINKING OF RE-WRITING FOR THE 1990 ST. JOHN'S PRODUCTION?

MW: Yes. And I sometimes wonder about that. You talk to people who have re-written scripts and then were disappointed. They say, "Oh, it's lost what it had in the beginning. It's so worked over."

JR: WHAT DO YOU FEEL NEEDS RE-WRITING?

MW: There are some parts that are just too obvious: character traits that I emphasized because people simply didn't seem to know who the characters were. I knew who they were. In rehearsal, actors would have found them. But in the writing stage, after being questioned a number of times by people involved, I began to feel there was a need for clarification. I felt I had to "show" parts of the characters and went overboard.

You know, I often wonder if in the rush to impose that structure, and make characters clearer I didn't lose the spontaneity of the piece, that part that makes the humour funny. . . .

JR: I SUPPOSE IT WORKS BEST WHEN IT PLAYS LIKE A HOCKEY GAME: FAST, FURIOUS AND YOU DON'T KNOW WHERE THE NEXT SHOT IS COMING FROM.

MW: Yeah. That would've been the key. I'm afraid I didn't feel particularly in control and didn't think that way.

JR: DO YOU THINK ST. JOHN'S AUDIENCES WILL REACT DIFF-ERENTLY TO THE PLAY?

MW: I don't know. It's really frightening. Part of me doesn't want to do it.

JR: WHY?

MW: I was such a solid part of the St. John's theatre scene for so long, and then when CODCO reformed in 1986 and I left the LSPU Hall as Dramaturge, I wasn't around much. I was also more than a bit disillusioned with theatre in Newfoundland and didn't do much live theatre. So now, three years later, I'm a little afraid to come back to the audiences. It's somehow different and less threatening when some of those people are at home, watching me on television, but the thought of having them sitting in the theatre, watching me live really scares me.

JR: ANY OTHER CURRENT PROJECTS?

MW: Yes. I'm doing a half hour piece for CBC Radio. I can't for the life of me remember the name of it. I always fall almost immedi-ately into a deep sleep whenever it comes on. Very dry. Very . . . I don't know: slow, flat, wide — prairie-like. The general theme of the series is "a journey taken" and seeing as I've been flat on my back for five months this year, that seemed the logical place to start.

And here's another terrible writing habit: during the last two months when I was on my back, I'd come up with all these seemingly terrific ideas and I'd write them down. Then I'd start to go with an idea and suddenly I'd stop and put it down. It's like a fear I have that if the idea is good and I'm running with it, it'll go bad if I keep going. Five good lines. Then I'll hit something that I'm not happy with and I'll put it down and leave it. Fear of the sixth line; so I'll have only half-page jottings till an outside force makes me pick the idea up again.

I read somewhere that the only difference between writers and other people is that writers write things down.

JR: DO YOU ACTUALLY SIT DOWN AND PUT PEN TO PAPER OR HANDS TO TYPEWRITER? OR DO YOU IMPROVISE OR ACT OUT THE WORK?

MW: When I'm writing I'm always "doing" the characters. I did that with all the hockey wives: I can't write them without acting them out. When I write without doing that and then read it back — it's never right. I have to get into character to write and also improvise to a certain degree, but I do it at the typewriter, not on my feet.

JR: DO YOU EVER MODEL A CHARACTER SO CLOSELY ON SOMEONE OR AN INCIDENT THAT THEY RECOGNIZE THEMSELVES AND GET ANGRY (OR FLATTERED)?

MW: The other full-length play that I wrote, *High Steel*, was a musical I wrote with Ron Hines, based on my mother's family and my brothers. They all worked on the building of the World Trade Centre in NYC and my grandfather helped put up the Empire State Building. All the men in the family had always done that kind of work and down in the States, they're called "the Fish." About half of the NYC union of the Steel Workers are ex-Newfoundlanders.

I wrote this saga about my mother's family, the Daltons. I called them the Costellos, not fooling *anyone* for a moment, of course. My mother came to the show and claimed that she was going to sue me because I stole all her best lines.

We performed it in St. John's for a month and it was a great success. The New York Local of the Ironworkers Union gave us a ten-thousand-dollar grant to produce it. We did have plans to tour, but it never happened. You know one of the great things about St. John's is that you can do everything: write, act, direct, produce. But that's also a drawback because you burn out so quickly. And if you've written a show, directed it, produced it and acted in it, sometimes you just don't have the energy left to work on getting a national tour going.

So that was the first full-length play that I wrote. I did the book and Ron did the libretto and music.

JR: WHAT WAS THE MOST TOUCHING MOMENT? THE FUNNIEST?

MW: The funniest moment was, of course, the wake at the end, where the husband, Mike (who isn't an iron-worker but has all these sons who are — like my father) is dead. It was based on my father's wake and I did get into a bit of trouble over that one! Tears, fights, screaming. . . . On stage it was hysterically funny.

My Aunt May, who brought me up and would be more lace-curtain Irish than shanty, was just horrified. It really was awful, but on stage . . . well, people just ate it up.

The character I modelled on my grandmother was quite touching.

A lot of the men would go to the States to work and the women would stay and raise the kids, keep the gardens and the hay fields and the cows and the "whatever else they were lucky enough to have" going. Now some men went and didn't come back and didn't send home any money. My Grandfather — who was purportedly a Tartar anyway — did just that: up and left Grandmom and the six kids for over ten years. Never sent home a cent and he was making seventeen dollars a day, working iron in New York (which at the time was a small fortune). My mother and her sisters went into service for room and board and *no* dollars a month because their mother couldn't afford to keep feeding them,. And then, almost eleven years after he left, Grandfather shows up and Grandmom says, "There's Rol coming up the gap. I must put the kettle on."

JR: SOUNDS LIKE *TERRAS DE BACALHAU*!

MW: Yes, doesn't it!

JR: DOES FAMILY FEED INTO WHAT YOU WRITE?

MW: Yes. Always. Partly because I didn't really have a family. My aunt brought me up. My father's two sisters and his brother, all unmarried and living in the same house, raised me. So I always felt like I wasn't part of my real family, who lived next door. When I was about eighteen months old, Mom and Dad had a very bad place to live: dark, dingy, and damp. And Mom had a bad back, as we all do, and she was pregnant with Greg. Then I got pneumonia and went into the hospital. When I got better and came home, it was so damp that Aunt May and Aunt Phine and Uncle Jack took me for a while and then they just kept me!

A few years later, Mom and Dad and the family moved back into the country, to Conception Harbour, and I would visit them for a week or two in the summers.

Now my aunts and my uncle were wonderful to me, but I still had that feeling of not completely belonging somewhere. I felt half-way between the two families. I guess that's why I've been consistently fascinated with families.

JR: IS NEWFOUNDLAND OR TORONTO HOME?

MW: Oh, definitely Newfoundland. I like Toronto, it's a nice cousinly kind of place, but it's not home.

JR: DO YOU THINK YOUR WORK IS UNIVERSALLY SUCCESSFUL BECAUSE IT'S SO SPECIFICALLY NEWFOUNDLAND-BASED?

MW: Absolutely. That's what I've always believed. "Parochial," "regional," "provincial": bullshit!

Why would you want to read anything that stoops to the lowest common denominator to make itself understood?

Look at Joyce's *Ulysses* — it changed the face of modern literature and it was about one day in the life of one man in Dublin, Ireland!

JR: TELL ME ABOUT PLAYING MOLLY BLOOM.

MW: Oh, I loved doing that. It introduced me to James Joyce's work. I went to theatre school, not university, so no one forced me to read Joyce. I'd picked up *Finnegan's Wake* in Grade Ten and put it right down! Getting to know Joyce's work was extraordinary. And Richard Ellmann's biography was such a way in.

I'm a very nervous performer — sometimes it actually *stops* me. I started the show with the "hell-fire and brimstone" speech from *Portrait of the Artist as a Young Man,* and once I got through that I was okay. Andy Jones directed me and Father Dinn (his character) kept getting in! But once I got into the two washerwomen from *Finnegan's Wake* I started to feel comfortable.

And then when I crawled into bed with Molly Bloom — or *as* Molly — I was away. It was my favourite part. Forty-five minutes, lying in bed, talking: what could be better?

JR: YOU'RE A CANADIAN WRITER BASED IN NEWFOUNDLAND IN A NORTH AMERICAN MARKET. YOU'RE A WOMAN WRITER/DIRECTOR/ PRODUCER/EDITOR IN A FIELD THAT'S STILL LARGELY DOMINATED BY MEN. YOU'RE A THEATRE WRITER IN A CREATIVE WRITING FIELD WHERE THEATRE IS A MINORITY PLAYER. DO YOU EVER FEEL MAR- GINALIZED? ISOLATED? OR DOES IT ALL ADD UP TO AN ADVANTAGE?

MW: Male-dominated?! In television that's how the world is run! Now we do demand a degree of respect as performers, but the male hierarchical structure is so apparent in the pecking order, even on our show.

It's all so shocking to me. Theatre in St. John's originally came about so organically, so naturally. Women were at the helm: me, Rhonda Payne, Donna Butt, Janis Spence, Marsha Woodford, Boo Noseworthy, Marlene Rice, Ann Anderson, Cathy Jones. We were writing the work, producing the work, administering and running the Hall.

JR: DO YOU FEEL THAT ST. JOHN'S IS A VACUUM?

MW: I've spent so little time in St. John's in the last three years, though I always feel like I'm there anyway. I don't feel as if I'm in a vacuum, no. At one point, when I was the programme *animateur* at the Hall, I did feel like I was on a treadmill. We'd produce one play, run it for three weeks and then we'd have to write another one. A play had a shelf life of three weeks, maximum, and then it was on to the next one. And you just couldn't keep that up. For the amount of work, the eighteen hour days that went into a collective, you wanted to see something come back. Two or three weeks wasn't gratifying enough to fuel the next collective. We needed time to play it, to have it seen. I began to feel like I was running very fast and going nowhere. But never a vacuum.

JR: YOU'VE WRITTEN OTHER FULL-LENGTH PIECES WITH MUSIC, HAVEN'T YOU?

MW: Yes. There was *Booze, Drugs and the Urge to Kill.* It was a late night cabaret piece that started from a country-and-western song I wrote with Ron Hines. I was in it too. It played for a week. I end up killing the guy I'm in love with at the end, by mistake, and go back on the booze.

JR: HOW DO YOU FEEL ABOUT OTHER PEOPLE DIRECTING YOUR WORK?

MW: Well, I've worked with Andy Jones and, of course, I trust him completely. And with CODCO, we all direct each other and that's perfect.

JR: YOU TOURED NEWFOUNDLAND WHEN YOU WERE EIGHTEEN IN *THE WIZARD OF OZ* FOR THIRTY DOLLARS A WEEK. HOW ON EARTH DID THIS MAKE YOU DECIDE TO MAKE THEATRE YOUR CAREER?

MW: What a nightmare! Touring Newfoundland wasn't a nightmare, and neither was the evening show, but in the afternoon I was playing the Wicked Witch of the West, and I just didn't want to be the bad person in the play! So here we were in Lamaline where kids were fainting with fear when *Toto* would come on. And these same terrified children, when I would enter as the witch, would hit me and stomp on my costume and threaten to beat the bearings out of me! Awful.

JR: AND THIS MADE YOU GO INTO THEATRE PROFESSIONALLY?

MW: Well, then at night, I'd perform in another play that was much more fun. And then the Good Witch got sick, so I got to play both witches, the good and the bad. I was great as the Good Witch. Why? Well, it was Andy, Dyan Olsen, Tommy Sexton, Bob Joy, Jane Dingle and others and we were travelling around, sleeping on gym floors having *just the best time*!

I think that a lot of Newfoundlanders are funny in a cynical, ironic way. My family was very much like that and so am I. Andy had another type of humour and I'd never met anyone who could do routines. He'd take off on a riff and I loved it. I wanted to be around that.

JR: AND IT WAS FAMILY. WHAT ABOUT THE SEED GRANT FROM PAUL THOMPSON AND THEATRE PASSE MURAILLE? HOW DID THAT HELP?

MW: Three hundred dollars. We used it to do *Cod on a Stick* which we wrote when I was at Ryerson Polytechnical Institute, in Theatre School. I was so terrified of performing back then (and I was worried that the show might not be good enough or funny enough) that I would actually act with my back to the audience, facing upstage! This was our own original work and I needed the confidence to realize it was working.

We got the money, I think, because Tommy Sexton and Dyan Olsen had gone down to audition for Thompson for *Under the Greywacke*, and he said he didn't have a part for them, but he'd give them a three-hundred-dollar seed grant to write something about Newfoundland!

JR: PASSE MURAILLE BECAME "CODCO WEST."

MW: Well, yeah. And, this is so odd, we started CODCO in Toronto, so we always came back with every show.

JR: WHAT FEEDS YOUR CREATIVITY?

MW: I read all the time. And my family. I don't go to the theatre much — when it's deadly I don't want to be there and when it's wonderful, it's so heart-wrenching that I'm not doing it. It's a no-win situation, isn't it? At home, anyway.

With *Hockey Wives*, I'd feed off a conversation I'd overheard, or a sentence. But then I went to Banff, and suddenly: nothing! I'm out there with the elks and there's nothing to feed off. So I'm going through old newspapers and reading about Hiking for Jesus and stuff and trying to figure out how I can make it work. For me it's better to be around people.

I lived up in Labrador for a time and wrote a play with the Innu, the Neskapi-Montagnais Indians and I came to Toronto right afterwards. And it was so clear. Of course you can't keep in touch in Toronto: because you can turn the lights on and off and the heat up and down you think that you've got control of your life. It's simple in Labrador to realize that you're a tiny speck in the wind and the rain and the snow. In Toronto, you're surrounded by the hand of man, the buildings and the man-made streets and you can begin to think that you are somehow other than what you truly are. It would be really easy to lose touch.

The Innu worshipped the Caribou at one time and still consider it important. They have a ritual they perform called the Mokoshon which is a feast surrounding the taking of caribou. When you kill a caribou you aren't supposed to take another until the hides are stretched and prepared and the bones must be put back into the river. They treat the animal with a great deal of respect even after death.

And then I went to a Catholic mass in Sheshatshit and it was only then that I had an understanding of what we, the Catholics, were up to with the bread and the wine. It was the same ceremony, except that we had more money and we were a few steps further removed from the ritual. That seemingly empty ritual had come out of a need to celebrate what we felt was giving us life, thousands of years ago. It certainly never felt like that to me as I was growing up. That same simple human need was there and I'd never seen it as starkly as I did up in Labrador.

JR: THERE'S A GREAT DEAL OF PAIN AND MISERY IN A LOT OF THE STORIES YOU TELL. IS THAT WHERE THE HUMOUR COMES FROM: THE MISERY?

MW: Pure misery? Oh yeah. Definitely. That's why people from Ontario often have such a tough time with humour! Because they're in the Land 'o Plenty. You know? They threw a seed in the ground and corn grew up. Now this is going to sound xenophobic, but people from Newfoundland, well, they put a spin on everything they say so that it's funny. And it seems to me to come from having to deal with some harsher realities: you've got to do *something* to make them more palatable. One way of making situations more bearable is through being funny and cynical and ironic.

JR: HAS IT BEEN DIFFICULT FOR YOU TO SLOT INTO THE ROLE SOCIETY IMPOSES ON WOMEN?

MW: Well, we're encouraged to listen to such an extent. And to ignore our instincts. It's a real fight to listen to those instincts and say, "Well, I'll act on my instincts and then take the consequences if I'm wrong." I just have to do what I think is right. If I listen, it always seems to work out.

It is nerve-wracking and you leave yourself out on a limb. But it's worth it. I think.

10. Playwright Carol Bolt

Gail Harvey

Carol Bolt was born in Winnipeg in 1941. She is currently an active member of Norman Jewison's Centre for Advanced Film Study. She is one of Canada's most prolific and award-winning playwrights and in addition to live theatre, has written for radio, television and film. She resides in Toronto with her husband (actor David Bolt) and their son.

And I don't have to beat you, Henry. Because all of us half-breeds, we're hunters. We got special knowledge of the future.

Gabe in *Gabe*

Well, of course, Jory can change the world if she likes, but don't expect anyone to notice.

Aunt Luel in *Shelter*

Selected published plays:

Shelter. Toronto: Playwrights Canada (copyscript), 1975.

Cyclone Jack. In *A Collection of Canadian Plays*, Volume IV, and in paperback with *Billy Bishop and the Red Baron* by Leonard Peterson. All published in Toronto: Simon & Pierre, 1975.

Playwrights in Profile: Carol Bolt. Toronto: Playwrights Canada, 1976. Includes *Buffalo Jump*, *Gabe*, and *Red Emma*.

Maurice. Toronto: Gage Publishing Company, 1977.

One Night Stand. Toronto: Playwrights Canada (copyscript), 1977.

Escape Entertainment. Toronto: Playwrights Canada (copyscript), 1981.

Selected produced plays:

Daganawida. Premiere at Toronto Workshop Productions, 1970.

Next Year Country. Premiere at Globe Theatre, Regina, Saskatchewan, 1971.

Pauline. Premiere at Theatre Passe Muraille, 1973.

Norman Bethune: On Board the S.S. Empress of Asia. Premiere at Muskoka Festival, 1976.

Desperadoes. Premiere at Toronto Free Theatre, 1977.

Star Quality (The "America" Project). Premiere at Actors Theatre, Louisville, Kentucky, 1980.

Love or Money. Premiere at Blyth Festival, 1981.

Ice Time. Commissioned by Theatre on the Move, 1986. Premiered 1988.

The Universe Is a Green Dragon. Premiere at Inner Stage, 1988.

Harvest. Premiere at Caravan Theatre (East), 1989.

Carol Bolt Interview

by Judith Rudakoff

JR: HOW MUCH DID THE COLLECTIVE PROCESS ACTUALLY SHAPE YOUR WORK?

CB: The shows I did at Theatre Passe Muraille were all, in a way, "true" collectives, even though the first one, *Buffalo Jump*, was a play that was already scripted. (It had developed out of a play that I had done before in Saskatchewan, a play that was very close to me: *Next Year Country*.)

When Paul Thompson suggested, "I think we should do this play as a collective," I was a little shocked but (and here's an indication of Paul's charm) I wasn't *horrified* by the idea! I never thought that the suggestion came because he lacked faith in my material, so I agreed, as long as we wouldn't simply use improvisations. I would watch improvs in rehearsal, and then go home and script the play. We would proceed that way.

The whole experience of working at Theatre Passe Muraille as a playwright after that was not as positive, because the writer on a collective doesn't really have that much chance for input unless the material is originally your own. If it's your material coming in to the process, then you have a strong idea of the thrust of the piece, of the metaphor.

I only did *Buffalo Jump* and *Pauline* as collectives at Passe Muraille. I really enjoyed working with those people, but I didn't like the process after *Buffalo Jump*, because there wasn't enough for me, as a writer, to do.

JR: IN THE EARLY STAGES OF YOUR CAREER YOU ALSO WORKED WITH GEORGE LUSCOMBE AT TORONTO WORKSHOP PRODUCTIONS.

CB: Yes. I loved working at TWP: it was really my first experience working in a professional theatre. The experience of working with George was wonderful. Anyone who has worked with him has found him infuriating and maddening and also, a real genius. As well, I got a chance to do an epic play at TWP with one of those huge companies that Luscombe used to have. I think there were thirteen, maybe fifteen people in the company (and only two of them were women!).

A good friend of mine, Diane Grant, was one of the two women, and in those days the women's roles were mostly the type where they would bring drinks to the men on stage, while the men pretended to be Che Guevera.

Now Luscombe really did want to give the women something to do besides come out of cakes, so I wrote a script with Diane in mind in which she got to play both a prostitute and a nun — a double character! And eventually, we actually went through with creating this piece about New France. A doomed play, you might think, but we were all a lot younger then! It got "poetic," which may not have been a good sign, though all the people in the company really loved it. Moments in it did work very well; there would be three or four minutes at a time when you were drawn in to the lives of the characters, their passions. But it didn't ever work as a complete piece. George knew this, even in rehearsal, and he tried to deal with the problems by going home every night and cutting, pasting, re-arranging the script into a different running order. This was before the days of word processors and every day, the first hour of rehearsal was spent pasting up the script in new orders. And it still didn't work!

Through it all, I still felt that I was fortunate to be getting the chance to watch very good actors say my lines.

Dress rehearsal finally came and the play was around three hours long, and even I remember it as pompous and pretentious and dull. . . . And Cedric Smith, a member of the company, came up the aisle in the theatre towards me and said, "Not bad." And I looked at him with the tears running down my face, and I said, "Yes, it was." And then he said, "Didn't you know that already?" I learned, from that experience, that there was a way to tell if a play is going to work or not.

JR: DID EITHER THEATRE PASSE MURAILLE OR TORONTO WORK-SHOP PRODUCTIONS HELP YOU IN ANY PARTICULAR WAY TO UNDER-STAND HOW BEST TO USE THE EPIC STRUCTURE YOU'D BEEN WORKING WITH?

CB: I don't think I learned about structure at Passe Muraille. Structure was the last element in most of the plays during the Paul Thompson years there. What was important then and there was the vitality that came from the immediacy of the experience and the actors' dedication to the process.

I started trying to put plays together with some semblance of order when I started working at Toronto Free Theatre, which I considered my spiritual home in the early days of the theatre. I was still breaking a lot of rules, of course!

Those plays were written for a company too and had a sensibility that everyone involved in the theatre understood. Toronto Free Theatre provided an encouraging atmosphere that any playwright would gladly die for.

JR: A LOT OF THE CHARACTERS IN YOUR PLAYS ARE ROOTED IN FACT, WHICH YOU USE AS A SPRINGBOARD FOR THE DRAMA.

CB: All the early plays were rooted in history. That was partly a political decision. At Passe Muraille and at Toronto Free, we felt it was important to create myth for our country. We were used to seeing stories of American and British culture; stories about their histories that were satisfying dramatically. We knew about their heroes, but seemed to think that our own, Louis Riel, for example, were dull. Obviously, he wasn't: he was a complete madman, but in those days, we hadn't discovered that yet, let alone get past the pre-conceived notions about Gabriel Dumont or the On to Ottawa trekkers or whom-ever else I was putting in plays in those days.

JR: WHAT MADE YOU DECIDE TO SWITCH TO DRAMATIZING IMAGI-NARY CHARACTERS?

CB: Well, eventually, after a number of those history plays (and there were many I wrote for young audiences, too, about people like Tom Longboat in *Cyclone Jack*) I said, "Well, this is a bit cowardly. I'm putting another person's story on stage." I'd concluded that audi-ences were more likely to be interested automatically because they're hearing about a "famous" person. Like Emma Goldman: people revere her, she's changed people's lives.

But I decided that if I really wanted to write, then I'd have to put something of myself in the plays, really take a risk. I thought that would be a real challenge: to see what happens when you write about yourself.

JR: AND THAT LED YOU TO *SHELTER*?

CB: Yes. Five Prairie women involved in an insane wedding shower for a woman who really doesn't want to get married and ends up trying to commit suicide in an armoire, while another woman is running for Parliament in her recently deceased husband's riding.

A lot of my family is in that play. The relationship between the women is based in part on my relationship with my cousin Linda. We were a year and a half apart in age and we had a rivalry growing up. And my relationship with my mother-in-law too. And sorting out how women relate to each other. I also wanted to look at how women's identity was being associated with and depended upon their association with men. Ten or twelve years ago, when I wrote the play, most Parliamentarian women were daughters or widows or in some way related to male Parliamentarians — Eva Peron Syndrome.

JR: THERE'S CERTAINLY ONE EXAMPLE OF HOW LIFE HAS CHANGED FOR WOMEN, ISN'T IT? HOW OUR MORALITY HAS, FOR VARIOUS REASONS, BEEN CHALLENGED AND WE'VE BEEN FORCED TO RE-EXAMINE A LOT OF GIVENS OVER THE PAST TEN OR TWELVE YEARS. HOW DO YOU THINK THAT MIGHT EFFECT A PLAY LIKE *ONE NIGHT STAND*?

CB: *One Night Stand* was, in the beginning, a technical exercise in structure. I'm an admirer of the thriller form and I wondered if I could write one. So I sat down with a pencil and paper and asked myself what would be a good thriller and technically interesting. At that time, *Sleuth* was popular. It was a two-hander with two men, so I first considered two women, then a man and a woman. Arbitrarily I chose the latter and thought that I'd try making it a love story in some strange way. Now in *Sleuth*, the two people dress up as other characters, so I couldn't do that, but I decided to have a corpse! And we'd put this character's name in the programme and the audience would think that she'd be showing up eventually and it would keep them hooked! Sharon to the rescue!

As a young person, I'd done a production of Arthur Kopit's *Oh Dad, Poor Dad, Mamma's Hangin' in the Closet and I'm Feeling So Sad* and I always loved the moment when the corpse fell out of the closet. So I decided to find an equivalent: the hide-a-bed sofa! And how did she get there . . . ? The writing of *One Night Stand* was in one way the result of trying to work out how the body got into the hide-a-bed sofa.

In the meantime, while I was pondering those elements, the book *Looking for Mr. Goodbar* by Judith Rossner was released. By that time, I'd decided that my play was about a pick-up in a bar, and here was this wonderful title: it just sings, and the book appeared to be about the same thing as my play. . . . But it wasn't. For me, *Looking for Mr. Goodbar* has always been a book about punishing a woman for her morality, for picking up a guy. I decided I wanted to write about an ordinary girl behaving in a normal way. Normal in a pre-AIDS society, anyway. Today, when casual sex is so dangerous, someone producing the piece might evaluate that and inject the concern into the text. I'd certainly make sure that Daisy and Rafe were shown to be practising Safe Sex. But the play is really about loneliness rather than morality.

It was fun to write and it changed my life. It was successful in a very commercial way.

JR: YOU WERE A MARKET RESEARCHER ONCE. HAS THAT HAD ANY EFFECT ON YOUR PERCEPTIONS?

CB: I did the statistical research for Dominion Bureau of Statistics census to make money to go to Europe. I lived in Vancouver then, the early sixties, and there were very few options for a university graduate with a Liberal Arts degree except, maybe, something called "junior executive."

In London I tried to get work and the DBS credit helped! I got a job at London School of Economics, as supervisor for a group coding responses to this rather posh study called the Robbins Report which surveyed every single undergraduate in England in 1958. Ten-page questionnaires full of questions like, "How much money do you make today?" and, "What is the meaning of existence?"!

I always found the range of response interesting.

JR: DO YOU THINK THAT MALE AND FEMALE ROLES HAVE CHANGED SIGNIFICANTLY SINCE YOU STARTED WRITING?

CB: Yes, I do. I remember, early on, Martin Kinch telling me that I wrote "like a man." He meant that as a compliment, and I took it as such at the time!

Last year, I wrote a play about Justine Blainey, the little girl who wanted to play MTHL hockey and went to the Supreme Court of Canada to win the chance. I don't think that could have happened twelve years ago. Nor would the average young girl have been that aware of her rights then. It's exciting to watch little girls in the audience at that play: their eyes are shining so brightly and they're straining to get closer to the action!

JR: HAS THERE BEEN MUCH CROSS-OVER BETWEEN YOUR WRITING CAREER AND THE ACTING CAREER OF YOUR HUSBAND, DAVID BOLT?

CB: Not really. We've been married for twenty years now and he's only done two of my plays: he played Most in *Red Emma* and Humph in the Bethune play I did in Gravenhurst. I wrote a play for him, but it hasn't been produced. It's called *Survival* and it came out of the experience of doing *One Night Stand*. It's about what happens when you change from the young idealist to the "old" idealist. The problem is that you think you want to change the world, and then you find that the world will pay you eight thousand dollars a year to leave it alone!

JR: HAVE THERE BEEN ANY PLAYWRIGHTS WHO HAVE INSPIRED YOU?

CB: George Walker. We started writing plays at around the same time and David was involved in George's plays as an actor, so I watched his work develop. He really is "inspiring" because he's been able to pursue his individual vision and make people understand it.

JR: YOU WRITE FOR ALL OF THE VARIOUS ENTERTAINMENT MEDIA. DO YOU FIND THAT AUDIENCES DIFFER IN ANY WAY?

CB: Yes, they are different. I've had a lot of valuable experiences with radio audiences, and they are extraordinary in that they get totally, totally involved: you really have to work to listen to a radio play. I can't usually do it! There always seem to be interruptions. That doesn't seem to happen with television. Maybe you have to make more of an effort to sit down and actually watch television.

But radio audiences are so much a part of the event. Every time one of my radio plays is broadcast, people stop me on the street, I get fan mail. And these are letters that actually talk about the plays, they are reactive. Radio audiences seem to feel more involved.

JR: IN VARIOUS INTERVIEWS YOU'VE SAID THAT YOU WRITE ABOUT ADVENTURERS, AND SEEKERS AND IDEALISTS. WHAT ARE THEY ON A QUEST FOR?

CB: Adventure!

JR: REAL OR IDEAL?

CB: Probably ideal. The people I'm interested in writing about, with the significant exception of those in *One Night Stand*, want to change the world. I'm really interested in the psychology of that attitude.

I wish that it were possible to change the world, but what I see when I look at the characters, Emma Goldman, for example, is not a "Hardy Boy" kind of character who can isolate what's wrong and then fix it. I see a complex woman who goes beyond what is reasonable in her quest. All my seekers have a flaw, like Bethune's egotism or Emma's romanticism.

JR: WHAT ABOUT GABE?

CB: Well, the way I characterized him is different than he really was.

I had originally written a "straight" play about Gabriel Dumont, an epic drama with a cast of about fifteen. TFT were interested in producing the play, but they only had a cast of five in their resident company: Chapelle Jaffe, Peter Jobin, Sol Rubinek, Brenda Donahue and Don McQuarrie.

My play originally had no women in it, but this was, I thought, an ideal group of actors to work with. So I told Toronto Free that I'd think it over.

I sat down that weekend and the metaphor that immediately occurred to me was that people in a modern story would re-play the old story. There would be scenes in the past to distinguish the stories. We originally conceived of these dream sequences being done with puppets.

The re-writing was quite fast and it became a totally different play. The five young people at the gas station who play out the story were completely new: Gabe and Henry Jackson and Louis and two women, a waitress and a sometime hooker. They were all Métis and knew the myth of Batoche and how the battle had been fought and almost won. They were all very romantic and visionary. Every one of those characters is so much in love with everyone else. . . .

So we went into rehearsal, and over the rehearsal period (longer than today's normal rehearsal period, thanks to those now defunct Local Initiatives Project Grants) of about four weeks we used big puppets that Miro Kinch designed. They were wonderful and we used them right into previews. Unfortunately, when you stood behind them to operate them, the audience couldn't hear any of the lines! By opening night, the puppets had become a lobby display.

In a way, the character of Louis Riel was based on my father. When my mother saw the play, she recognized that and was enchanted. I was quite happy with *Gabe* too. It's the only play of mine that ever got totally positive reviews, but even so, it isn't done a lot. Its language is beautiful, but very profane and harsh. Maybe that's why.

JR: WHAT IS MORE IMPORTANT TO YOUR CHARACTERS, TRUTH OR IDEALS?

CB: Ideals. Maybe this is the market researcher in me talking, but "what is truth?" If you ask someone a question and it's of any import, then probably you'll get a whole range of opinion in the answer.

Now I'm not espousing a "liberal" viewpoint here: I think there is right and wrong. I hate it when people say, "Oh, well, he's just doing his thing . . . " or whatever. It's the individual's responsibility to decide which is which.

Even if you consider history — I've done a lot of historical research for my plays — you'll find that the same event is described in as many different ways as you have sources. If you get to the primary sources, you'll likely find that there's a whole other story *there*, which becomes *your* story.

JR: WOULD YOU CALL YOURSELF MORAL, IMMORAL OR AMORAL?

CB: Moral.

JR: AND YOUR PLAYS?

CB: Amoral. I hope.

JR: IS DISENCHANTMENT INEVITABLE ONCE SHELTER IS DESTROYED?

CB: No. I think enchantment is always possible even if shelter has been destroyed. People whose value system is destroyed by externals are missing the whole point of existence. History proves that that's true: people go through horrible situations and finally become better people, stronger. Though obviously one would never choose to go through something atrocious like the Holocaust, the stories of growth and heroism come out of events like that. Living in "Scarberia" with a swimming pool doesn't make you a better person.

JR: SO WHEN YOUR CHARACTERS MATURE AND GO INTO THE WORLD WHERE THEY ARE FORCED TO DEAL WITH REALITY, DO YOU THINK THEY FACE REALITY AND STRENGTHEN THEIR IDEALS IN ORDER TO SURVIVE?

CB: I don't think any of them ever do face reality. They always say, "Well, I see that the cloak makers are on strike, that the Regina riot happened, that the pick-up is a murderer. . . ." They always create a fantasy where their counterpart can be redeemed. Because they're romantics.

JR: HOW VITAL IS THE ROMANCE TO SURVIVAL?

CB: Very. For me.

JR: HOW DOES ALL THIS FIGURE IN *ESCAPE ENTERTAINMENT*?

CB: It's about romantics. It was inspired by my experiences with Toronto criticism, specifically with Gina Mallet, the *Toronto Star* theatre critic at the time. My knowledge of her was minute and I certainly didn't research her, but what I saw was a person who had come to Toronto from New York. What I made my character feel was that she was a big town person in a small town place. And that seemed to me to be an interesting starting point for a character. I felt great sympathy for the character. I started playing around with what might happen to that character if she reviewed not theatre, but movies. I thought that the Canadian film industry at that time was pretending to be big time while it was still very small town.

The reaction was, I think, totally uncalled for! I don't mind people saying that they think my plays are bad, but this one ranks with *Winter Offensive* as one of the plays that has gotten the worst reviews in the history of Canadian theatre!

Tim Bond directed it and he remarked to me after I'd seen Gina Mallet's review, "Well, you didn't think she would like it, did you?"

JR: WOULD YOU DO IT AGAIN, GIVEN THE WISDOM OF HIND-SIGHT?

CB: Yes. At the time, it was quite devastating. But I'm glad I did it. I saw it last year in Vancouver and it got a totally different response. The problems in the script were addressed but people liked it! It was a normal theatre event rather than some kind of cleansing of everybody's soul.

JR: WHAT ABOUT *DESPERADOS* AND THE CRITICAL RESPONSE TO IT?

CB: I don't think it's a good play. It came out of writing *One Night Stand*. Some people's reaction to that play seemed to be that I had given up a career where I had been writing "wonderful" plays (of course, no one had ever told me that they were wonderful before *One Night Stand*) to do this commercial shit. That was frustrating, so I wrote a play about just that kind of rejection. It was also about money and how money corrupts.

I remember one man (who is probably a really nice man) yelled "Boo!" at the end of the play. It was quite shocking. *Desperados* is a raw, angry play and I don't think it's of any real value. There are dramaturges, however, who really admire the text and I remember people in rehearsal telling me, "This is the best thing you've ever written." Good actors, good director, and the script was "relatively there." At that time I just couldn't get past rage at how society was set up to make the audience understand why they should be there watching people do horrible things to each other.

And the Toronto theatre scene at that time, the early eighties, was changing. We'd been writing plays for seven or eight years at that point. There were new playwrights, and audiences were building. And not only did they want to see what they'd come to expect: they wanted something new and challenging as well. For me, as a writer, what I wanted to tell them just then was not precisely what they wanted to hear. Which was fine. . . .

As it happened, I got the chance to work a lot in film and television over the next many years. And I got to remove myself from the spotlight. After *One Night Stand* I got quite a bit of recognition. Now writers are usually really shy and I for one wasn't comfortable with walking down the street and people knowing who I was. At least, not to that extreme degree. I found I wanted to get away from that lack of anonymity, away from people forming opinions of me that had nothing to do with me and were only based on what they'd read about me in newspapers. I found that really disturbing. I was glad to be able to back off.

There were people who were overly concerned with why I'd even written *One Night Stand*. It didn't concern me at all: very simply, I wrote it because I love thrillers.

And I also want to be known as the writer who wrote *Escape Entertainment*.

JR: WHAT'S MORE IMPORTANT TO YOU: TO TEACH OR TO ENTERTAIN?

CB: To entertain.

JR: IF I WERE GOING TO NAME THE QUALITIES THAT EPITOMIZE THE CANADIAN HERO, I THINK I'D SAY UNSHAKEABLE IDEALS AND STAMINA. HOW WOULD YOU DEFINE THE CANADIAN HERO?

CB: I think Canadians are very good at being heroes. Terry Fox, Ken Taylor. Now they're heroes in a way that's not the same as those we're used to seeing in American or British movies. The search for the Canadian Hero (in film more so than in theatre) is one that has been fraught with difficulties: in English Canada the stories have been real downers. It's traditional that the English Canadian Hero looks for Truth and Beauty and doesn't find it.

JR: OR DIES. OR GETS MURDERED.

CB: I don't think that's as true in French Canada. Nor is it the same in terms of Canadian plays written over the last few years. The search to define or find Canadian Heroes seems more subtle. There aren't any big, heroic dramas where everything works out and there's a happy ending. But you don't get that vision in any really modern literature any more.

JR: DO YOU PREFER WRITING FOR FILM OR THEATRE?

CB: It depends on what I want to accomplish. In film, there's a problem for the writer in terms of artistic control. I think if you want the kind of control or input you get in theatre when you're writing for film, then you have to be prepared to take on other, additional responsibilities. You have to direct or produce.

In general, the film process is that the writer produces something called "The Script." ("Blueprint" is the polite term for it.) The director and producer will then feel very comfortable with changing the script and shaping it into a piece that expresses their vision of what should be said. Unless you have a really honest and creative collaboration on the go, you, as a writer for film, place yourself in a lot of jeopardy.

Film writing is certainly exciting because it's dangerous and because the rewards, financial and also in terms of impact, are great. And, perhaps, more immediate than in theatre.

In theatre, the audience is there, but it's smaller and more specialized. You've reached, in a way, the converted. I'm a political writer and I want to change people's minds about issues. In film, the audience may not know your work or the themes that concern you. They haven't gone to your plays for the past decade, so you have to convince them anew each time.

If you want a pure experience, for a writer, theatre is much purer. I'd hate to have to choose one or the other, film or theatre. Or radio. Or television. All very different. I'd hate to give up any of them, because they all give me something.

JR: YOU'VE WRITTEN A GREAT DEAL OF THEATRE FOR YOUNG AUDIENCES TOO.

CB: Yes. I don't know why that is. I began working at Young People's Theatre years and years ago with Susan Rubes and the collaborations were extremely happy and productive. I did some really good shows with Tim Bond, Jane Vezey, Paul Vigna. I always wanted that to continue. That audience was so important in a real way.

JR: WHAT INTERESTS YOU MORE, PROBABILITY OR POSSIBILITY?

CB: Possibility. George Walker comes to mind immediately when I think of probability. His vision of the future is so totally black. I prefer to think idealistically, that the world might get better, even if that defies logic.

JR: WHAT REPRESENTS POWER TO YOUR CHARACTERS?

CB: For Emma Goldman, power is not something that consciously concerns her. She is powerful. She's charismatic and manipulates her friends and she does that naturally, naively. That's probably true of Gabe as well, come to think of it. Certainly Laurel in *Escape Entertainment.*

JR: THEY ALL HAVE GREAT CONVICTION ABOUT WHAT THEY'RE DOING. THEY ALL ACT IN INNOCENCE WITH AN IDEALISM THAT TRANSCENDS EVERYTHING ELSE.

CB: Yes. I was thinking about Emma today, actually, because of a film piece I'm working on at the Centre, and I discovered that it's about the same thing I always appear to write about: the Fascism of the Left, where people get so absorbed in a vision that the end justifies the means.

JR: THAT THEME REALLY APPLIES TO MUCH IF NOT ALL OF YOUR WRITING.

CB: How come I didn't notice that before?

JR: TELL ME ABOUT YOUR CURRENT INVOLVEMENT IN NORMAN JEWISON'S CENTRE FOR ADVANCED FILM STUDIES.

CB: I wanted more power in terms of film-writing. I was in a situation where people would ask me to do a project and I'd accept even when I may have had something more interesting to me in mind. I wanted to be able to develop projects for film that I could initiate. I decided that one way to go would be directing. Or producing film. Or at least taking some responsibility in those areas. Co-producing, for instance. Good idea, but I didn't really feel qualified. Or willing to invest the time to sell myself around the world as a producer. So I decided to take a sabbatical with the intention of finding out how the business is organized and how I might fit into it in a creative way other than writing.

JR: HAS THE TIME BEEN A GOOD INVESTMENT?

CB: Oh yes. Definitely. It's bizarre *and* delightful to go back to school in your late forties.

JR: YOU SEEM TO COME TO EACH PROJECT WITHOUT ANY PRE-CONCEIVED NOTIONS.

CB: I try to come at each project as if it's fresh, always new. And, as we've discovered in this conversation, always the same!

In the hothouse atmosphere of the Centre everything is analyzed and that's very interesting. Our first creative project was a five minute film which was then critiqued for two weeks by very different people: Arthur Penn (director of *Bonnie and Clyde*) and Frank Pearson (screenwriter of *Cool Hand Luke* and *Dog Day Afternoon*). And finally, Stephen Frears from *Sammy and Rosie Get Laid* came in for a day. And at the end of this process where there was at least a meeting or a script conference every day, I had to then deal with all the input! And convince myself that it's not all gospel truth but just opinion. You always have to filter criticism you're getting. Somehow. That has been a new experience for me: the ongoing analysis while I'm writing. It's painful at times, but finally, it's exciting to look at that kind of input.

JR: HOW DO YOU STRIKE THE BALANCE BETWEEN BEING THICK-SKINNED ENOUGH SO THAT THE CRITICISM CAN'T DEVASTATE YOU

AND THIN-SKINNED ENOUGH TO BE ABLE TO DIGEST AND INCORPOR-
ATE THE COMMENTS?

CB: I don't know. It's all really a logical function; it has nothing to do with sensitivity. If you examine, for example, a simple comment like "the script is confusing," you have to take into account all the various elements: Who has said this? Why does the confusion disturb this person? Is that a negative element of the script? What style are they coming out of and how does that affect their opinion of the script? It's all relative and criticism has to be placed in a context.

JR: DOES THE BANFF PLAYWRIGHTS COLONY DO THE SAME THINGS FOR THEATRE?

CB: My experience with Banff has been that it's much gentler. Banff isn't aiming to make writers better writers (except in a subsidiary way), but rather to make plays better plays. The emphasis is really on the work.

JR: OVER THE COURSE OF YOUR PLAY-WRITING CAREER THUS FAR, HAS BEING A WOMAN AFFECTED YOUR INFLUENCE OR SUCCESS?

CB: Sharon Pollock once said in an interview we were doing together that in a way, we were both really lucky because when we started writing, theatres could produce our plays and get both a Canadian and a woman in their season in one shot! So we were a minority, but it didn't necessary work against us. That was part of our "charm."

JR: HAVE THINGS CHANGED TODAY?

CB: Oh yes. Now, theatre in our country today is based on developing and producing Canadian plays. We have a solid audience in Toronto, for example, that we didn't have twenty years ago, an audience that *expects* to see new Canadian plays every season.

JR: TELL ME ABOUT *THE PENNY UNIVERSE.*

CB: It was the first play I ever wrote. I wrote it in a Dramatic Writing Course in university. I used to read it with my friends around the kitchen table, while drinking bottles of home-made sake (made by my neighbour Frank Davey — a wonderful poet!), after straining the fruit flies out of it.
We thought it was quite wonderful.

JR: WAS IT?

CB: I don't know. I destroyed it. And the reason I destroyed it was that I took it in to my writing professor and he said: "Well, your play has no plot, no character and no action." And I wept and he poured more tea. He thought the dialogue was interesting. So I tore it up and went to England.

JR: DID HE PASS YOU IN THE COURSE?

CB: Oh yes. So much for plot, character and action. . . .

JR: DO YOU THINK THERE'S A FUTURE IN WRITING PLAYS?

CB: Sure. What else is there?

11. Playwright Joan MacLeod

Michael Cooper

Ms. MacLeod was born in 1954 in Vancouver, where she worked with handicapped people for the Mainstream Society between 1978 and 1984. A radio version of her first play, *Jewel*, was Canada's entry in the 1988 Prix Italia. Ms. MacLeod is beginning her fourth year as playwright-in-residence at Toronto's Tarragon Theatre.

(imitating Elvis) *Good evening ladies and . . . ladies. It's a pleasure. Elvis Presley is here!*
(singing) *Love her tender, love her tender*
Never let her . . .
Lover her tender, lover her tender
Lover her, love her tender . . .

Are you watching me?

Jhana in *Toronto, Mississippi*

Produced and published plays:

Toronto, Mississippi and *Jewel*. Toronto: Playwrights Canada, 1989.

Produced plays:

Amigo's Blue Guitar. Premiered in Toronto at the Tarragon Theatre in 1990.

Joan MacLeod Interview

by Rita Much

RM: YOU WERE WRITING POETRY FOR A NUMBER OF YEARS BEFORE YOU STARTED WRITING PLAYS. WHAT PROMPTED YOU TO MAKE THAT TRANSITION?

JM: Actually, I wrote prose before anything else. I worked on a novel, off and on, for about five years. And while I was working on it, I started writing poetry because the novel felt so big and complicated. Then I learned that, sometimes, you can finish a poem in a day, and I think I got a charge from being able to contain and finish something. So that's partly how I got more serious about poetry. I've written both prose and poetry since I was a kid and when I was in graduate school and started publishing, it was with poetry that I was first successful.

RM: WHEN DID YOU BECOME INVOLVED WITH THEATRE?

JM: I went to Banff, to the School of Fine Arts, to attend the Advanced Writers' Studio. The Playwrights' Colony was running at the same time and I became friends with some playwrights. I began attending their workshops because, for one thing, it seemed like they had a lot more fun than the poets: they got to work with people. I felt an immediate kinship and by the end of my six weeks there I was hanging around with the playwrights all the time. And I got very curious.

The poets had to do a public reading so I asked one of the actors in the Playwrights' Colony if she would like to read my work, a long poem called "John Buchanan," which was based on my grandmother. I thought it would be good for me to hear some stuff out loud, because most poets don't get that opportunity. The reading was very successful and, at age thirty, a light went on in my head. I suddenly realized that my work is best out loud. It sounds very silly, but it was something that had never occurred to me all through my twenties when I was trying to write pretty seriously. My novel is written in the first person as are most of my poems which have a really strong narrative line. I think I was really grooming myself for drama and just didn't know it.

RM: YOUR DRAMATIC LANGUAGE IS VERY LYRICAL. ONE CAN REALLY SENSE A CAREFUL CHOICE OF WORDS, DICTION, ON YOUR PART. DO YOU THINK THAT WRITING POEMS FOR YEARS INFLUENCED YOUR PLAYS IN ANY WAY OTHER THAN THE LYRICAL ELEMENT IN THE LANGUAGE?

JM: Well, with poems you have to nail something down really quickly, and I think the same thing happens in theatre. You have to learn how to compress things, to make things very clear and very original very quickly.

RM: THE SYMBOLISM IN YOUR PLAYS REVERBERATES IN THE WAY THAT SYMBOLS OFTEN DO IN POETRY. YOU CAN'T PIN THE SYMBOL DOWN TO ONLY ONE MEANING. THERE ARE MANY REVER-BERATIONS AND CONNOTATIONS FOR THE READER. IS THAT AN IN-HERITANCE FROM THE POETRY WRITING?

JM: Probably. Symbols are something I'm never aware of when I'm writing. They sort of spring from the work organically, whether it's a poem, a play or a novel. In *Toronto, Mississippi* I suppose you could say Elvis is symbolic of romance or of self-destruction, but when I was writing the piece Elvis was just someone King, the character who plays the Elvis impersonator, loved.

RM: THERE'S A FOCUS IN YOUR PLAY-WRITING ON LANGUAGE. WHAT ROLE DOES THE VISUAL PLAY?

JM: It's funny, because we just sold the film option for *Jewel*. I was shocked that anyone would think of making a movie of it — it's a monologue! And then after meeting with this film-maker last week I realized that when you break it down the writing *is* so very visual that adapting the work to the screen becomes easy. The monologue reads like a treatment. It's just describing a whole story, and every second sentence is giving you a big visual clue: exactly how the top of the desk looks and so on.

RM: DO YOU TAKE GREAT CARE WITH SETTING IN A PLAY? DO YOU TRY IN AN EARLY DRAFT TO GET A CLEAR PICTURE OF THE SET AND BLOCKING?

JM: No, not at all. I think my visual sense is very poor at the moment. I think the reason is my background as a poet. I'm used to just having the page to work with. So *Jewel*, my first dramatic piece, sort of all takes place on the page. With *Toronto, Mississippi* I started working out loud for the first time. I realized that with Jhana, the hyperactive, retarded character, the way she moves influences the way she talks. When I was writing, I'd get up and march around my apartment and I'd hug myself and she'd move so quickly that the language started doing the same thing. In the new play I'm working on now, *Amigo's Blue Guitar*, I've had to force myself to think visually, to consciously picture the stage, because it's something I'm still not used to doing.

RM: *JEWEL* IS A DRAMATIC MONOLOGUE. DOES THAT FORM HAVE A SPECIAL APPEAL FOR YOU? WILL YOU USE IT AGAIN?

JM: Not for a while, but I think it felt like the best bridge into drama, since it was a single voice and the language is poetic. Now that I know a little bit more about dramatic structure I realize that it's much easier to have more than one character. You get two people talking and energy happens.

RM: THE PLAY TAKES OFF ON ITS OWN.

JM: That's right. With *Jewel* I found it hard to get things to happen, to make it active, because there is only one character.

RM: IN ADDITION TO WRITING POETRY AND STAGE PLAYS YOU'VE WORKED ON AN OPERA WITH COMUS MUSIC THEATRE AND YOU'VE TURNED YOUR HAND TO RADIO DRAMA AS WELL. IN FACT, *JEWEL* WAS MADE INTO A RADIO DRAMA FOR CBC RADIO. DOES ONE FORM HAVE A SPECIAL APPEAL FOR YOU? OR CAN YOU MOVE QUITE FREELY FROM ONE TO THE OTHER?

JM: I feel quite at ease moving around.

RM: WHICH DO YOU PREFER?

JM: Drama. I think *Toronto, Mississippi* is my strongest work, and I want to continue in that vein. My new play has six characters and three acts and I'm thinking of writing a two-hander.

RM: DO YOU FEEL THAT ONE PARTICULAR FORM IS A BETTER FORUM FOR WOMEN WRITERS? DOES ONE OFFER, OR CONSTITUTE, A BETTER PLATFORM FOR A WOMAN WRITER?

JM: I don't think so. I don't think there is a difference.

RM: I UNDERSTAND THAT DURING THE REHEARSAL PERIOD OF THE PREMIERE PRODUCTION OF *JEWEL* YOU LOST THE ACTRESS WHO WAS TO PLAY MARJORIE AND THAT YOU STEPPED INTO THE ROLE AT THE ELEVENTH HOUR. WHAT WAS IT LIKE TO DO A ONE-WOMAN SHOW AND TO PERFORM IN YOUR FIRST STAGE PLAY TO BOOT?

JM: Well, in retrospect it was a great experience; at the time, I was terrified.

RM: HAD YOU ACTED BEFORE THEN?

JM: Twice. When I was in Banff in 1985 I wrote the first draft of *Jewel* and performed it then. But it was only thirty minutes long and we all knew each other. And then we took it to the Fringe Festival in Edmonton that summer. Claire McCord performed the play for a week, but then we got two extra dates that she couldn't do, so I played Marjorie. However, the crowds were really tiny, eleven or so, and mostly friends.

RM: I READ THAT AFTER THE EXPERIENCE OF PLAYING MARJORIE IN THE TARRAGON PRODUCTION YOU DECIDED NOT TO ACT ANY MORE.

JM: Yes. It's hard work and I felt lucky — I sort of got by. I would rather write than act. I think writing is a lot more pleasant. Doing *Jewel* at the Tarragon taught me a great deal in a short amount of time. That whole experience of "the show must go on" was marvellous and it boosted my confidence to be able to handle it: to know what a run feels like; to know what a Tuesday night means; and to do two shows on Saturday. It felt good to find out how hard it is and what actors go through.

RM: YOU HAVEN'T DIRECTED ANY OF YOUR PLAYS. DO YOU WANT TO IN THE FUTURE?

JM: No. I'm sure one gains a certain kind of knowledge by directing one's own plays or the plays of other people, but in my case it would be at the expense of a lot of other people. For me it would be like doing math. I'd be scared and I don't think I'd enjoy the process.

RM: HAVE YOUR FAMILY AND BACKGROUND INFLUENCED YOUR WORK?

JM: Very much. I have one older brother who also writes and parents who have always been very supportive. My father is a real story-teller. If I have any talent it probably comes from him.

RM: WHERE ARE YOUR PARENTS FROM?

JM: Both my parents are from Glengarry County, which is a little farming community between Ottawa and Montreal, right on the Quebec border. It's half Scottish Presbyterian and half French Catholic. I had a grandmother who lived with us until I was fourteen and who spoke Gaelic. Actually, both my parents spoke some Gaelic. It's an unusual background in some ways. My parents married late — my father was almost forty-seven when I was born — and I think that being raised by parents that much older made me in part develop the writer personality a bit.

RM: IN WHAT WAY? DID YOU START WRITING VERY YOUNG?

JM: Yes. I remember always wanting to be a writer. I remember being four or five and sitting on my father's knee and talking to him in rhyme, because that impressed him. I was always making up stories that I performed for my family. While growing up, I was terribly proud of my parents because they are very kind people, but at the same time I was really embarrassed because they had white hair when I was in grade one. I think anything that makes you take a step back and worry about everything makes you a writer.

RM: DO YOUR PARENTS WRITE?

JM: My father went to a creative writing course for senior citizens and wrote his memoirs, which were great. They all like to try to write, I think, though no one else does it professionally.

RM: WHICH PLAYWRIGHTS HAVE INFLUENCED YOU? ARE THERE ANY THAT YOU CAN SINGLE OUT AND SAY, "YES, I'VE LOOKED AT THEM AND I WANT TO DO THAT," OR "I CAN DO THAT, BUT BETTER"? AND DID DAVID FREEMAN'S *CREEPS* HAVE ANY IMPACT ON *TORONTO, MISSISSIPPI*?

JM: I was well under way with it before I read *Creeps* so it didn't influence my play in a direct way. The people who have influenced me the most are friends. In Banff the person who introduced me to theatre was Alan Williams and he still influences my work a lot. Actually, I've just given him the first act of my new play for feedback. He's smart, he's been working in theatre for a long time, and I respect his work. He's also hard on me; he wants me to write well and I know I get honest answers from him. Probably one of the reasons I started with a one-person show is that it was his forte and that is what I was used to seeing. His heightened use of language in *Cockroach Trilogy* also made an impact. "Hmm, that's interesting," I thought. I'd never heard anything like that before.

RM: WHO DO YOU LIKE TO READ?

JM: I read a little of everything: Judith Thompson, David French, Sharon Pollock. And I love Sam Shepard. I read a lot of him. Actually, it's prose writers who interest me most.

RM: CONTEMPORARY PROSE WRITERS?

JM: Yes. Margaret Laurence, Margaret Atwood, Alice Munro. Reading all of them when I was eighteen, nineteen just turned my head around. Laurence and Munro were both writing about a landscape, physical and emotional, that I knew intimately. I don't think I understood before that writing could be about the events in my own day, my own life. Reading Munro and Laurence taught me to use the personal, or start with the personal, and then to make it bigger, more accessible.

RM: SO YOU'RE HEAVILY ENTRENCHED IN THE CANADIAN TRADITION.

JM: I guess so, though I'm a fan of American writers from the south like Flannery O'Connor and Faulkner. There are so many levels to O'Connor's work: black humour, spirituality, complex human relationships. As for Faulkner, *The Sound and the Fury* was very important to me in the writing of *Toronto, Mississippi*. I went back and read the book when I began the play. I should also mention that Bobbie Ann Mason's *In Country* has influenced *Amigo's Blue Guitar*. I very much admire her way of transforming popular culture — Bruce Springsteen, shopping malls, video arcades — into literature.

RM: YOUR PLAYS AREN'T OVERTLY FEMINIST. WOULD YOU CALL YOURSELF A FEMINIST WRITER?

JM: Oh, yes.

RM: WHAT DOES THE TERM MEAN TO YOU?

JM: I have a hard time with it, in a sense. I certainly live like a feminist. When I first got to Toronto, the first place that I sent *Jewel* to was Nightwood because I'd heard there was this "women's theatre," and I was really excited about it. And they said it was good writing but that it wasn't their cup of tea because they felt it wasn't a feminist piece. And I felt really hurt by that. I think *Jewel* is very feminine: it's about a woman's strength. It's also a play that has really gotten through to people. I've received stacks of letters on it, from widows in mill towns out in B.C. to guys in northern Alberta. There's something about the work that gets through and that I'm proud of.

RM: DID YOU SUBSEQUENTLY GO TO NIGHTWOOD THEATRE TO SEE THE KIND OF SHOWS THEY DO?

JM: Yes, I've seen a few now and I like what they do very much. I think they have some really talented people working there and I've talked through my initial problems with them. I hope I can work with them sometime. I feel my work portrays women in a strong and human light. It's always women who respond the deepest to my work.

RM: WHEN YOU WRITE A PLAY ARE YOU CONSCIOUS OF INCLUDING A MESSAGE OF ANY KIND TO THE WOMEN IN YOUR AUDIENCE?

JM: No, I'm not conscious of anything like that.

RM: MANY WOMEN WRITERS IN CANADA FEEL THAT MALE PLAYWRIGHTS IN CANADA DICTATE THE ACCEPTED STYLE OF WRITING PLAYS. DO YOU AGREE?

JM: I don't think there is a difference in male/female styles of play-writing.

RM: HAVE YOU EVER FELT THAT YOUR PLAYS WEREN'T ACCEPTABLE BECAUSE THEY WERE WRITTEN BY A WOMAN?

JM: I haven't had any direct experience with that at all. At the same time theatres in this country are run by men. I feel lucky. I've been in theatre for only three years but both my plays have done well. I would feel very differently if I couldn't get them on some-where.

RM: DO YOU THINK THERE IS A DISTINCTLY MALE AESTHETIC OR IS REALLY GREAT ART GENDERLESS? DOES IT TRANSCEND THE BOUN-DARIES OF SEX?

JM: I hope so. Good art is good art. However, most of what I read and feel closest to is work by women. I don't know what that means.

RM: DO YOU EVER WORRY THAT YOUR AUDIENCE, SPECIFICALLY THE MEN IN YOUR AUDIENCE, WON'T UNDERSTAND OR FULLY AP-PRECIATE YOUR WORK BECAUSE YOU ARE WRITING AS A WOMAN AND SO FROM A FEMALE PERSPECTIVE?

JM: I always feel more secure about giving my work to a woman to read. I know that usually she is going to respond more warmly. So I do worry a little bit about that. But I don't often feel misunderstood. Many men like my work and probably the person who understands my work the best is Urjo Kareda at the Tarragon Theatre here in Toronto with whom I sit and talk from the first line of a new play.

RM: DO YOU HAVE A PICTURE OF A CERTAIN KIND OF AUDIENCE WHEN YOU WRITE?

JM: No. In fact, when I'm in the theatre waiting for a perfor-mance of one of my plays I often feel I have nothing in common with the audience. That's not true, of course.

RM: WHERE DO YOU GET THE IDEA FOR A PLAY? HOW DID *JEWEL* BEGIN?

JM: I was in Banff, in the Music Theatre Studio Ensemble, and I was supposed to write a libretto though I barely knew what the word meant. All I knew was that opera had to be big! I wrote one scene that wasn't bad, so we set it to music. And then I just kept on writing until eventually one female voice got stronger and stronger. I realized that it was a monologue and that the story had to be told in that form.

RM: WHEN I READ IT FOR THE FIRST TIME I THOUGHT THAT YOU MUST HAVE BEEN DRAWING ON YOUR OWN EXPERIENCE. DO MANY PEOPLE TELL YOU THAT?

JM: Yes, and I do draw on my own experience. I did live up north for a couple of years when I was in my early twenties, and as a result the novel takes place up there and *Jewel* is set in the same sort of territory. I also worked in a pipeline camp for a winter when I was twenty-two, so I drew on that and more importantly I knew what it was like to have a boyfriend who worked on the rigs.

RM: THE SITUATION AND THE LOCATION ARE BOTH VERY EX-OTIC, VERY REMOVED FROM THE ORDINARY.

JM: Yet when I wrote *Toronto, Mississippi,* Toronto was very exotic to me. My new play is set on the West Coast, probably because Vancouver, my home town, is now somewhat exotic to me as a result of my distance from it these past few years. Once that sharpness happens, I know I can write about it.

RM: YOU WORKED WITH THE HANDICAPPED FOR APPROXIMATELY TEN YEARS. DID YOU EVER THINK THAT ONE DAY YOU WERE GOING TO WRITE ABOUT THEM?

JM: Yes. I wanted to write about handicapped people, mentally handicapped people, for a long time. I tried writing a poem and a couple of stories but they didn't work. Then I wrote *Jewel,* which got me an invitation to the Playwrights Unit at Tarragon, for which I had to write a play. I said, "This is it — I'm finally going to write about the handicapped."

RM: WHY ELVIS? IN AN INTERVIEW YOU SAID THAT HANDI-CAPPED PEOPLE OFTEN BECOME OBSESSED WITH PERSONALITIES. ARE YOU AN ELVIS FAN?

JM: I'm definitely an Elvis fan.

RM: DID YOU DO RESEARCH? DID YOU GO TO ANY CLUBS FEA-TURING ELVIS IMPERSONATORS?

JM: Oh, yes, and it was fun. I got to read all kinds of trash literature in the name of art. I once worked with a handicapped woman who loved Elvis. She was very lonely and had wall-papered her room with pictures of him. When she was down she would put him on the stereo to hear him sing about loving her. She had also just started working at a sheltered workshop and was bored and discouraged. Listening to Elvis, or better yet singing along with him, or best of all *being* Elvis was a lot more fun than anything else in her life. Then, just after he did *White Dogs in Texas,* Alan Williams, another Elvis fan, visited me on his way to Graceland. He brought me a few Elvis records and some material to read and before long I was hooked. It was then that I realized that since Jhana was partially autistic she would imitate behaviour all the time and that if she was going to be obsessed with someone why not make him an Elvis *impersonator.* At first I thought it would be too corny to have the Elvis impersonator actually show up in the play but then Jhana's father suddenly showed up for dinner and didn't leave. That's what got the play going: his refusal to leave is what ups the stakes for everybody. As you can see, I'm not very organized about the way I write. I never know what's going to happen a page ahead.

RM: WHAT IS THE MOST IMPORTANT THING AN ACTRESS PLAYING JHANA SHOULD DO?

JM: That she has the same sexuality, needs, loves, frustrations, as anyone else. She just thinks a bit more slowly. If you get rid of your slickness, the polite, civilized veneer, you'll find the Jhana within.

RM: DO YOU WRITE QUICKLY OR IS WRITING A LONG, DRAWN-OUT PROCESS?

JM: It's a long, drawn-out process though at times I'm a binge writer. I try to write a minimum of four hours a day, but a lot of the time that just means that for four hours a day I'll be feeling bad because I'm not writing. And then all of a sudden I'll go crazy — I wrote *Jewel* in a weekend. Of course, I knew the world of *Jewel* very well because I'd written five drafts of a novel about it.

RM: DO YOU REWRITE DURING THE REHEARSAL PROCESS?

JM: Yes. On *Toronto, Mississippi* I wrote a new prologue two nights before the opening and we cut a half an hour altogether. It was just too long. I rewrite rather a lot and Tarragon is set up for that. We have a week of previews so that we can rewrite. The whole process there is geared toward a new work and toward a playwright being in rehearsal.

RM: DOES YOUR HOME LIFE, YOUR DOMESTIC LIFE, IN ANY WAY INTRUDE ON YOUR WRITING, OR ARE YOU FAIRLY FREE?

JM: I'm pretty free. I live by myself and can write when the spirit moves me. I've also been writing full-time now for nearly three years. Before that I had to work as a dicta-typist for seven dollars an hour. When I first got to Toronto I was broke all the time.

I hope I can do it all. I'd love to have a kid one day. I think writing is a job that, once you're established, you can combine really nicely with raising a family because it's very portable and you don't have to punch a clock. Sometimes you can use the loneliness of being on your own to write.

My first year in Toronto was horrendous. I ripped the ligaments and cartilage in my knee two months after I got here. I had to go to physio every day and I needed two knee operations. I ended up borrowing money from my parents in order to survive which was pretty demoralizing, as I was thirty-one at the time. But in the midst of this I wrote *Toronto, Mississippi*.

I had no control over my life — financially, emotionally or physically — so I began writing a play in order to create a world that I could control. I took all the pain of that winter and very consciously turned it into something joyful. I'd say, "I'm going to have fun with Jhana, she's going to be a gas today." I've never been so aware of using my own pain or joy or whatever and putting it into my work.

RM: YOU SAID IT WASN'T DIFFICULT TO GET YOUR FIRST PLAY PRODUCED. HOW DID YOU GET INVITED TO THE TARRAGON PLAY-WRITING UNIT?

JM: Alan Williams told Urjo Karedo that I was moving to Toronto and that he thought I was a good writer. The day after I sent them *Jewel* they called to invite me to join the Playwrights Unit. I was overwhelmed because I was so used to waiting months while a publisher sat on my poems.

RM: IS BEING A WOMAN IN A MALE-DOMINATED PROFESSION A PROBLEM FOR YOU?

JM: No. But my experience is limited. I'll have a better idea about the sexual dynamics after this year when I leave the Tarragon nest and see my work in other places. A lot of women are doing my work: Martha Henry is directing *Toronto, Mississippi* at the Grand Theatre. Teri Snelgrove is directing *Jewel* in Vancouver, and Glynis Leyshon, who runs the Belfry, is directing *Toronto, Mississippi* in Victoria. In a few months I'll know what it is like to work with a female director. I like what Andy McKim and I have done but I also feel a little bit like I got married a virgin since he's the only direc-tor I've worked with.

RM: IN *TORONTO, MISSISSIPPI* BILL REMARKS THAT FEMALE WRITERS "HAVEN'T HAD MUCH OF A VOICE AT ALL UP UNTIL NOW." DO YOU HAVE ANY VISION ABOUT WHAT THE FUTURE WILL BE FOR WOMEN WRITERS IN CANADA?

JM: I think it's going to be terrific. I think that the best prose writers in this country are women, and that feels immensely exciting. And to a large extent the best people writing for the stage right now are women, too. Despite cutbacks, a Conservative government and free trade, as well as the importance placed on the big and glossy in theatre today, I feel I am in good company when I look around at the women writing for the stage right now, women like Judith Thompson, Colleen Murphy, Sally Clark, and Linda Griffiths. I feel a part of a very rich community. I feel lucky.

RM: WHAT ABOUT THE ISSUE OF REGIONALISM. WOULD YOU DESCRIBE YOUR PLAYS AS REGIONAL? FOR EXAMPLE, IN *JEWEL* ONE GETS A VERY POWERFUL SENSE OF THE ISOLATION OF THE NORTH.

JM: The isolation *is* tremendous. The place where my plays take place is always important and there's always certain kinds of in-jokes. But I hope the work transcends any regional quality. The radio version of *Jewel* was Canada's entry in the Prix Italia, which is the international television and radio awards. This means that it was being read and listened to by sixteen different countries. So there's something about *Jewel* that makes sense outside of Canada while at the same time it is, I think, uniquely Canadian. My new play is very West Coast.

RM: DO YOU SEE YOURSELF AS BASICALLY A WEST COAST WRITER?

JM: Well, it's funny, because I never would have thought that until I moved out here, and now I realize how West Coast I am. I mean, probably even the way I'm sitting on this chair is West Coast. I think it's significant that three of four productions of *Toronto, Mississippi* this season are in B.C. There's something about me that they're responding to that I don't quite know about. It will be curious to find out what that is, especially since I've had no success at home. I've never had anything put on there.

RM: MARJORIE IN *JEWEL* AND JHANA IN *TORONTO, MISSISSIPPI* ELICIT A VERY PRIMITIVE, GUT REACTION FROM THE READER. WOULD YOU SAY THAT YOUR PLAYS HAVE PRIMARILY AN EMOTIONAL APPEAL, RATHER THAN A CEREBRAL AND INTELLECTUAL ONE FOR THE AUDIENCE?

JM: Yes. The strongest part of my work is the emotional.

RM: IS THIS CONSCIOUS OR DELIBERATE ON YOUR PART?

JM: It's not conscious. It's just what I do best, what interests me the most. I think my work is getting "smarter"; I think I'm getting more confident about what I have to say. There are parts of *Toronto, Mississippi* that deal specifically with ideas and I really enjoy them. And I feel that there is going to be a lot more of that in my new work. I think that in the last ten years I just didn't have the confidence to play with ideas. I always knew that I could get through in an emotional way and I've never had a problem being passionate. I suppose being the "smart girl" came a lot a harder. I was afraid of the label.

RM: WHAT STRIKES ME AS CURIOUS ABOUT PLAYS BY WOMEN WRITERS WRITTEN IN THE LAST TEN YEARS — BRITISH, AMERICAN AND CANADIAN — IS THAT THERE AREN'T MANY TRAGEDIES. BOTH *JEWEL* AND *TORONTO, MISSISSIPPI* COULD EASILY BE TURNED INTO TRAGEDIES. AT THE END OF *JEWEL* MARJORIE COULD JUST GO OFF THE DEEP END AND IN *TORONTO, MISSISSIPPI* SOMETHING ABSOLUTELY TERRIBLE COULD HAPPEN TO JHANA OR EVEN TO BILL, WHO BECOMES A VERY POWERFUL CHARACTER IN TERMS OF ELICITING EMOTIONAL RESPONSE FROM THE AUDIENCE. AND YET BOTH PLAYS END WITH A VERY DELIBERATE AFFIRMATION OF LIFE. IN BOTH THE VERY STRONG

WOMEN MAKE A STAND, A DETERMINED STAND. MARJORIE DECIDES
TO LIVE AND THAT'S OBVIOUSLY A VERY COURAGEOUS AND POSITIVE
ACT; AND MADDIE SAYS "NO" TO KING AND ALIGNS HERSELF WITH
BILL. WERE YOU EVER TEMPTED AT ANY POINT TO TURN EITHER PLAY
INTO A TRAGEDY?

JM: No, because I feel an obligation to be hopeful. I hate
saying that because it sounds so corny, but that's part of the reason
I want to write. I mean, we do mess up and life is hard, but people
manage. People do amazing things. After sitting in the archives at
CBC listening to tapes of the *Ocean Ranger* widows, I had to write
something about affirming life. As for the character of Jhana in
Toronto, Mississippi, I wanted to express my happiness that people
like her are alive and a part of my life. There are a couple of
mentally handicapped people who I love the way I love my good
friends or my parents and I wanted to show that. I wanted to upset
the cliché and show that a person like her is fun to be around. In
my new play the central character is a really unhappy eighteen-year-
old guy, but he's going to get through the pain. I have to figure out
what turns him around.

When I was in my twenties all my work was very dark. There's
still lots of darkness but I think finding the light is a big challenge.
I've learned a great deal about humour during the last few years.
There was no humour at all in my work until I got into theatre. I
had written a couple of poems that were pretty funny and parts of
my novel were funny but I have had to acquire the confidence to be
funny. Of course, when we're young we are often very serious about
ourselves, and then once we hit our thirties we realize that many of
our concerns don't really matter in the long run.

RM: WHAT DOES THE TITLE OF YOUR FIRST PLAY MEAN?

JM: It's a terrible title. It's not strong. "Jewel" actually refers to
a wedding band. Marjorie says the word three or four times and at
the end she talks about removing "the perfect jewel."

RM: WHAT DID YOU WANT IT TO REPRESENT FOR HER: HER
HUSBAND, THE LOVE THAT SHE KNOWS HE HAD FOR HER?

JM: Yes: the image each has of the other. In one of the first
lines I wrote I talked about the husband going down in the water
"like a dark jewel." I later cut the line but for some reason the
image stuck in my mind.

RM: WHAT WOULD YOU CALL IT IF YOU HAD TO RENAME IT?

JM: Well, the radio version is called *Hand of God.* It's a bit
better, but it's not great either.

RM: IN YOUR FIRST TWO PLAYS YOU DEAL WITH THE IDEA OF THE HOMECOMING. THE HUSBAND DOESN'T ACTUALLY COME HOME IN *JEWEL* BUT THAT'S WHAT IS LONGED FOR. HE'S ALWAYS ABSENT, AND SHE'S ALWAYS WAITING FOR HIM, WAITING FOR THE MESSAGE, WAITING FOR THE RETURN, WAITING FOURTEEN MONTHS AND HOPING THAT HE IS STILL DRIFTING. IN *TORONTO, MISSISSIPPI* THE FATHER DOES COME HOME AND THERE'S HOPE FOR A BIT THAT HE MAY RECONNECT WITH MADDIE AND BE A RESPONSIBLE FATHER. IS IT A COINCIDENCE THAT BOTH PLAYS INVOLVE THE THEME OF THE HOMECOMING OR DOES THE THEME HAVE SPECIAL MEANING FOR YOU?

JM: I feel embarrassed that you've pointed it out because I wasn't aware of it. It's very astute; it's quite true. My novel is called *Waiting for Home* and it's also about that. So is my new play, *Amigo's Blue Guitar*.

RM: IN WHAT WAY?

JM: It's all about homes. An eighteen-year-old boy called Sander lives on a gulf island farm with his father, who came up to B.C. as a draft-dodger twenty years earlier. Sander hasn't been happy and he keeps thinking that the world will change when he gets to university, that a big event will transform his life. He ends up sponsoring a refugee from El Salvador who comes to stay with him. The father's mother, who is from Oregon, also comes to stay because she's a bit crazy and has to be taken care of. But she keeps wanting to go home, and the refugee's goal is to flee Sander's place and set up his own home.

RM: SO FAR IN YOUR DRAMATIC WORK YOU HAVE FOCUSED ON THE FAMILY.

JM: Very much so. In my new play it's the brother-sister relationship that is really important. It just feels natural to write about the family. It's not something I think much about. In the case of *Amigo's Blue Guitar* I didn't at first know how to get across Sander's social awkwardness and repression. Then suddenly a mouthy and confident older sister walked into the play and everything fell into place.

RM: MANY WOMAN PLAYWRIGHTS WRITE ABOUT THE FAMILY. DO SUBJECTS USUALLY ASSOCIATED WITH THE MALE WRITERS — POLITICS OR WAR, FOR EXAMPLE — HAVE ANY APPEAL FOR YOU? DO YOU SEE YOURSELF AT SOME POINT IN TIME WRITING A HISTORY PLAY?

JM: I'm not really interested in that. However, I see all of my work as political. *Jewel* arose out of the fact that when I worked in the oil fields I learned that accidents were being covered up. So when the *Ocean Ranger* went down I was really curious about it and read everything I could get my hands on. I wrote *Toronto, Mississippi* because I wanted people to change their thinking about mentally handicapped people. And the motivation behind the new work is that we are developing refugee policies in Canada that appal me. I work with a refugee group in Toronto and I sponsor refugees. So my work always feels political, and it always feels personal.

RM: WHY DID YOU CHOOSE TO MAKE THE HANDICAPPED CHARACTER IN *TORONTO, MISSISSIPPI* FEMALE? ELVIS DID HAVE A DAUGHTER, OF COURSE, BUT DID YOU EVER CONSIDER MAKING THE HANDICAPPED CHARACTER MALE? YOU MIGHT BE ACCUSED OF SUBSCRIBING TO THE STEREOTYPE VIEW OF WOMAN AS VICTIM.

JM: I always knew the character was a woman. Jhana started out as a combination of two mentally handicapped people I know, one male and one female. I think she has a lot of male in her.

RM: DO YOU FIND IT EASIER TO WRITE FEMALE CHARACTERS THAN MALE CHARACTERS?

JM: It has been in the past. But it was fun to create Bill in *Toronto, Mississippi*, who was the first male character I had written.

RM: HE'S VERY WITTY AND WIT IS SEDUCTIVE.

JM: He's also quite goofy, but people don't notice that as much. During the intermission of a public reading of the play in Banff I overheard two women in the bathroom saying that they thought Bill was the sexiest character they had ever heard.

RM: BOTH MARJORIE IN *JEWEL* AND MADDIE IN *TORONTO, MISSISSIPPI* ARE VERY STRONG. I THINK MADDIE DESCRIBES HERSELF AS BEING "AS SOLID AS A ROCK." IS IT SIGNIFICANT THAT MARJORIE'S HUSBAND IS AN ABSENCE IN HER LIFE (EVEN WHEN HE WAS ALIVE HE WAS USUALLY FOUR THOUSAND MILES AWAY) AND THAT MADDIE'S EX-HUSBAND IS A WANDERER? WERE YOU TRYING TO WRITE ABOUT A COMMON EXPERIENCE OF WOMEN TODAY?

JM: Yes. I live by myself and I write about what I know. Maybe I'll write differently in a year's time. Women are on their own a lot more than our mothers were, I think. Most of the women around me are on their own.

RM: WHAT ABOUT REVIEWS? ARE YOU INFLUENCED BY CRITICS?

JM: I hate saying this, but I stay up all night and go to the newspaper box, and worry. I've been pretty lucky with reviews, though, and I'd never change the way I write for critics. I think I hold my breath and cross my fingers and hope they are in a good mood when they see the show.

RM: DO YOU THINK THAT IN GENERAL MALE CRITICS SOMETIMES FAIL TO UNDERSTAND PLAYS BY WOMEN OR THAT THEY ARE BIASED AGAINST PLAYS BY OR ABOUT WOMEN?

JM: Yes. I wish there were more female critics in Toronto. One review of *Toronto, Mississippi*, for example, was in some ways a good review, but it was such a bizarre interpretation of the play, and so incorrect, that we couldn't use it to promote the show. The man who wrote it just didn't understand the play. I felt like he didn't pay attention, or something. In addition, neither the *Star* nor the *Globe* said it was funny. On opening night people laughed from the very beginning but the humour was never mentioned, and that feels like sloppy reporting to me. I agreed to be in the Chalmers' Committee this year partly in order to enter the enemy camp. I want to impress on critics that their comments affect the playwright's ability to pay rent and get a second production.

RM: WOULD YOU LIKE TO BE A CRITIC?

JM: No. I think the only kind of writing I can do is creative writing. In school I was always terrible at writing essays. I'm just not interested.

RM: YOU ARE A WRITER-IN-RESIDENCE AT THE TARRAGON THEATRE FOR THE THIRD YEAR IN A ROW. DO YOU WORK WITH NEW WRITERS?

JM: Yes. The Tarragon usually takes on six new writers a year and there are always two or three writers-in-residence who will informally discuss their work with them.

RM: HAS THE CLOSE INTERACTION WITH OTHER WRITERS DIRECTLY INFLUENCED YOUR OWN WORK? HAVE YOU LEARNED MORE ABOUT THE ART OF PLAY-WRITING?

JM: What I've learned is to work at theatre, to immerse myself in it. I love going to the read-through the first day of rehearsal, attending the dress rehearsal and the first preview, watching the last performance of the run and talking with designers and tech people. When I wrote *Toronto, Mississippi* I shared an office with Judith Thompson, who was writing *I Am Yours*. As you can imagine, it is a very rich and nurturing environment.

RM: WHAT DO YOU THINK IS YOUR GREATEST ASSET AS A WRITER? WHAT ARE YOU DISSATISFIED WITH?

JM: I think one of my assets is the way I use language. I've got a good ear for its rhythm, and images are usually clear, perhaps because of my background in poetry. My weakness is structure, though I think I'm getting better at it.

RM: CAN YOU DESCRIBE THE STRUCTURE OF YOUR NEW PLAY?

JM: I'm fooling around with it. There are many more scenes in it than there were in *Toronto, Mississippi*, so I'm looking at the energy that can happen when you've got short, fluid scenes and multiple locations. I'm using exterior scenes for the first time. My first impulse was to set it in a living room, like my first two plays. Hopefully, the work itself will dictate the structure. I think that's the best way.

RM: DO YOU HAVE PARTICULAR GOALS AS A PLAYWRIGHT? ARE THERE CERTAIN SUBJECTS THAT YOU KNOW YOU ARE GOING TO WRITE ABOUT AT SOME POINT?

JM: Not really. The main plan is to keep writing well and to take my time. Now that I've had a little success, I'm scared of just pumping them out. I want to write a screenplay at some point, as well as to finish a book of poems. I'd like to be a good novelist, though that would be down the road a bit. As for subjects, I'm putting all of myself into the play I'm currently working on and can't think much beyond that.

RM: DO YOU SEE YOURSELF TEACHING PLAY-WRITING AT SOME POINT?

JM: Actually, I've been offered a job at the University of Victoria and I think I'll take it for a year at some point. I won't want to write for a while after I finish the new work and teaching would be great. I went to school there, so it would be like going home.

RM: ARE YOU AMBITIOUS?

JM: Yes, I am. I made a big commitment to writing when I moved out here three years ago. I knew I had some talent and decided to take myself seriously. It has become really important to me just that my work be seen and that I connect with an audience. Making contact with the public means a lot to me.

RM: DO YOU HAVE ANY ADVICE TO GIVE TO YOUNG PEOPLE WHO MIGHT BE CONSIDERING WRITING FOR THE THEATRE?

JM: To finish things. I wrote a three-hundred-page novel that didn't get published but it gave me confidence to actually finish it and I learned a great deal about aesthetic unity. So many people with talent start things they never complete. The fun part of writing is starting something, feeling inspired, but unfortunately it's only about five percent of the job. Most of the work involves rewriting and rewriting and rewriting.

RM: DO YOU EVER SUFFER FROM WRITER'S BLOCK?

JM: Oh, yes. When I worked full time as a life-skills teacher with mentally handicapped adults I didn't write for three years. At the end of an eight-hour day the last thing I wanted to do when I got home was to write. And I got blocked after *Toronto, Mississippi*. I didn't write for six months because I felt so tired and drained.

RM: THE KEY, THEN, IS TO PERSEVERE.

JM: Absolutely. Budding writers should finish things and recognize that a large part of writing isn't fun. It's very hard work and it's also lonely.

RM: DO YOU ALSO RECOMMEND THAT YOUNG WRITERS FOLLOW YOUR PATH AND BECOME INVOLVED IN AS MANY ASPECTS OF THEATRE AS THEY CAN?

JM: I certainly do. The text forms the basis of theatre but you have to understand what other people's jobs are and what they can do for you. I had no idea that actors could make something better than it was on the page. Watching Brooke Johnson, the woman who initially played Jhana in *Toronto, Mississippi*, bring that part to life was probably one of my greatest thrills as a creative person.

12. Playwright Sharon Pollock

Born in Fredericton, New Brunswick in 1936, Sharon Pollock wrote her first play in 1967. She has been Artistic Director of Theatre New Brunswick and she was recently appointed to the position of Associate Director at the Stratford Festival in Ontario. Ms. Pollock won the Governor General's Award for Drama in 1981 for *Blood Relations* and in 1986 for *Doc*.

She was looking up at the camera. She was smiling a bit. You could see her teeth. . . . She looked as if she was waiting. Just waiting.

Catherine in *Doc*

I've mastered the art a seein' the multiple realities a the universe, and more than that. I have embraced them, though they be almost always conflicting, but equally true. . . . Now, how far is it — fifteen feet, or the abyss, or nothin' between us?

Mr. Big in *Whiskey Six Cadenza*

Produced and published plays:

Blood Relations and other plays. Edmonton: NeWest Press, 1981. Includes *Blood Relations*, *Generations* and *One Tiger to a Hill*.

Walsh. Vancouver: Talonbooks, 1983.

The Komagata Maru Incident. Toronto: Playwrights Canada, 1985.

Doc. Toronto: Playwrights Canada, 1986.

Whiskey Six Cadenza. In *Plays by Women.* Edmonton: NeWest Press, 1987.

Produced plays:

A Compulsory Option. Produced by the New Play Centre, at the Vancouver Art Gallery, 1972.

Out Goes You. Produced at Vancouver Playhouse, 1975.

Mail vs. Female. Produced at Lunch Box Theatre Calgary, 1981.

Getting It Straight. Produced at Factory Theatre, Toronto, 1990.

Sharon Pollock Interview

by Rita Much

RM: WHAT DO YOU LOOK FOR WHEN YOU GO TO THE THEATRE?

SP: As a playwright I don't feel obliged to see everything and what I want to see in the theatre changes over time. At the moment I'm interested in imagistic techniques. Unfortunately, the further one gets away from Quebec the less opportunity one has to see them. Basically, I want to be engaged and I want to be provoked in some way when I go to the theatre. I find it difficult to watch a play without de-constructing, taking it all to pieces. I can't just experience the event holistically. I'm always looking at the work on many different levels. I'm looking at what the playwright's doing, at the text, at what I think the director has contributed, and I'm thinking, "Why have they made this choice?" or "Gee, I really disagree with that choice but I understand why it is they made it." It's very seldom that I can find something that allows me to just be carried along with it, which is what I want when I write a work. I don't want someone sitting there looking at all the parts.

When I have been carried away it wasn't usually related to a terrific production, now that I think about it. Sometimes a really stunning performance does it for me. John Murrell's *Great Noise, Bright Light* did it because it was the very first play I saw that seemed so truthful to a place that I was very intimate with — Alberta during the early Social Credit years. I had a wonderful rush. I thought there were things wrong with the production, things I knew John was still working on, but I felt that I was experiencing it in a way that the Greeks experienced work because of a shared knowledge of a time, place and history. A few productions of Beckett's work have moved me deeply, John Neville's *Endgame* in Halifax, for example. And sometimes work by young writers and performers in which there is a wonderful sincerity and commitment that radiates forth from them can move me. Interestingly, all of the shows I've talked about are from ten or so years ago. I don't know whether there's a scarcity of moving scripts or productions or whether I've been choosing the wrong shows or whether I've over the years erected certain barriers that don't allow me to give of myself in that particular way as readily.

RM: WHAT IS A SHARON POLLOCK PLAY?

SP: All of my plays deal with the same concern. I think I write the same play over and over again. It's a play about an individual who is directed to or compelled to follow a course of action of which he or she begins to examine the morality. Circumstances force a decision, usually the authority (family, society, government) is removed emotionally or geographically from the protagonist, and it usually doesn't end very well. It doesn't resolve in happiness. I think that is a very Canadian thing, actually, that comes from living in Alberta or the Maritimes and feeling that Ottawa never seems to understand what it is that is required in these places. It also has something to do with being a woman. Male society defines appropriate behaviour and action for women and I can never conform to that without denying aspects of myself.

Another identifying mark is perhaps language. I have a good ear for dialogue but it's an enhanced dialogue. A poetic quality permeates the language in my plays. Curiously, *One Tiger to a Hill*, which I think is the least characteristic of this, is going to be produced at Stratford, a very language-oriented place.

RM: YOUR EARLY WORK (*WALSH, ONE TIGER TO A HILL, THE KOMAGATA MARU INCIDENT*) WON YOU THE TITLE, FOR A WHILE, OF "SOCIAL PLAYWRIGHT," A LABEL TO WHICH YOU HAVE OFTEN OBJECTED. IS THERE A MORE SUITABLE LABEL FOR YOUR WORK?

SP: Actually, I feel that every play should be committed to social comment. What I mostly objected to was that the term was very narrowly applied to my history plays, as though a history play was somehow a lesser work. Then I would say, "Well, what's *Macbeth* but a history play? What's *Richard III*?" I sense when people defined me as a social playwright that they seemed to be saying that a social playwright is not quite a real one — that the real one is not a political playwright. They made me feel that I had a hidden agenda or ideology, and that my artistic choices were being determined by my adherence to a specific political ideology. I think it's strange that when I moved from the public to the more private arena, the label was dropped, yet I think *Doc* is full of social comment, as is *Blood Relations.*

RM: DO YOU STILL BELIEVE THAT THEATRE CAN BE AN INSTRU-MENT OF SOCIAL REFORM?

SP: Oh yes. Of course, nothing happens overnight. But I believe that if it's not a critical eye that's being brought to bear on the subject, it's a wank-off, that you're not doing what you should do.

RM: IN AN INTERVIEW YOU GAVE IN *HOME-MAKER'S* MAGAZINE IN MARCH OF 1980 YOU SAID THAT IF YOU DIDN'T WRITE YOU WOULD BE IN JAIL. DOES ART, THEN, CONTAIN YOUR ICONOCLASM?

SP: We think of art as creation, but it's also destruction. It's destroying what you see around you and then creating your own version of it. The act of destruction is an essential part of art because of its energy and the ego or gall that says, "This isn't good enough. I don't accept this." I was saying yesterday on a panel discussion at the 1989 P.E.N. Conference that the most important things that I had to contribute as a playwright were curiosity and irreverence, a healthy disrespect for everything, even what I write.

I think of myself looking at the world around me saying, "This isn't right." In my head is the image of what the world is supposed to be. If I hadn't come from the middle class and had a certain kind of education and certain kinds of opportunities, I believe that my act of saying, "This isn't good enough" would, since I'm female, take the form of destroying myself. If I were a man it might very well take the form of illegal activity of some kind. But I have certain tools and skills and so I have found a way of saying the world should be different in a way that society accepts. If in my next play I could construct the perfect image of the world, I wouldn't have to write another play.

I think all artists are criminals. They should be engaged in the act of tearing down and reconstructing.

RM: THOUGH YOU LIVED IN THE WEST FOR MANY YEARS YOU WERE BORN AND RAISED IN THE MARITIMES. HAVE YOUR ROOTS THERE INFLUENCED YOUR WORK? WERE YOU TAKEN TO THE THEATRE WHEN YOU WERE A CHILD? WERE THERE ANY WRITERS IN YOUR FAMILY?

SP: My mother wrote for herself. I never thought that writing or any of the art forms were something I could do. It never entered my mind. I've always been a voracious reader. I think that reading was an escape for me. My mother belonged to all of those Book-of-the-Month clubs and I remember reading anything that came into the house. My father tells me that I went through all of the books at the Fredericton Library.

RM: WHAT WERE YOU LOOKING FOR?

SP: I have no idea. I still read anything and everything. For me there is nothing worse than coming to Toronto at eleven at night and finding I have nothing to read. In desperation I'll read the hotel room Bible. Once I even stumbled my way through part of a French translation.

When I was a child we frequently visited Montreal. My father would always order me a pink lady and we'd go to night-clubs to see stand-up comics. When we went to New York we'd see musicals: *Oklahoma, Peter Pan, South Pacific*, that kind of thing.

But I didn't see myself as going on the stage. When I finished school and went to university I didn't have a compelling ambition to do anything. I thought I would get married, which I did at the end of my first year. I'm appalled when I think about it but that was the reality for me. I went to university because it was inconceivable that one didn't go unless one's father couldn't afford it. I remember telling my father just before Christmas during my first year at university that I didn't know what it was I wanted to be and that what I was discovering was how much I liked knowing things. The accumulation of knowledge is what interested me. As far as a career goes, I believed, and I think many women today believe this, that my contribution was to dedicate my life to making it all better for a man. The more screwed up the man, the more attracted the woman is to him.

RM: WHAT FIRST DREW YOU TO THEATRE?

SP: I belonged to the Drama Club in high school and when I went to private school I participated in some concerts. I remember playing Santa Claus in one. I suppose I liked hiding behind the roles I performed. I felt that I was performing all the time anyways so going on the stage was natural. Then when we moved to a place outside of Toronto I joined an amateur theatre club, as an escapist leisure activity, I suppose. It was only after I left my first husband that I became involved in professional theatre. I returned to New Brunswick where my father suggested I become either a teacher or a nurse — those were my two choices. But the Beaverbrook Playhouse was being built and I remember walking by one day and chatting to a man called Alexander Gray, who had once been a part of Joan Littlewood's company. He was starting a company of his own, the Company of Ten, and was putting together a subscription season. They were looking for someone to run the box office, so I took on the job. I auditioned for a part and soon became fairly involved with the company. I then realized that my idea of theatre was very narrow so I threw myself into reading tons of plays and commentary and dramatic theory.

After I left New Brunswick the poverty of working in the theatre and the lack of a Canadian voice — there were no Canadian works — propelled my career on. In other words, I had to work to survive so I looked for work that was meaningful to me as a woman and a Canadian.

RM: WHAT IS YOUR MOST VIVID MEMORY OF TOURING B.C. AND ALBERTA WITH THE PRAIRIE PLAYERS IN THE SIXTIES?

SP: We did a production of Jellicoe's *The Knack* which won a number of awards at a Dominion Drama Festival. I won best actress and Michael Ball won best actor. We lived off that play for one summer. I remember playing in Nelson at some arts-oriented college that was packed with people sitting on the window sills and so on. Our sets wouldn't go up so we performed the show in a corner of this room as opposed to the stage. We always travelled with a minimum number of lights, perhaps eight. But here we couldn't access the lighting equipment on the stage so what happened was that all but two lights, that were focused on the bed, burned out. I have a vivid memory of all of us trying to get as close as possible to the bed. We comforted ourselves with the thought that at least we'd earn some money for once, as the place was so full. When we went to get the cheque we learned that it's necessary to make certain of the ticket price before signing the contract. I think we earned about $1.98 because the tickets were sold for about a quarter. Every place we went we learned something more about how we could get screwed financially and artistically.

RM: HAVE YOU GOT PLANS TO RETURN TO THE STAGE IN THE NEAR FUTURE? WHAT KINDS OF ROLES WOULD APPEAL TO YOU?

SP: I like to do something once in a while to keep acting fresh for me. When I was acting a lot in the sixties the role determined how important acting was to me. Most of the time I had to take any old part because I needed the money. Of course, now age is a factor for me in considering what roles I should play.

I'd like to play Medea. I think. The character is so very large; it resonates in a powerful way. Here we have a woman who does the very worst "unnatural" thing male-run society thinks she can do. It would be fascinating to try to find a way to present that act as rational, given her choices. I'd like the chance of showing the audience the tremendous pain that drives Medea to kill her children. The appeal of the role is that Medea is a woman *in action.* She's not passive or weak. Whenever we see powerful women we turn them into witches. Think of the big, ugly step-mother in fairy tales. I'd like the challenge of showing a powerful woman who isn't a witch.

As for other roles, I've often thought that *King Lear* could be made intriguing if Lear were a woman. I'd also like to direct *Hedda Gabler* — since I'm too old to play Hedda — to see how it can be made more relevant to today's audiences.

RM: DID YOU HAVE DIFFICULTY GETTING YOUR FIRST PLAYS STAGED BECAUSE YOU ARE A WOMAN, AND A CANADIAN?

SP: I think I was lucky. I got a lot of support from people at the beginning of my writing career. If I were starting out today with *Walsh* as my first play it would be far more difficult. It's a history play with a large cast and a native component and it makes a political statement. I don't know of any major regional theatre that would produce a play of this size and nature by an unknown playwright.

As for being a woman playwright, well, playwrights who are just starting out are generally powerless and women are powerless. So a woman just starting out might actually not see the inequities because the role is a powerless one anyway. What happens to her is cloudy, not always clear. I certainly believe that I always thought I had to have a lot of reasons to back up my work. I always had to know more than anyone else in order to put my case forward. I didn't have legitimacy in my very person, which I think a man has. I also think that the more successful a woman playwright becomes, the more powerful she is and the more she works within the power structure of theatre, the more obvious to her the sexual discrimination is. In the way certain male directors may express a difference of opinion, for example. It seems to me that men are applauded when they demonstrate assertiveness and vision and move towards that vision, but women are compelled to do things more obliquely. Women can't be direct, they can't show off. I know that I have conversations with my board the nature of which would be entirely different if I were a man. I've had thrown at me that my artistic perceptions and choices are dictated by my femaleness. Choices men make are thought to be universal. As Artistic Director of Theatre New Brunswick I'm very conscious of having to "power dress," to wear the female equivalent of a man's three-piece suit, which is a symbol of authority in our society. Since power is not associated with women I feel I need to dress powerfully to assert my authority. My experience and expertise are not enough.

RM: HOW MUCH HAS BEING THE MOTHER OF SIX CHILDREN IMPINGED ON YOUR WRITING CAREER?

SP: I was writing for a living so writing was not something I had to squeeze in between cooking dinner and another job. And the chaos of a large family wasn't too much of a problem because I inherited my father's ability to look as though I am paying attention while I'm thinking about something completely different. I couldn't stand it when my father did this but I know I can tune out the world around me when I want to. One of my daughters would say, "You're not listening to me," and it was true! I wasn't. I'd make appropriate, or sometimes inappropriate, noises every once in a while and focus on something else: an idea for a play, a news item, anything.

There *was* a certain amount of resentment against the children's father and patriarchy in general for the child-bearing burden imposed on me, but I got rid of the resentment eventually by living alone. I can't seem to live with a man without immediately feeling responsible for his happiness, internal and external. I get this feeling that I should make all the bad go away and then I resent the responsibility I've taken on. I can't be bothered to live with anyone now and I'm happy I have only myself to take care of, that I don't have to support anyone emotionally and spiritually, apart from my children, who support me.

RM: DO YOU LIKE TO BE REGARDED AS A FEMINIST PLAY-WRIGHT?

SP: Yes, it is important. I certainly don't understand how a woman with any sense of justice can not be a feminist, but I object to those people who think that "feminist playwright" means that there is a hidden ideology by which aesthetic choices are being governed. I don't see it as a limiting term at all.

RM: DO YOU SEE YOURSELF AS A ROLE MODEL FOR THE NEW WAVE OF WOMAN PLAYWRIGHTS IN CANADA? CAN YOU GIVE THEM ANY ADVICE?

SP: I don't like labels, as you mentioned. Others may see me as a role model. I don't see myself as that. Everyone has to find his or her own way, one not patterned on anybody else. Advice? In the terribly difficult act of creation and communication, in the search for a platform, remain true to yourself.

RM: ARE YOU INFLUENCED BY WOMAN PLAYWRIGHTS IN CAN-ADA AND ABROAD? WHO DO YOU READ?

SP: I read Caryl Churchill. I enjoy Margaret Hollingsworth's work, which isn't very mainstream in the way, say, Ann Chislett's work is. I find Sally Clark interesting, as well as Judith Thompson. I'm going to direct Wendy Lill's *Memories of You*, at Theatre New Brunswick, which I think is very powerful writing. I'm also attracted to the piece because the feeling I had at the end of the play can't, I think, have been what Lill intended me to feel. I walked out saying, "What a stupid bitch!" about the main character who destroys every-thing because of a passionate commitment to an asshole, and I don't think I was supposed to feel that. I hope to discover what Lill intended. That's exciting. And if that's what she intended, I have to find the larger meaning.

RM: WHAT WAS THE MOST SURPRISING OR UNUSUAL PRODUCTION OF ONE OF YOUR PLAYS?

SP: I've often been surprised in productions of my plays when an actor or director has taken a particular tack and opened a door for me. "Oh yes, that's in there!" I'll say. "That's a perfectly valid way to do that and I hadn't thought of it that way." After I saw a black man playing TS in an English production of *The Komagata Maru Incident* I cannot see that piece without thinking the part of TS should be played by a member of a visible minority because it changes the reason why he tells the story in a way that makes it far more interesting. Another example is Guy Sprung's use of the set in his production of *Doc* at Theatre Calgary, which was quite wonderful.

You see, for me the actors and directors and designers don't serve the playwright. They serve the document, which is what I call the text. A playwright who demands that his or her vision of the work be served risks losing the possibility of unknown factors of the work surfacing. The first production of a play is a journey of discovery and exploration because the playwright often doesn't know, hopefully, all that is there. Of course, the playwright's insight into the work shouldn't be disregarded. The playwright has had a longer association with the document than anyone else and so she ought to be able to use the document, to direct others to it as a resource, so the others can find the answers to all the questions that arise in the rehearsal period. The work is larger than the person who created it. All the playwright is, ultimately, is the means to the end.

RM: DO YOU PREFER TO DIRECT YOUR OWN WORK?

SP: People tell me I don't respect the playwright enough when I direct my own work. I'm always very interested in what other people can bring to it. For example, what was so wonderful about working with Guy on *Doc* was that he seemed to truly believe that whether I knew it or not every word that was put there existed for a reason. To have a director who trusts the structure and trusts what it is you're doing is marvellous.

It's a frightening prospect to direct a first production but I do find I'm moving towards that, possibly because there aren't many good directors around.

RM: IS THERE A DIRECTOR YOU HAVEN'T WORKED WITH WHOM YOU'D LIKE TO DIRECT ONE OF YOUR PLAYS?

SP: I find Richard Rose interesting as a director, and I think the kind of work I do he might direct rather well. Some of the younger directors seem exciting — Larry Desrochers in Manitoba, for example. It's strange that woman directors don't immediately jump to mind; I know the relationship between me and a woman director would be different. I'm certainly looking forward to Jackie Maxwell directing my new play *Getting It Straight*.

I think I'm fairly open in the choosing of a director for my work. Perhaps it's because I hear the voices in my head as I write but I never say the lines out loud unless there's a problem with rhythm. Then I might speak the lines under my breath to see where the bump is. And I think that that is a great advantage because until an actor speaks those lines they've never really existed outside my head; consequently, I give more space for the director and the actors to bring in what it is they have gotten from the work.

RM: AS ARTISTIC DIRECTOR OF THEATRE NEW BRUNSWICK DO YOU OFFER SOMETHING THAT A MALE A.D. DOESN'T? DOES YOUR SEASON DIFFER IN ANY MEANINGFUL WAY?

SP: Anything I bring reflects the fact that I am a playwright as well as a director. I also can't help but notice that I chose a significant number of plays by women or plays about women for my two seasons: *Crimes of the Heart, Memories of You, Moon for the Misbegotten, Agnes of God, The Road to Mecca.* I didn't deliberately choose plays by or about women. I chose works that speak to me and which I thought would speak to the audience there.

I believe there should be more female artistic directors. However, it's difficult for woman directors to work their way up to the position because few get work on the main stages across the country. How can a board take you seriously unless you have a certain kind of visibility or profile? My two guest directors are women this year, Marti Maraden and Susan Cox. If I were to have only men's names cross my desk I would query that. I'm also aware of our multiculturalism: a black Canadian will play the role of Mary in *Salt-Water Moon*, for example. And I make a point of asking guest directors to be aware of the total talent pool.

RM: WHAT DO YOU HOPE TO ACHIEVE IN YOUR NEW POSITION AS ASSOCIATE DIRECTOR AT THE STRATFORD FESTIVAL?

SP: I don't know what it will achieve for me. I believe that is a wish there to critically assess what has happened in the area of Canadian work and by that I mean Canadian plays. I believe there is great support — the desire and the will — on the part of the Artistic Director for Canadian work and I hope to act as a resource for him in whatever way possible.

RM: IF YOU COULD BRING A NEW AUDIENCE INTO THE THEATRES WHO WOULD YOU BRING?

SP: Members of the multi-cultural community, visible minorities, young people. Unfortunately, our theatres are built around the subscription season so we're promising we'll do stuff that is like the stuff the audience liked last year, but better. Our success rate is determined by how many of those we can get back. The kind of programming that will attract the present subscribers is often not the kind of programming that will attract the new audience. I think we might have to bite the bullet and accept that our audiences will be increasingly conservative, and so then will our programming, and that those audiences will represent that segment of the population that is best able to pay the full price of the ticket — only we will be subsidizing it. I don't know whether I really believe there is the desire and the will on the part of the major companies to change that. Unless the boards change, we can't make the change. Part of me feels that it's impossible, in fact, to create within the structures that have evolved in our theatres. What we really need to do is put people who are in "people services" on the boards: librarians, social workers, nurses, artists, or else do away with boards as presently structured.

RM: YOU HAVE TAUGHT PLAY-WRITING AT THE UNIVERSITY OF ALBERTA AND THE PLAYWRIGHTS COLONY AT BANFF. CAN WRITING BE TAUGHT OR WAS YOUR JOB REALLY THAT OF DRAMATURGE?

SP: I don't think you can teach play-writing. If they are honest gatherings, they might operate in a way as a consciousness-raising experience. People might come out of a writing course with more knowledge of themselves and the world around them as the result of examining and trying to create dramatic texts and forms of drama. You don't turn out writers. You only hope you don't destroy any.

RM: DO WE NEED MORE DRAMATURGES IN CANADIAN THEATRE?

SP: No, because of the way the dramaturge is used in Canadian theatres. The dramaturge is usually defined as the person who stands in place of the playwright, sometimes in a rehearsal process, because they really don't want the playwright around or the playwright is too weak to speak for him- or herself or the playwright is too emotional or neurotic. So they get this extra person on their side. When the going gets tough the playwright can be thrown out and this extra person steps in to mediate on behalf of the text or the playwright. That really offends me. What I'm looking for are some other artists connected to the theatre on a full-time basis who can tell me, "You're crazy," or, "No, this is a better idea." I want an on-going dialogue about what it is I'm trying to do, and I want it with directors, designers, actors, not literary editors.

I think in our search for new material we go along with a lot of stuff that is too far removed from a draft that we or a dramaturge can properly assess. There are a million good ideas and the worst thing is to come across a play that has a wonderful idea but isn't a play yet. Later you discover that it never moved from the idea stage, or it moved in a direction you never anticipated. Then, because of this strange feeling of commitment to the work, hardly anyone has the guts to say, "Sorry, it's not for us."

RM: YOU'VE FREQUENTLY REMARKED THAT YOUR PLAYS HAVE A GREAT DEAL OF HUMOUR IN THEM. DO YOU WANT TO WRITE AN ALL-OUT COMIC PIECE?

SP: I think comedy is much harder to write than tragedy, but I don't choose the form. The story chooses the form and the story usually begins with a question inspired by something I've read or heard. I never know where the next play will come from. I don't try to foresee it in terms of subject matter or form. I have certainly thought of writing a comedy because so many things seem absurd or insane and what can you do but laugh at them? Sometimes I think my life is a comedy and my work more tragic.

RM: WHAT IS THE GREATEST CHANGE THAT HAS OCCURRED IN YOUR WRITING?

SP: There is a greater trust and much less of a need to control. When I began, and maybe it's because I was dealing with events that were documented and because my writing was in some way a response to a lack of control in my life, I needed to control every aspect of my writing. I used to feel I had to have a clear view of what the work meant or was saying or what my point of view was, so as to communicate it to others. Now I feel as if I trust much more what is unknowable about my work as I'm writing. I feel that there can be more "space" in what I write. I don't know if that's the right way of putting it. I don't need to know so much about it in order to write it. At the same time I have to know everything about everyone who is in the play and I have a scenario and so on.

I also have a greater awareness of structure now, or how the angle of observation, which is how I define structure, gives fresh insight into old stories or old situations that are recognized. It's much easier to think up new stories, which are really old stories, than it is to think up new structures. But I've never been able to begin to put the dialogue on the page until I was able to understand the way in which I was going to tell the story and that always comes to me in a moment when I suddenly have a sense of the entire work. I can't tell you what it is but as I start to write I know that this "fits" and that doesn't. I think that in the future I'll be playing more with structure or ways of telling the story.

RM: CAN YOU DESCRIBE YOUR NEW PLAY, *GETTING IT STRAIGHT?*

SP: It's about a woman in an asylum who tries to reconstruct how she thinks she got there. In a sense the play suggests that the ways of knowing — logical, rational, sequential — don't seem to have worked and that perhaps there are other ways of knowing, that women are particularly open to because they give birth and raise children, that are more valid and which should be listened to however they come to people.

RM: IN WHAT DIRECTION IS THEATRE IN CANADA GOING IN THE 1990S?

SP: Greater conservatism. What I want to see is greater opportunities for artist-generated projects of whatever scope and scale the work dictates, with meaningful financial support. Boards and buildings are presently restrictive to creation.

DATE DUE

11/29/95			
GAYLORD			PRINTED IN U.S.A.